Brotherhood of Murder

Books by John Guinther

Moralists & Managers:
Public Interest Movements in America

The Malpractitioners

Winning Your Personal Injury Suit

Philadelphia: A 300-Year History

The Jury in America

Thomas
Martinez
with
John
Guinther

Brotherhood
of Murder

How one man's journey through fear
brought The Order—the most
dangerous racist gang in America—
to justice

McGraw-Hill
Book Company

New York St. Louis San Francisco Auckland Bogotá
Hamburg London Madrid Mexico Milan Montreal New Delhi
Panama Paris São Paulo Singapore Sydney Tokyo Toronto

1 2 3 4 5 6 7 8 9 FGR FGR 8 9 2 1 0 9 8

ISBN 0-07-040699-5

LIBRARY OF CONGRESS CATALOGING-IN-PUBLICATION DATA

Martinez, Thomas.
   Brotherhood of murder.

   1. Order (Organization) 2. Martinez, Thomas.
3. Defectors—United States—Biography. 4. Assassination
—United States—Case studies. 5. Fascism—United States
—Case studies. I. Guinther, John. II. Title. III. Title:
Brotherhood of Murder.
HS2330.073M37 1988   322.4'2'0973   87-26263
ISBN 0-07-040699-5

Book design by Kathryn Parise

This book is dedicated to my lovely wife, Susan,
and to the memory of my dear mother, who passed away
January 3, 1987, and whom I miss very much.

—*Thomas Martinez*

Contents

PART I: The Coming of Carlos

PART I | The Coming of Carlos

1 | The Machine Gun and the Bible

As I went down the escalator, I passed the woman going up. Our gazes met but, as had been prearranged, we showed no recognition of one another. Upon stepping off the escalator, I saw directly ahead the luggage-arrival section of the airport. My descent to it, I realized, had a symbolic quality, since—if our plans worked out, hers and mine—I would soon be going underground with Bob Mathews as a member of his secret Order.

While I waited for my bag, I reflected how big city airports all seem to look alike, and this one in Portland, Oregon, and the one I had departed from seven hours earlier, Philadelphia International, were no exceptions. I said to myself, find your way around one, find your way around them all. That was a deliberately irrelevant thought: to scare away my fear.

I watched as the suitcases from my flight began to come sliding down the ramp. Bob had said he'd meet me here, but he was no-where in sight. I spotted my bag heading toward me. As I stooped to retrieve it, I glanced up and there he was, showing no more sign of knowing me than had the woman on the escalator. He knows something's up, I thought, as he walked away.

I grabbed my bag and followed him into the lobby. Standing near the entrance was a man with a sweater over his arm, and I was aware that Bob, who was about ten feet ahead of me, gave him a quick look as he went by him and out into the parking lot.

I fell into step behind Bob. A heavy rain was coming down. I was bare-headed, Bob in a wool cap with flaps pulled over the top. I was so much bigger than he that I could almost have protected him from the downpour just by hovering over him. Lean and lithe, clean-cut handsome, he had dark brown hair and dark brown eyes that ordinarily had a sparkling quality but this evening were reddened by exhaustion.

His first words were, "I don't like that aerial," nodding to the one pointing upward from the rear of a black Lincoln Continental.

"Bob, they're made like that," I said, seeing along with him the man in the car; he was reading, or pretending to read, a newspaper.

Motioning me to walk alongside him, Bob mumbled, "Mumbo jumbo, mumbo jumbo, mumbo," as if to indicate to any watchers that he was talking to me casual state-of-the-weather talk.

Then, with a little skip of a motion, he headed me back into the airport. "Doesn't feel right to me," he said, and led us to a stairwell I hadn't noticed on our way out. Glancing back, I saw that the man with the sweater was walking in our direction. Halfway down the steps, Bob halted, his hand going inside his coat. "Let him come," he said looking back at me.

"What's wrong?" I said as I wrapped the strap of the bag I was carrying around my wrist, intending to hit his gun arm with it if the sweater man appeared above us.

We waited for thirty seconds or so, and when nobody came, we returned to the lobby. The sweater man was nowhere in sight. I waited until we were back in the parking lot before I asked, "Bob, are you alone?"

He said, "Yes," and then startled me by running over behind a wall, from where he could watch a man who was sitting on a bench. Protected from the rain by an overhanging roof, the man seemed intent on the newspaper he held unfolded in front of him. "There was another one there earlier," Bob whispered.

I had no doubt who the man was, no doubt what would happen to me if Bob decided I knew him. I said, "Come on, man. It's pouring. I'm getting all shook up. What's going on?"

He continued to study the man, saying only: "This is why I'm still here. Because I'm careful."

Apparently, however, he was satisfied—for the moment anyway—and he led me across the lot to a car. We had just reached it when a skinny man with red hair and a straggly moustache came over to us. Thinking he might be a cop, I said, trying to sound tough: "What do you want?"

Bob laughed and said, "It's okay, Tom; he's with us," and I laughed, too, as if I were pleased, but I wasn't. Bob had said he was alone—it reminded me of the lie Walter West was told just before he was killed six months ago.

The redhead got into the back of the car as Bob slid into the driver's seat, me next to him. As we started, Bob said to the redhead, "See if that little gray Volvo pulls out," and, hell, it did, and as it did, Bob took out a handgun and laid it beside him. Looking back, I saw the redhead fix a silencer onto a machine gun.

We continued to drive in no apparent direction, Bob's glance all the while flicking back and forth from the rear-view mirror. As offhandedly as I could, I asked, "Who is this guy, Bob?"

"Reds," he said, "but call him Sam. Sam, this is Spider," my code name; I'd gotten it because of a spider I had tattooed on my shoulder. From underneath the seat, Bob pulled out his machine gun, also with a silencer, and laid it next to him on top of his Bible.

No one spoke. We drove in silence for nearly half an hour before finally turning down a dirt road fronted by a sign saying DEAD END. I heard the twigs cracking and the pebbles bounding against the wheels and that was all.

After making a U-turn at the end of the road, Bob brought the car to a stop. He and the redhead sat waiting and I did, too, waiting for the headlights of the Volvo. Glancing behind me, I saw that the redhead had placed a hand grenade on the seat, shifting the weight of his machine gun as he did. He's used to handling weapons, I thought. One gun he'd had in his possession, I knew, had been used five months earlier to murder a man named Alan Berg.

* * *

The dead end in Portland was thirty years and 3,000 miles from the reasons I ended up there. Reasons, but one reason mostly: For my entire adult life, I had been a racist. I don't mean I was one of those people who make little anti-Semitic jokes or complain when a black family moves into the neighborhood. I was the genuine article. I had belonged to the Ku Klux Klan. I had belonged to the National Alliance, an American version of the German Nazi party. I had friends in the Aryan Nations, which is exactly what it sounds like. Some of the people I knew in the racist movement were tough street kids from big cities like me, others were good old boys from little towns in the South, but some were doctors, lawyers, executives, or college professors.

Whatever our differences in background, each of us, I had found, had an attribute in common. We felt the presence of a force in our lives more powerful than we. The force exploited us. It sought to do us harm. It blocked our way to success and happiness. When, in our search for a means to combat this evil power, we turned to organized racism, we learned that, far from being inferior to the force, we were under attack by it precisely because we were superior. Our superiority sprang from the fact that we were white. Only as part of an Aryan whole, we discovered, could we defeat the force; individually, we were nothing.

Few people enter the racist world with the expectation that they will be led to commit crimes. Many never do. Nevertheless, as the wine of superiority is imbibed, the inferior self that is doing the drinking can take a drunkard's step, then a second (perhaps not yet an illegal one), then a third, a fourth, and then on and on, easy step after easy step until, as happened to me, that self is backed into a corner, frightened and desperate, crying out: But I didn't mean for this to happen.

Some people come out of that corner violently, as Bob Mathews did. By the time our destinies crossed for a final time in Portland, he had already led a rampage of robbery and murder across the United States in the name of Aryan supremacy.

The Order was the name he gave the little band of zealots he headed, although almost as frequently—and more aptly—he referred to his gang as the Bruder Schweigen or silent brotherhood. Not for it the way of beer-gut marchers shouting white power slogans, not for it robes and hoods or burning of crosses. It proceeded instead by stealth, with guns and bombs, murder its ultimate moral act, terrorism its method.

Bob's Order is gone now, in part because of the way I came out of my corner. But the idea he let loose remains. It teaches that organized racism, because it is so tiny in its membership, can only force the nation to accede to its goals by frightening its people into submission through random acts of violence. That teaching continues to be practiced, even as I write, by men who, as Bob did, carry guns, plant bombs, plan assassinations, and commit robberies to finance their efforts.

I shall begin my story—and his—by describing my life before I got to know Bob and by relating the little I know of his life before we met as members of the National Alliance. Mine tells the tale of a working-class white boy from the big city who is threatened by what he sees; Bob's of a middle-class white boy from rural America, threatened by what he doesn't see.

2 | Whitetown

People who know something about Philadelphia will know a great deal about me as soon as I say I'm from K&A. K&A stands for Kensington and Allegheny Avenues, where the old Market Street El-evated rattles along overhead. It's a busy corner, with its sooty gray bank building, its fast-food restaurants, its small, tired-looking and second-rate retail shops under the El, but it's more than a corner. It's both itself and the spread of life around it. I think most big cities have a K&A under one name or another. Whitetown is one name, by which is meant not suburb white or upwardly mobile white but white white, working-class white, K&A white.

The neighborhood of which K&A is the hub is called Kensington—ask a Philadelphian where he's from and he's more likely to name his neighborhood than his city—and right to the south of us was Fishtown, and Port Richmond nearby (it used to be called—no one remembers why—Point No Point), and Tacony and Bridesburg, Holmesburg and Olney, which was once a German-American enclave, and a few blocks from where I lived as a boy a little section we called Jewtown.

Once, a long time ago, in the days before the American Revolution, Kensington was a green place of forests and little dairy farms. Each day the farmers would lead their cows along the cobbled streets of the little village of six blocks square that was Philadelphia then. In long rows, as an old picture shows, the farmers would line up the cows, one in front of each house on a block, the wives in their long homespun dresses and peaked caps emerging, flower-painted pitchers in hand, to obtain, each from her cow, her day's supply of milk.

Not only are there no cows in Kensington now; there's little grass and few trees. Factories came, and the owners built workers' houses on the green land; there's street after street, row after row, of them now, tiny houses, most of brick, grimy brick, hard to see the red any-more.

Life's never been easy for the Kensingtonians. Most who live there today are of Irish descent, most are Catholics, and a good many can trace their path to America back to the 1840s, when the potato famine in Ireland brought them here. At first, the menfolk, for the most part, worked on the docks at Port Richmond, often replacing freed blacks—replacing them because they were white and also because they'd work for even less money than the blacks would. (I am telling what I know now, not what I knew when I grew up; when I was a boy we never heard about whites taking jobs from blacks.)

As the manufacturing plants began to multiply after the Civil War, life got better in Kensington. Even when that meant twelve-hour work-days (twenty-four when there was a shift change), jobs were both more plentiful and more secure than they had been when the docks were the main source of employment. And if the wages were often shorter than the hours, that also improved when the unions came. But the Second World War came, too, and after it, bit by bit, the factories moved to the suburbs. Some folks moved along with them, but most stayed because Kensington—even if jobs were harder to get now and even harder to keep—was still home.

By the time I was growing up, the drug dealers had already begun their invasion of K&A; the aging corner boys, grown sullen and sour, now talked deals as they pocketed their unemployment checks. On the back streets, huddled in the lots, at the rears of playgrounds, the blue-eyed, blond-haired lads sniffed glue and stared vacantly.

And all the time the sound of the El, its constant coming and receding roar—every five minutes it seemed—twenty-four hours a day, seven days a week. It's the sound of your life when you're a K&A boy, so much so that you don't think much about it because it's always there, except you know deep down that you are told something about the value outside people put on you when you're the kind of person who lives with all that noise, that noise that runs over the decayed main street you shop on.

All that's bad. It's what Kensington was, what it was becoming, what it became even during my short life. But that's not all of Kensington. That, rather, is what outsiders see, the ones who write books about it, the sociologists, who see the faces of the people and find only hate and despair in them.

But when the folks there look at themselves, what they see, what I saw of myself when I was growing up there, is much different. We, they and I, see people who are honest and thrifty and think it is a good thing to work hard and save to buy one of the little houses, people who sit on their steps in the summer and talk neighborhood talk. When I was a boy, we'd have block parties to which the man who worked for Oscar Mayer would bring the hot dogs, and people like my dad, who was a baker, would bring the rolls, and the Schmidt Brewery workers would see to the beer. You'd have good times and innocent times with the folks you knew, and you wouldn't think, during the block parties or talking on the steps while the Phillies game was on the radio in the living room, you wouldn't think about the blacks moving into Jewtown just a couple of blocks down the Pennsy railroad tracks from your home.

My family consisted of my parents and my two brothers, one ten years older than me, the other seven. Despite the differences in our ages, I was especially close to my middle brother, Lee. I tagged after him and he looked after me, and I thought he was the wisest person in the world. When I was eleven, Lee joined the army. His desertion of me, as I saw it to be, left me with an anger I couldn't express, a desperate longing for his return, and a need, I now think, for someone to replace him. Even when I became an adult, there were times I'd find myself holding conversations with an imagined Lee, as if, that way, I'd happen on good advice about the problems facing me. The real Lee was, by then, thousands of miles away, a career soldier, permanently stationed in Germany.

As is true of most families in Kensington, my father was the ruler of the house. My mother was a continuing gentle and nurturing presence, but she always stood back, deferring to my father. Among my earliest memories is seeing his cat-o'-nine-tails on the hook on the kitchen wall, the feeling of it being used by him on my bottom. I was frightened of him, revered him, and spent most of my childhood trying, unsuccessfully, to find ways to please him. (Not that I felt put upon. On the contrary, I knew from an early age that I was luckier than most. Some kids had fathers who drank and cursed and beat their wives and hit their children just because they were there. That's Kensington, too, but it never happened in my house.)

My father started life with great promise and came on hard times. He was of Spanish and Swedish parentage, Catholic, a brilliant student, graduating at the age of sixteen from Central High—then Philadelphia's public school for gifted boys—but his family was poor and he had to go to work right after graduation, then into the Navy for World War II, and he never did get the chance to further his education. After I was born, in 1955, misfortune struck. We owned a house outside of Kensington, but lost it and all our money, too, when my father became seriously ill. To his shame, we were forced to move to a public housing project. By the time I was five, he had recovered his health, obtained a job as a route man for a bakery, and had bought us our little house in Kensington, not far from Jewtown. During his illness he had turned to the Church for help, but when the priests told him his problems were no affair of theirs, he stopped being a Catholic and we boys, as a result, were brought up in the Protestant faith of our mother—which was why I went to public rather than parochial schools.

Until I started junior high school, when suddenly they were everywhere, I'd hardly ever met any black people. They kept away from K&A. In the entire six grades at my elementary school, we had just four black kids, three boys and a girl. I have no strong memory of them as individuals, but I knew, even then, that you didn't make friends with them.

I don't know exactly how I knew that. I didn't get it at home. There was no racist talk there. But when you're a child, you're a sponge, sopping up everything around you, so that you often know things in your soul before you know them in your mind. If I had to put my finger on a single source for that soul knowledge, it was the word "nigger." That's the Kensington word for blacks, as in other White-towns, North and South. It's not the word itself—when you're little, one word's much like another—but the tone in which it was said. You heard that tone being used by people who looked like you, adults you had been taught to respect, and you got a message about people who didn't look like you, who could be talked about in that scornful manner.

The year I began junior high, 1967, was also the year Philadelphia began busing black children to hitherto predominantly white schools. Ours was one of those selected. Hearing of that decision, many of our Catholic parents, who until then had been satisfied with the pub-lic schools, decided to send their children to the sisters, and some non-Catholic parents followed suit. By the time the school year be-gan, enrollment in our public junior high had shrunk by nearly half; the arriving black children filled all the empty white seats.

From the day of the first class, hatred became the major subject in the curriculum, the only subject the children, black and white, boys and girls, seemed willing to learn together. They, the boys especially, carried out these learning sessions in the hallways, in the gym, in the locker rooms, on the playground, with insults and punches and shov-ing. We whites had our triumphant moment each day after school when the buses came to pick up the blacks. As they marched into them—most often under police protection—we had the sense of hav-ing repelled them from our neighborhood.

Until the next day. I think I knew even then that it was a battle we'd never win. The enemy was too powerful.

My senior high school, Thomas Edison, was nearly all black by the time I got there. The state of the building conveyed the contempt the system had for anyone unfortunate enough to have to go there: dark and dirty corridors, few and battered textbooks, falling plaster. In keeping with the appearance of the building, we were supervised by a faculty of listless men and women who often acted (and so we perceived them) as though they had been punished by being sent to teach at Edison.

It was a dangerous place to be, and not just for the rare white student like me. Though I didn't realize it then, black youngsters who didn't belong to the gangs that roved the corridors at will—the Zulu Nations, the Valley Gang, the Eighth and Butlers—were also at risk. (The corner of Eighth and Butler has changed since then, and not for the better; it is now the city's major cocaine hub, with kids, most of them Puerto Ricans these days, some not even in their teens, selling crack through the windows of the long lines of cars, many with out-of-state license plates, that pass through day and night.)

I didn't last long at Edison. Murder was the reason. One Friday, a white boy from Kensington was stabbed to death by a black gang member who was in my homeroom. A racial fight broke out in Jewtown that weekend. Rocks and bottles were thrown. The police had to break it up; I was in the middle of it. On Monday, during one of my classes, a pal of the boy who had done the knifing called over to me: "Hey, Turtle, you still from Kensington?" I knew why he was asking that, so I said, "Nah, I don't hang nowhere anymore." And he said, "You're a liar. We're going to put a homicide on you after class." Ten of his fellow gang members stood up and left the room. My teacher laughed as if this was funny. I waited a few minutes and then asked to be excused to go to the bathroom. I ran out the first exit I saw.

That was the last day I ever spent in school.

Fearing my father's wrath, I didn't tell him I had quit school. When he finally found out, he called me a bum, just as I had expected he would. In both my expectation and then the reality, he had given me a grievance to nurture, the first in a long line. My grievance had less to do with his failure to understand why I had fled school than with his assumption that I was lazy. That was unfair. Even while I was still in school, I had held down a part-time job in a bakery. My ambition in life was to become a baker, just like my dad.

The only good part of my adolescence was wrapped up in a girl named Susan. I was fifteen, nearly sixteen, when we met; she was thirteen and small and slender and pretty. Her younger sister was chronically ill with kidney disease—she was the poster child one year—and Susan, because her parents worked, eventually had to quit school to look after her.

Susan looked after me, too. She had strict moral standards, despised drugs and alcohol, and at thirteen was much more mature than I was at sixteen. She led me away from the boys I hung out with, from the beer drinking and the pot smoking. Her parents, however, saw me as a bad influence, not understanding that the opposite was true. Susan was told she could no longer see me. That decision became my second grievance. Bitter, I went back to my old ways, and when I saw Susan out with other boys—you'd see that, too, in Kensington, it's a small town in a big city—I couldn't stand it and I joined the Army.

I lasted only a few months. At that time, in 1973, the Army guaranteed recruits that they would receive training in a skilled trade of their choice. I wanted to learn baking, and that's what we agreed to, but when basic training was over I found myself assigned to building bridges. They had broken their contract with me—the lying bastards, I thought—and I demanded out.

Out I went and back to the partying, weekends in Atlantic City, girls, even got my own apartment. Oh, I was a man now. One day I ran into Susan at the laundromat. A few months later, we were married. I had another job in baking—donuts this time—bringing home $112 a week, and soon we were expecting a baby. Life was good. I was off the Kensington corner for good and nowhere near the one in which I'd eventually find myself cowering.

Bob Mathews, by that age, however, had already taken the first steps toward his.

Will-o'-the-Wisp

During the three years of our friendship, Bob Mathews never, save by the most fleeting of references, spoke to me of his childhood, or what it was like to be him growing up. Because of what eventually happened between us, I have not been able to ask those who might know most about him for fear of endangering them or myself. I have, however, learned some parts of his story.

One of three sons, just as I, Robert Jay Mathews was born in the tiny Texas town of Marfa. Its one claim to fame is the will-o'-the-wisp lights emanating from nearby marshes and which dance always a breath from those who would pursue them, tantalizing, false, a chimera in the night.

Bob's family was solidly middle-class, the father a reserve officer in the Air Force who reached the rank of colonel by the time he retired a year or two before his death in 1983 when Bob, two years my senior, was thirty years old. His mother, whom I met briefly, struck me as fastidious—Bob's compulsive neatness may have come from her—sensitive and rather forlorn. His brother John, perhaps seven years older than Bob, was a college graduate who became a school teacher in the little town in Washington State near where Bob lived most of his adult life. Bob pointed him out to me one day, describing him, with tight-lipped and bright-eyed tension, as "liberal scum."

When Bob was in his early teens, perhaps a little before that, his father was transferred to Phoenix, Arizona. His posting was to provide Bob's only protracted exposure to big city life. But I don't think the hatred of blacks and Jews that would consume his life could have been prompted by the Phoenix environment. The Jewish presence there was minuscule, the black not much greater—less than 5 percent of the total. (By contrast, at that time, blacks made up 35 percent of the Philadelphia population.) Neither was Phoenix a traditional Southern city with a long history of bigotry and hatred toward minorities. Yet, as early as junior high school, possibly while still living in Marfa, Bob had established contact with the right-wing John Birch Society, and was feeding on its literature.

When Bob was about to graduate from high school, Colonel Mathews, perhaps worried about the direction his son's life was taking, prevailed on Arizona Senator Barry Goldwater to sponsor Bob for an appointment to the U.S. Air Force Academy. Unfortunately for Bob and the people who would die because of him, he didn't get admitted because of low grades in mathematics.

Even had he been accepted, however, he might not have enrolled. By then he had become involved with an Arizona tax resisters league called the Sons of Liberty. He may have been one of its founders, and clearly he was one of its leaders. That someone so young would be in a leadership position in a group consisting mostly of adults may seem surprising, but even then Bob apparently had the ability to attract people older than himself to his causes. Later on, the majority of members of The Order would be his seniors, several of them old enough to be his parents.

Some tax resister groups believe in peaceful protest, but others have an ugly and violent edge to them. Members of the militant groups typically are also survivalists who, heavily armed, may take to the wilderness to await a cataclysmic end to the world, in which God will unleash the final battle between the forces of Good (always them) and Evil (usually the Jews).

Exactly where Bob's group fit into the tax resister spectrum isn't clear, but it doesn't appear to have been one of the habitually violent ones. Nevertheless, according to a letter Bob wrote in 1984, the Sons of Liberty were sufficiently lawless that Bob himself became a target of the IRS, which, he wrote, attempted to assassinate him. Since Bob's fictions tended to have some basis in fact, this bizarre claim almost certainly did also. Considering the tactics of tax resister groups, quite possibly the Sons of Liberty and the police were involved, at some point, in a confrontation, and shots may have even been fired. Whatever the actual event, it seems to have had a traumatic effect on Bob, providing him (based on his letter) with his first proof of government's malignant power and also apparently of the ineffectiveness of tax protesting as a means of confronting it. (In later years, when he had money to hand out to racist groups by the hundreds of thousands of dollars, none went to tax protestors or survivalists.)

Around 1975, Bob moved to Metaline Falls, tucked away in the far eastern corner of the state of Washington. With his father's financial help, he bought a patch of forested land, cleared enough of it to set on it two house trailers, in one of which his parents subsequently lived. At some point, his brother John moved to Metaline Falls, too. While John taught school, Bob supported himself and his bride, Debbie, by working in a nearby cement plant, where he met and became friendly with an older man, Ken Loff, who later became one of the original members of The Order.

Except for Loff, Bob kept largely to himself. After work, he didn't stop at the taproom for a few beers with the boys, and rarely did he take his wife out for an evening. Instead, night after night, year after year, he went into his room to read, and I don't mean he just read: He studied.

A favorite source for educating himself was the *National Vanguard*, a magazine put out by William Pierce of the National Alliance. Its "scientific" racist articles appealed to Bob strongly; he wrote Pierce letters filled with praise. Wilmot Robinson's *Dispossessed Majority*, a similarly pseudo-learned Aryan supremacy tract, was, Bob once told me, his strongest early influence. *Mein Kampf*, as might be expected, was also a subject of his study, as was Oswald Spengler's *Decline of the West*, which he seemed to know practically by heart. I believe he also made his way through Simpson's *Which Way Western Man?*, which is even longer and duller, though no less anti-Semitic, than Robinson's book. The book he hadn't yet read was Pierce's racist novel, *The Turner Diaries*. When he did, it became the blueprint from which he created The Order and its deeds.

Picture him then, Bob Mathews as a very young man, with his bright mind and not much education, hiding away every night in his little room in his little town in the middle of nowhere, poring over his tomes with their tiny print and their big secrets, the secrets that would save the world outside Metaline Falls. If only someone would listen.

A lonely man he was, perceiving a huge threatening outside world. But was he also a dangerous man alone in his room? I don't think so, not yet, not beyond retrieval, but I also don't know how much hate you can ingorge, how many fantasies of violence you can entertain at night, before you lead yourself to murder in the morning.

4 | The Klansman

By the time I was twenty-one, I was ready for David Duke, a self-styled genius through whom I would enter the world of organized racism. I met him, in a way, through Tom Snyder, who had a TV talk show at the time. By then I had quit my job at the donut shop, because the man who had hired me had not come through on his promise to cover me under Blue Cross, which I needed for the baby. Like the Army, he had broken his contract with me, so out I went. After I quit, I couldn't find work that paid a living wage. This infuriated me: Blacks and other minorities, I heard, if they wanted jobs, got them for the asking. "Affirmative action" it was called, and I was its victim. Never once did it occur to me that perhaps the real reason I couldn't find a decent job was that I was a tenth-grade dropout.

An event that occurred just before I heard David Duke on TV added to my bitterness and to my willingness to accept his message.

By then, Susan and I had been reduced to living on unemployment compensation, or "compo" as it was popularly known. When a system has a nickname that everybody understands, it usually indicates how important it is to them. "Compo" was important to us

Kensingtonians. As the economy and jobs got scarce, many of us had to learn its rules; how to stay on, how to get back on once we were off. All that became part of our folk knowledge, just as too many black families had to learn to live with welfare and its bureaucratic rules.

One day I received a call from a man at compo, who said: "Martinez? You want a job? It pays $10 an hour." I'd never made anywhere near that. Excitedly, I told him I did. When I arrived at his office, he took one look at me and said in surprise: "You Martinez? Where did you get that name?" I told him my father was Spanish. "Well, you won't do," he said. "This place is only hiring Mexicans and Puerto Ricans on a government contract." Outraged, I demanded he send me anyway, and reluctantly he did. When I got there, the boss said, "You can't have this job. There's a mistake in sending you here. It's all Spanish-speaking." Pointing to the sign over his head that declared the company didn't discriminate on the basis of race, I said, "There's no mistake, mister. If you don't hire me, I'll file an action against you." That got me the job, but I didn't stay long. The boss was right; the other workers spoke only Spanish and spent most of their time, I found to my disgusted satisfaction, smoking joints and reading girlie magazines. Such an inferior people! I quit. What a great country America is, I thought: If you're white and want a job, you get one only if you have a Hispanic name.

It was in that frame of mind that, a month or so later, I happened to turn on Tom Snyder the night David Duke was interviewed. Duke was a young man—only a few years older than me—and ruggedly handsome, looking like a young Robert Redford in the way Bob Mathews looked like a macho version of Donny Osmond. As Duke was talking of how the government had money to bus black kids to school but not a penny for the working-class white man, I thought: "Damn, this guy is right. This guy is right! Who is this guy?"

He was, he told Snyder, the Grand Wizard of the Ku Klux Klan. In school I'd learned that Klansmen were vigilantes, an image that was favorable to me from the cowboy movies I had seen at the Midway Theatre when I was a child. I also knew, whether from school or elsewhere, that they wore robes and hoods, took secret oaths, had secret rites, which meant to me that they possessed a secret knowledge. That attracted me, and so did Duke, so smooth and articulate; and when he told Snyder he had an IQ of 173, I thought: A person that bright has to know what he is talking about.

The following day I called the television network and was connected with a member of Snyder's staff, who readily gave me Duke's address in Metairie, Louisiana. I wrote him immediately, asking for information. By return mail he sent me his magazine, *The Crusader*. It was nicely packaged, containing none of the ranting about "kikes" and "niggers" that are the common coin of most racist publications. Rather, the articles focused on my pet bugaboos, affirmative action and busing. It met my needs. It explained why I wasn't getting anywhere. I had been right all along. It wasn't my fault.

I sent him a check. About a week later I called him, asking for more literature. He sent it, along with an application. By then I was in a state of awe that someone so important, who'd been on national television, would take the time to speak to me. I filled out the application and mailed it, and that was all there was to it. I was now a full-fledged Knight of the Ku Klux Klan.

At that time there were perhaps three dozen Klan organizations in the United States, each more or less independent of the others, but the big three were the Invisible Empire, the United Klans of America, which claimed to be the original, and Duke's Knights of the KKK. (Subsequently, Duke was forced out as head of the Knights; he went on to start the National Association for the Advancement of White People.)

In my chapter we had nearly two dozen members, most from working-class areas in Philadelphia like mine, though quite a few were from Bucks County to the north, where people like us had moved, both to be near the factory work available there and to get away from the blacks. My closest friend in the Klan was a fellow from Bucks whom I'll call Jack Martin; I don't want to give his real name, because he is no longer involved in racist activities. For the most part, he and I and the others made our contribution to the cause by handing out literature on street corners in places like Kensington and Olney, which still had a substantial German population, and for the most part we were well received, too. Some folks had never met a KKK member before, and they usually seemed impressed, which impressed me with me, too.

Not that the people who appeared to approve of the Klan were likely to join. In a way, it was like the Depression of the 1930s, when it was the communists explaining how the government was going to hell and people were starving because of the capitalist system, and a lot of folks then would nod their heads and say, "Hey, yeah, that's right, man," but they didn't join either. Still, we were getting the word out.

Many Klan members, however, I soon discovered to my disappointment, weren't interested in working for the cause of true white Americanism, or for much of anything else either. As I began to attend conventions of various Klans around the country—I had a decent paying job in a dye factory by then and could afford it—I learned that eager toilers in the vineyard like Jack and me were considerably outnumbered by the beer-and-shot types who had joined the KKK so they could flash their cards in bars; it gave them respect. Just getting them to pay their dues could be a major undertaking, as I found out when I tried.

Although most of those in my chapter were around my age, at the conventions I met a number of old-timers who had been active in the early 1960s. I'd spend hours sitting among them, listening to them relate how they planned their attacks and brag about the "whompings," as they called them, that they had "put on" various blacks and their white followers in organizations like the Southern Christian Leadership Conference. But they were sad, too. They were sad the blacks had stopped marching. They wished they'd start again, so they could get out their baseball bats and lead pipes and start having fun again.

My own keenest sense of participation—when I thrilled to the sense of power the ritual gave me—came when I stood in hood and robe (cost, $30, payable to the Klan) among dozens of men similarly clad, strong in our white anonymity, in a field at night, the grass under us, the crickets chirping (me a city boy not used to grass, and never having heard crickets), in our hands the torches, above the crosses burning, the cries rising from our throats: "White culture! White culture! White America! We want a white America!" I felt then as though I had been transported back to a past that was all good, right after the Civil War when just a dozen men got together one night and created the Klan. I was part of that history; I was going to make it this history.

The late 1970s was a good recruiting time for the KKK and groups like it, especially in the South. That was because Jimmy Carter was President. His appointment of Andrew Young as ambassador to the United Nations was a grievous blow. You might expect that, we thought, from a Northerner like Hubert Humphrey, but Carter was a Georgian. That made him a "nigger lover" and, worse, "a traitor to his race." To me, Carter embodied all the worst traits of radical liberalism, and I was surprised, after I left the racist world, to learn that real liberals saw him as a conservative. Ronald Reagan, on the contrary, was bad news for racists. When a right-winger gets to be President, it's hard to convince other right-wingers that they have to join the KKK or the Nazis if they want to save the country.

To one extent or another, we were all zealots, but for me racism had become an obsession. At my job, during breaks and lunch hours, I never mingled with my fellow workers, but went off by myself to read my magazines and books; by then I think I was subscribing to every racist periodical in the country. At home, when I wasn't holding Klan meetings in my living room, I'd delve into the mass of literature I kept there. I forbade my family from watching "The Jeffersons," not because it had black actors but because of its interracial couple. Other times, I turned on programs because I expected them to be "liberal" and make me furious, a feeling I found I increasingly enjoyed. As I became ever more immersed, all my old interests—attending rock concerts at the Tower Theatre, jazz at the Bijou—seemed trivial to me, a waste of time, and the more I fed my racism, the hungrier I became for more.

I learned who the great leaders were, the ones to be revered. The Reverend Robert Miles, whom many considered to be the greatest, I met at a Klan rally. He was pastor of the Mountain Church in a nearby town in Michigan called Cohoctah, and soon after, if he wasn't already, he became one of Bob Mathews' mentors. Miles preached a weird doctrine called Dualism, which teaches that Yahweh (Miles' word for God) and Satan were once equals in a battle that they fought in space, and when Yahweh won, He made the mistake of exiling Satan to Earth, where he had to stay forever unless he could trick the Caucasian people to his side, in which event he would win with the help of his evil allies, the Jews.

I brought Susan to the Michigan rally with me because I wanted to prove to her (she had her doubts) that my new friends weren't a bunch of crazies. We were honored by being permitted to stay with Mr. and Mrs. Miles, and Susan was quite taken by him. We all were. He was such a kindly, gentle man, the stereotypical grandfather figure. When we met him, he had just spent six years in Marion Penitentiary after being convicted of conspiring to blow up school buses.

Even before the time of the Michigan rally, however, my fervor for the Klan, though not for racism, was declining. It was no longer satisfying my need for action. True, we'd pass out our literature, put our cards under doors, contact people whose names Duke forwarded to us from among those who responded to his various media performances. But that was it. The rallies were great, the cross burnings, the hoods and robes, the rhetoric, the sitting around with the old-timers listening to them reminisce. But I began to realize that it was only talk. I wanted to turn the whole country around, and where was I, I thought, but with a bunch of yappers who had no program.

Jack Martin had begun to feel the same way. He introduced me to a man named Alan, who was a member of the National Alliance. The NA wasn't just talk, Alan told us. It had a program. I was twenty-five years old. I was ready to become a Nazi.

5 | The Circle

It was on an evening in October 1983 that nine men met in a wooden building that had been constructed at the rear of Bob Mathews' property outside Metaline Falls. There the men formed a circle and greeted one another, right arms outstretched in the Nazi salute. As Bob spoke, the others repeated his words: "I, as a free Aryan man," each recited, "hereby swear an unrelenting oath upon the green graves of our sires, upon the children in the wombs of our wives, upon the throne of God almighty, sacred by his name, to join together in holy union with the brothers in this circle."

Upon completing the words, the men stood silent while a woman placed a baby boy on the floor in the center of the circle. She withdrew. Bob continued and they repeated: "From this moment, I have the sacred duty to do whatever is necessary to deliver our people from the Jew and bring total victory to the Aryan race."

Bob concluded the ceremony by saying for himself as their leader: "Let me bear witness to you, my brothers, that should an enemy agent hurt you, I will chase him to the ends of the earth and remove his head from his body."

The Order was born. Two weeks later, on October 28, Bob, accompanied by two of his followers, held up the World Wide Video Store in Spokane, Washington. Their take: $369. It was hardly an auspicious beginning for what would become the single most profitable crime spree in American history.

CHAPTER

6 | The Christian
Identity Cult

Each of the men who formed The Order's fatal circle were either members of or had connections with a religious cult known as
Christian Identity. I had heard of Identity when I was in the Klan,
but had little direct knowledge of it until I got to know Bob and his
confederates. The primary reason for my ignorance was geographic: I
was from a big Eastern city and Identity churches were for the most
part located in rural areas in the Mid- and Far West.

Different cults appeal to different people—Hare Krishna to some,
Christian Identity to others—but they all, I think, trade on the same
basic appeal: By accepting our Truth, they say, you prove yourself to
be a superior being—others may not be capable of understanding,
but you are. That can be a seductive invitation, and once you have
accepted it, you aren't likely to want to question any of the details of
the Truth that is now revealed to you, even those you might have
recognized as illogical or totally senseless before you joined the cult.

In the case of Christian Identity, it was founded in the late eighteenth century by a man who was a lunatic. His name was Richard
Brothers. On a certain date in 1795, Brothers prophesied that God

would come down from His throne in heaven and proclaim Brothers "prince of the Hebrews," because he was God's nephew. God, it turned out, doesn't practice nepotism, and He never got around to proclaiming Brothers anything, but that didn't stop the prophet or his followers. As the theology developed, its basic truth became that the Jews could not be the remnants of the Biblical nation of Israel. Rather, the Western Europeans (or, in some versions, the Anglo-Saxons alone— Brothers was English) held that singular honor. They were the true lost tribes, and some of them had trooped over to the New World, which was also the New Eden. Brothers' teaching, therefore, invested Aryans with the Biblical mantle of righteousness that the Jews had usurped with their claim of being the Chosen People.

For about a century, Christian Identity teaching was forgotten, only to be resurrected in California—where these kinds of things do tend to get resurrected—during the early days of the civil rights movement by an emotionally disturbed Methodist minister named Wesley Swift, who added some flourishes of his own to Brothers' doctrine. According to Swift, the Jews not only aren't the natural heirs to Israel but are, in actuality, the sons of Cain, who himself was the product of a love affair between Satan and Eve while Adam wasn't looking. Cain's children subsequently hied themselves off to the woods, where they mated with animals to produce the lowly non-white or "mud people."

After accomplishing that remarkable feat, the Jews went on (just as the Nazis put it) to bring about virtually all the evil the world has known, though for some reason they didn't really get their act together until the nineteenth century, when they came up with Marxism, went on to foster the American Civil War (the wrong side won) and every major war since, with the forces of darkness continuing to win, as with the Allied victory in World War II. When not busy being communists and international bankers (viciously plotting to do Midwest farmers out of their land), the Jews took time off to bring us the mortally dangerous "Dear Abby" column, the "Have a good day" greeting, which is a Jewish code signal to slaughter Aryans, and those strange check-out markings found on packages of food in the supermarket. The Jews' ultimate goal, however, was not to put the mark of Cain on Ivory soap, but rather to mongrelize the Aryan race out of existence, thereby depriving it of its New Eden.

This was being accomplished at the present time by encouraging interracial marriages and by "financing the blacks to take over most of our major cities," according to a Christian Identity "church" in Arkansas calling itself The Covenant, Sword and Arm of the Lord. Most of the CSA members were survivalists, who supported themselves on an encampment of several hundred acres by selling guns and offering a "Christian martial arts" course in urban warfare, even though they claimed their only goal was to live in peace in the wilderness. At its height, the CSA membership was probably less than a hundred.

A somewhat larger organization—with probably 200 congregants, though rarely more than fifteen or twenty attended any Sunday service—is the Church of Jesus Christ Christian in Hayden Lake, Idaho. It got its name from the belief that Christ was not a Jew but a "Christian," i.e., an Aryan descended from Abel rather than the Jew-breeding Cain.

Though there are several claimants, the generally recognized leader of the Identity movement is the Church of Jesus Christ Christian's pastor, Richard Girnt Butler. A self-styled minister, he is a retired aeronautical engineer who worked for the Lockheed Corporation, during which time he became a disciple of Swift. To learn what kind of person Butler is, look at his book shelf, where you will find the Bible and *Mein Kampf* placed next to each other. Or visit the classes that the children of the congregants are required to attend and hear them recite the pledge of allegiance in which they declare: "We are one Aryan nation under God."

Aryan Nations is the name Butler gave to the secular wing of his church. On his 20-acre property, surrounded by a six-foot-high barbed wire fence and patrolled by Doberman pinschers, military training goes on, the young men in their fatigues using posters of Menachem Begin for target practice. Constantly the recruits are exposed to pseudo-religious, survivalist rhetoric in which, for example, motorcycle gangs, such as the Hell's Angels, are revered as the new Apostles.

One of the main activities of the Christian Identity movement appears to be the accumulation of weapons. A few years ago in California, before Bob Mathews started The Order, two Identity members were caught with what was then the largest cache of illegal weapons ever seized in American history. (The stockpile was so huge the arresting officers had to use an airplane to photograph all of it.) They're ready to kill, too, or at least some of them are. It would be a Christian Identity member who in 1985 put out a contract on my life.

Nazis, American Style

At the 1981 National Alliance convention in Arlington, Virginia, a young man came hurrying up to me, declaring: "Hi! I'm Bob Mathews! Tom, I've heard a lot of good things about you, about your recruiting in Philadelphia." He was a little overweight in those days, his hair longish; he wore a goatee. His smile had delight in it, in himself and in you, and it remained with him in all of its charm from the first day I knew him until the last when so much else about him was gone.

Along with the smile came a way of speech that could have a hypnotic, soothing quality, the voice a sing-song tenor, yet one that could simultaneously manage to bubble with enthusiasm. He also wrote poetry—not very good poetry except that it had the same kind of driven eloquence as his speech, derived from the enthusiasm that colored and directed both the brightest and darkest sides of his life.

That first meeting with him, I got a taste of the eloquence, not on matters racial, but from his description to me of the natural beauties of the countryside around Metaline Falls.

Nearly three years later, when he was pressing me to join The Order, I visited Bob there and he wasn't wrong in his description. There was a sweeping grandeur to the mountains, just as he said, and the little valleys, the abundance of wildlife—we were driving one day and a big bear came lumbering casually across our path, quite a sight for a city boy like me—and the town of Metaline Falls itself was as if it had a troop of Dutch ladies who went about scouring it every morning; I'd never seen a place that clean.

(Cleanliness was a fetish with Bob. On the same occasion we saw the bear, he stopped the car on the mountainside and agitatedly got out. At first, I couldn't understand what he was upset about, but then he pointed to the cliff where I saw, partway down, a paper bag caught in the top of a tree; it had torn, causing the contents to litter the ground below. Bob raged at people who would throw trash out of their cars that way. I agreed with him, I thought it disgusting, too, but the extent of his fury took me aback. "I'd like to kill anybody who does things like that," he said.)

Standing a few feet from us as we talked was the man who led the National Alliance, Dr. William Pierce. At the moment his back was to us, as he conversed with an advertising agency executive from Chicago, an insurance company vice-president from the South, and a public school teacher from Ohio. All three men, like Pierce and Bob and me, were Nazis.

Pierce, who was in his mid-forties when I joined the NA in 1980— the same year Bob did—was an unprepossessing man physically, something I have found to be generally true among the six racist cult leaders I have met. Pierce was typical: moonlike face, bland expression, spectacles. He could easily have been taken for a bookkeeper, and while he was not exactly flabby—like the Aryan Nations' Butler—he did look as though he should get out from behind his desk and down to the gym to work out more often.

It was only when he spoke that the steel in him showed. He had a clipped, monotonal way of talking, like a drill being turned in your flesh, one slow revolution after another, his phrasing and his tone never admitting of doubt. That, I think, is an approach that all cult leaders seek. Any uncertainty they show, they realize, can lead to doubt and doubt to disbelief.

Pierce first entered the world of organized racism in the early 1960s.

He used the same portal of entry as did Bob and many others I met, the John Birch Society. At that time, the Georgia-born Pierce was an assistant professor of physics at Oregon State University, having received a Ph.D. from the University of Colorado a year or two earlier.

When he was about thirty, Pierce left college teaching to join George Lincoln Rockwell, whose National Socialist White People's Party, the pioneering neo-Nazi organization, had been founded in 1959. There, Pierce served as editor of Rockwell's quarterly, *National Socialist World*. Following Rockwell's assassination by one of his followers in 1967, Pierce stayed on for a while under the new leader, Matt Koehl, who started his career in anti-Semitism, just as Bob had, while a high school student.

After briefly operating a mail-order gun business in the late 1960s, Pierce had a falling-out with Koehl and, along with several of Rockwell's original founders, joined an organization then known as the National Youth Alliance, located near Rockwell's old headquarters in Arlington, Virginia. The NYA had its beginning as Youth for Wallace, formed during Alabama governor George Wallace's 1968 campaign for President. The behind-the-scenes power in the NYA was Willis Carto, head of the far right-wing, Washington, D.C.-based Liberty Lobby, publisher of an anti-Zionist magazine called *Spotlight* and also publisher of a book that teaches terrorist urban warfare tactics.

After wresting control of the group from Carto, Pierce briefly continued the policy of recruiting solely on campuses, often through the device of placing little ads in college newspapers. Somehow Bob saw one of those ads; that's how he came to the National Alliance, as it was now called. By that time, however, as my joining shows, Pierce was taking members wherever he could get them.

Those who responded to the ads received a copy of the *National Vanguard*. Like the paper Pierce had edited for Rockwell, the *Vanguard* was filled with long, dull articles of a pseudo-scholarly nature designed to prove Aryan superiority and the Zionist conspiracy. As Bob declared, they were "very intellectual."

More explicit expressions of Pierce's beliefs were found in the NA *Bulletin*, which, unlike the magazine, was distributed only to members. In the July 1980 issue, for instance, Pierce quoted one of his own speeches, in which he said in part: "Some may engage in individual activities, like the Pennsylvania sniper who dispatches inter-racial couples with his rifle. *We certainly don't want to discourage that last activity...*" (italics added). In 1983, a federal Court of Appeals rejected Pierce's efforts to obtain tax-exempt status for the National Alliance. In its decision, it noted that the NA "repetitively appeals for action, including violence...to injure persons who are members of named racial, religious, or ethnic groups."

Pierce's favorite word, one he used over and over again in those grinding speeches of his, was "cadre." To defeat the Jews, to defeat the conspiracy that attempted to hold "stout-hearted Aryan men" in thralldom, a chosen few was all that was necessary. With the right men, all would proceed in perfect "order"—another favorite word of his, and the name he gave to the conspiratorial group that overthrew "the System" in his novel, *The Turner Diaries*. Rigorously disciplined, absolutely obedient, perfectly indoctrinated, the cadre—or The Order—would make victory inevitable. That was the conception Bob Mathews adopted for his own when he created his Order.

The qualifications for cadre status, however, were never made clear. By the time I joined the National Alliance, the membership had taken on a hodgepodge quality. Although some of the aging Youth for Wallace types remained—among them doctors, lawyers, professors, engineers, chemists—I was not the only corner boy who had drifted in from the old cities of the North, along with our Southern cousins, good old boys who, like me, had tired of the Klan. Geographically, the Far West was heavily represented, particularly by young men like Bob, who lived in isolated areas. I sensed from some of them that they had joined the NA primarily out of boredom; they hoped it would give them something to do. More numerous, or at least it seemed that way—they made more noise—were the young rebels, often from well-to-do families, who joined the National Alliance in the 1980s just as they would have the Weathermen or similar leftist groups had they been born ten to twenty years earlier. To such youngsters Bob Mathews, as daring and charismatic as Pierce was not, would be perceived as a leader to emulate and follow.

I also appealed to these privileged young rebels. I was from the working class—rough-hewn, tough and street-wise—which made me a symbol to them of the underprivileged white world they had previously known only in their suburban fantasies, but which they were now determined to save from the blacks and Jews. One who seemed especially to admire me was the intellectually gifted Billy Soderquist, eight years my junior, who had probably been made fun of when he was a boy because of his chubby, baby-faced appearance; he joined the National Alliance when he was sixteen. Another of my admirers was Billy's best friend, the sweet-natured Richie Kemp, a six-foot-five star on his high school basketball team. One would later be described by the U.S. Justice Department as a "cold-blooded murderer" for The Order; the other was marked for death by it.

8 | What I Learned about the Jews

O n an evening in mid-November 1983, Bob Mathews and several of his followers prowled unmolested through the corridors of the Olympic Hotel in Seattle, Washington, searching for places to plant a series of small bombs. The devices were timed to detonate later that night when the Baron deRothschild was making a speech in the hotel ballroom. In Bob's mind, Rothschild was *the* Jew, the symbol of international banking controlled by the Zionist conspiracy. At the last minute, however, Bob called off the terrorist act, and the men sneaked out of the building. The reason he made that decision is unclear; his only later comment was that something hadn't felt right to him. Six months more would go by before The Order would claim its first victim, and he would be, not a baron, not even a Jew, but an Aryan, a believer in the teachings of Christian Identity.

One of the first actions Bob took when he organized The Order in October 1983 had been to write out an assassination list of the nation's enemies, almost all of whom were Jews. Henry Kissinger and

Norman Lear, the television producer, were at the top, along with Rothschild. The Jewish radio talk show host, Alan Berg, would not be added until the following spring.

No blacks made the list. This may have been because Bob's reservoir of hatred was entirely for Jews. (I have often wondered if he ever met one.) When he talked about them, a little bubble of saliva would form at the corner of his mouth, the dark eyes almost seeming to dance. Blacks, on the contrary, were for shrugs, the little sigh of superiority. They could be murdered later, perhaps by beheading as foretold by Dr. Pierce in *The Turner Diaries*.

The distinction Bob made also reflected an ideological one of the period. By the early 1980s, racists generally no longer regarded blacks as an organized threat to them, as they had been when Martin Luther King, Jr., was alive. That is, blacks were dangerous but principally as sex criminals—papers like the *Thunderbolt* regaled us in every issue with tales of huge black men raping white virgins. The perception had changed sufficiently that, by the time Bob formed The Order, racists were even welcoming certain blacks as allies, most notably the Muslim minister Louis Farrakhan, whose anti-Semitism matched their own.

I was more typical of the average white working-class American bigot. As I grew up I had almost no contact with Jews; they were of little concern to me. Indeed, as it happened, the few images I had of them from home were favorable. My mother occasionally spoke of the "nice" Jewish neighbors she'd had when she was a girl, and when I was about ten, both my brothers were working for Jewish merchants about whom they also spoke favorably. It was not that I hadn't been exposed to anti-Semitism in the neighborhood. I doubt if anyone from a background like mine could have avoided that. I knew Jews were sometimes called "kikes," that they were supposed to be cheap, that in some vague way they "ran things," but I did not see them as a threat to me.

Blacks were. They had tried to take over my school when I was in junior high, had offered to kill me when I went to one of theirs, were given favored treatment for the pitiful handful of jobs for which I, as a dropout (at their hands), was qualified. They were loafers, they were criminals, they were, that is, inferior.

It was because of my need to believe in black inferiority that I became an anti-Semite. The path I took, I think, is a common one—Bob's, through books, an unusual one—among those youths who join racist organizations or who are influenced by their propaganda.

In part because of my environment, but in a larger part because of my utter ignorance of American history, by the time I was twenty I had concluded that a terrible series of events had mysteriously overtaken our country. The drug culture had emerged to attack and destroy our children; divorce had become rampant, leading to the dissolution of the family, children again being the principal victims; American manufacturing, in ever greater numbers, was fleeing abroad, leaving honest white working men like me competing for fewer and fewer jobs. Simultaneously, the civil rights movement had furthered the plight of the white man by giving the violent and inferior blacks access to the few remaining traditionally white jobs.

These two sets of events—our social and economic dissolution on the one hand and the civil rights movement on the other—seemed to me obviously related, with the blacks somehow at fault for both. Yet how? My dilemma was a monumental one, for if the blacks had succeeded in becoming powerful and dangerous on their own, how could I continue to believe that they were inferior?

The only conclusion I could draw was that someone must have helped them. Quite apparently, the government had, but that wasn't a satisfactory answer, since it created an even more difficult puzzlement: Why would our government deliberately seek to weaken our country?

When I joined the Klan, I was told by both my new friends and its literature that international Zionism was somehow at the heart of all our problems. The message, however, was a diffused one, as it might not have been if I'd lived in the West and been exposed to Christian Identity's virulent anti-Semitism. With the Klan, on the contrary, the black problem was in the foreground, because its leaders recognized that those they were likely to attract, young men like me, felt economically threatened by blacks and so they pandered to those fears. The Jews, who did not compete for the same jobs we did, hovered only as a background menace.

In the National Alliance, the opposite was true. The hate focused nearly exclusively on the Jews. Blacks were merely creatures of the Jews. Thus, every activity in which I had seen blacks apparently playing a leadership role—from drugs to civil rights demonstrations—was actually orchestrated by the Jews or Zionists (the two terms were used interchangeably).

The Jewish or Zionist program—spearheaded in this country by the Anti-Defamation League of B'nai B'rith—had as its goal nothing less than to destroy the fabric of American white culture. (In racist lexicon, Jews are never considered to be white people.) The Jews would succeed, too, unless the one remaining remnant of patriotic Americans, the Aryan right wing, stood up to them. The Jews recognized this and were bending all their efforts to defeat the courageous but outnumbered Aryan warriors.

I never quite swallowed the whole of this ideological rigamarole. I didn't believe in any eventual pitched battle between the Jews and the Aryans as the National Alliance called for. As best I can recall, its idea of warfare always struck me as a fantasy, one I didn't want to have occur. I didn't believe in killing people. However, because the rest of the ideology told me what I wanted to hear, I accepted that wholeheartedly. It was good to know, I found, that I had been right all along in thinking the blacks inferior. I could now continue to look down on them—even hate them for their criminal and brutish behavior; I especially liked the "brutish" part—without treating them as an enemy worthy of my superior concern. For my true enemy I had a worthy foe, the endlessly crafty Jews.

From the National Alliance I even learned that, just as the Jews had gained control of the government to foster the destructive civil rights movement, just as they had gained control of the drug business, so had they infiltrated the legitimate business community. One of their most nefarious schemes had been to send American manufacture abroad in order to do whites out of their jobs. So that was how that happened! It was such an obvious explanation, I wondered why I hadn't thought of it myself. Perhaps it was because, as Dr. Pierce explained, the Jews had been able to cover up their plots by also gaining control of the media. (One of his leaflets, tens of thousands of which have been distributed, explains how that happened; it's called "Who Rules America?")

*　　*　　*

Bob Mathews was just a month away from beginning his war against the Jews when I next saw him at the September 1983 National Alliance convention in Arlington. During the two years since our first meeting, we had kept in touch, by letters, by Christmas cards, by exchange of various news clips from the racist press that proved the Zionist conspiracy. We were friends, but he was at one end of the country, I at the other, and I would not say we were close. Yet, in a way I could never quite define, I had the sense of being courted by him, that he admired me, valued me more than I did him, so that I wasn't surprised that, at the convention, it was he who sought me out.

He had trimmed down over the two years, the goatee shaven off, the hair now cut short. He seemed bursting with an energy that led him to grab at my sleeve, as if by so doing he could press his energy—his sense of self—into me. "I have to see you! Alone!" The voice rose. "It's very important!"

When we got to my room, he seemed, at first, more relaxed. He told me, in a by-the-way fashion, that he was planning to sign his property over to Pierce. That stunned me. I told him, "You'd be crazy to do that, Bob. What if he turns your wife and kid out, or decides to build a Goddamn army there?"

"An army?" he asked, and I sensed a moment's drawing-back, followed by a rush of words, barely connected, about the glory of the United States, how much he loved its green fields and its majestic mountains, how he worshipped the innocent and loving nature of its beleaguered white citizens who were being defiled by the Zionist conspiracy and its black lackeys. Then: "I'm not going to be alive for very long, Tom," he interrupted himself, gazing up at me in a sad and trusting way, as if I could make it not happen. "I've only a short time to go."

He began to sob. "Oh, Tom! Tom! All I've ever wanted is for my little boy, all our children, to grow up and be free." I put my arm around him. "We must save our land for them." I patted his shoulder. He kept crying.

By the time he left, I was shaken. I had never had a man break down like that in front of me. Bob, however, departed the room completely calm, quiet and thoughtful in his demeanor, and I was as startled by that almost as much as I had been by his weeping. It was as if he'd switched something on and then off, and once off, it was completely forgotten.

I followed him down to the convention floor. And there he was, transformed again, standing at the podium, bright of eye, the voice singing. His listeners, as if at a church revival meeting, swayed in their seats along with the rhythm of his words. "Revolution!" he cried. "We no longer talk! The time for war has come!" They rose, still swaying, clapping. I think that I, stunned, was the only one who didn't.

Three weeks later, he formed The Order.

The Revolution Begins

I next heard from Bob in early December, this time by letter. By then, the aborted attempt on the life of the Baron deRothschild was two weeks in the past—I'd not learn of it until the following summer—with Order members busying themselves at other tasks. Plans were underway to rob a bank, though the main activity, I now know, was taking place at the printing plant located at the Aryan Nations compound. What was being turned out there was not racist literature: It was $50 bills.

Bob's letter made not even the most indirect references to any of these activities, unless, in it, he was reflecting the uncertainty he felt about the likelihood of their success; the tone was somber, the mood despairing. When I showed it to Susan, her reaction was the same as mine had been when he wept in my hotel room: that he was planning to commit suicide.

In my concern, I phoned him. Much as his calmness had astonished me after his weeping, so now did the exuberance of his mood. He seemed amazed that I would have taken his letter "that way," but was delighted that it had caused me to call him. I had the impression he had only a vague recollection of its contents. "Do you still have the faith, buddy?" he asked, his voice perky, light. More insistent: "Do you?"

"Kind of," I responded, and went on to tell him about the money problems that had arisen with the house I'd just purchased. He was interested. He was sympathetic. He sounded worried that his good friend should be worried. I only later realized that he had immediately perceived how my financial difficulties could be useful to him.

On December 20 he called back. He had a surprise, he said, one he hoped would please me. He planned to drive to Philadelphia early in January and would like to visit me during his stay. His tone, if anything, was even more self-possessed than in the previous call, both confident and calm, the voice of a man who was at the top of his form and aware of it. As soon as I got off the phone, I began to plan how I'd take him around, show him the historic sights, the Liberty Bell, Independence Hall, the art museum steps that Rocky had run up in the movie. I'd show him a good time, I thought.

Less than a week before he was due for his visit, I had another call from him, this at 2 a.m. His tone was clipped, no how-are-you-and-Susan pleasantries this time: "Tom! You have the number for Dale Strange, don't you?" I said I did. "Okay, you call him, okay? Call him and tell him just this: 'The revolution has begun.'" Without a break, he spun on, voice speeding now: "Hell's bells, Tom! The government, they crashed a cross lighting of Bob Miles and Butler in California. Now we're at war."

The raid had occurred on the property of Frank Silva, an original member of The Order. Among the fourteen people arrested, in addition to Silva, was Randy Evans, also an Order member, Miles, and Butler, who had driven all the way down from Hayden Lake just to attend the fun. The charges were subsequently dismissed but, even so, the judge had made it onto Bob's growing assassination list after he described Bob's allies as "slimy, no-good, yellow-bellied scum."

I told him I'd do as he asked, and he rang off with the same abruptness that had marked the entire call. Perhaps I should have been excited to learn, at two in the morning, that a revolution had begun. I wasn't. I had heard that cry of wolf from my racist friends before. What did strike me, negatively, was that Bob would want me to call

Strange about it. He was a former deputy sheriff in Philadelphia who had gone off to the woods with a handful of followers after he had appointed himself an Identity minister. He and his troops strutted about in army fatigues, wore clerical collars, kept their hair long in ponytails. Each of them was expected (I think required) to have two wives.

Since Christian Identity in general and Strange in particular had never appealed to me, I decided, despite my promise, not to follow Bob's wishes. I figured he just didn't know the kind of person Strange was. I went back to sleep.

10 | The Drunkard and the Time Bomb

When I had told Bob my faith was at the "kind of" stage, I was speaking the truth, though not when I blamed my house problems for my loss of enthusiasm. I had quit the National Alliance shortly after the 1983 convention, was on my way out when Bob wept on my shoulder, as my warning against his giving his property to Pierce suggested.

For the better part of three years, my commitment to the NA had been a fervent one, the emotional rewards I received from membership more substantial than any I had gotten from the Klan. Had I been able to, I would have given my full time to its programs. As it was, at least once a month, Jack Martin and I journeyed to Arlington and spent the entire weekend at headquarters. At night we slept on the floor; during the day we policed the place, worked in the mail room, in the computer room, made sure the security system was in order, did whatever we were asked, sometimes under the direction of Mrs. Rosemary Rickey, a sweet grandmotherly lady who had been involved in the right wing all her life and who was Pierce's secretary. Other times, which were the best, Pierce was on hand and I had the opportunity to spend hours in the great man's company, listen to him pontificate, ask him reverential questions. (Jack frequently complained that Pierce liked me better than him, and I'd always deny that to Jack but it made me proud that he would say it, and secretly I knew it was true.)

Even at home, I was busy about my master's business. On the weekends that I wasn't at headquarters and on most weekday nights, I went door to door in Kensington and Olney selling the *Vanguard*. It's a pro-white paper, I told people, and almost invariably they responded that they approved of that, and perhaps even gave me a donation. My first full day of canvassing, I brought in $60. Each evening, when I got home from my tour, I'd sit for hours more in my kitchen stamping copies of the paper with the NA's local PO Box number. We obtained a newspaper dispenser and set it up at the corner of K&A, selling an average of twenty copies a month that way. Under my leadership, our cadre—there were only ten of us—soon was bringing in $150 a week. The major part of the total came from my efforts.

My work did not go unnoticed. Apparently I was one of the best fund-raisers in the country, because nearly every issue of the NA *Bulletin* mentioned my name, described the fine work I was doing, the money I was bringing in.

At NA conventions, Pierce asked me to hold workshops on recruiting techniques, and I did. My hotel room became the recreational center of the convention, twenty to thirty people crowding in at one time. It wasn't unusual for members I didn't know to introduce themselves to me as Bob had in order to tell me how they'd read about me: Glad to meet you, Tom, they'd say, what a privilege to meet you, Tom; and even at home, people from all over called me just to say hello. It was a heady experience: Anonymous corner boy becomes famous, and not just in this country but abroad, too, where the National Alliance had members who belonged to various underground Nazi groups. Everything was finally working out for me. Life was good.

I didn't bother to consider that fewer people came to an NA convention, about 150, than resided in a couple of blocks of Kensington— or that the dues-paying membership for the entire world was 700 tops.

My disillusionment with the NA began to creep up on me during the spring and summer of 1983, although the actual event that led to my quitting the NA seemed not only unrelated but in direct contradiction to the change occurring in my feelings.

That episode, the propelling one that drove me out of the NA, took place on a Saturday in July 1983. That day, Jack and I had attended an NA meeting in Bucks County. On our way home, we stopped for something to eat at a Roy Rogers restaurant in Horsham, a Philadelphia suburb. While we were sitting at our table, Jack used the word "nigger." A middle-aged white woman in the booth behind us overheard; whirling around, she gave us a tongue-lashing for using that kind of language. We shouted back at her that we had a right to talk any way we wanted in private; the woman, leaving her slender, blond-haired teenage daughter in the booth, went off to get the manager. As she disappeared, I said to Jack, "I'll throw her out of the Goddamn window if she doesn't shut up." Hearing that, the girl began to cry hysterically. At that moment the manager, a black woman, arrived at our booth, the mother in tow, and asked me what the trouble was. I felt embarrassed to have to tell her the word we used—"You know, it's like black, or Negro, except..."—and when I admitted to the word, the manager laughed as though she were amused. Jack and I got up, in something of a self-righteous huff, and left, not knowing she had already called the police. We had just driven off when we heard a siren behind us and found ourselves being motioned over to the curb. The officer wanted our addresses because of the "problem" at the restaurant. Jack and I looked at each other in amazement: Why, it was just as it said in the *Thunderbolt*, the time would come when a white man couldn't even use the word "nigger" in public without being harassed by the Jew-controlled constabulary. It was happening to us, right now. We were furious. We also ended up with a summons.

Justice may not move fast most places in the United States, but it does in Horsham, and within a week we were in front of a magistrate, listening to how I had threatened the woman, the daughter adding that I was drunk. I shouted, "She's a liar! She's a liar!" and the girl began to cry again in her fear of me. Jack and I were found guilty of issuing ethnic slurs and of disorderly conduct and fined $350 apiece.

The fine was a great deal of money for me, and almost immediately I contacted Dr. Pierce, assuming that he'd take care of it just as he had for our state organizer, Alan, when he was fined for beating up a Jew who had the nerve to complain about him putting up anti-Semitic posters. But Pierce was having none of it; not only did he refuse to pay the fines from the treasury, he wouldn't give us even a couple of dollars from his own pocket. At the convention in September, he made a speech declaring that the organization would be bankrupted if it came to the financial rescue of every member who got in trouble with the law.

Not everyone agreed with Pierce. During the convention, sympathizers, including Bob, came to the room Jack and I shared to give us donations. We recouped the entire cost of our fines that way.

By itself, my resentment at Pierce's treatment of me would not have been sufficient for me to leave the NA, or if it had, my response probably would have been to shift my allegiance to another Nazi organization, most likely Matt Koehl's. By then, however, that was no longer possible for me. Doubt had entered my mind, and because of it, I was taking my first tentative steps, very reluctantly, away from the ideology that had dominated my life and given me such satisfying emotional rewards.

As I see it now, for a cult to maintain its hold on its members, it must shut out from them, as much as it can, the exterior world. This is achieved in several ways. Primarily, members are encouraged to associate only with one another, since outsiders may bring with them ideas that challenge or contaminate the truth the cult teaches. Members are also assigned activities that both isolate them from the outside world and give them a feeling of accomplishment within the cult. The marches, the hoods and robes, the burning crosses, of the Ku Klux Klan have as their purpose not to convince outsiders of the verities of the racist cause but to provide the demonstrators with the fantasy that they themselves have power. Much the same purpose is behind the military training that goes on at the Aryan Nations, the Covenant, Sword and Arm of the Lord, and elsewhere. The purpose of the training is not actually to prepare the membership for war—the leaders know that way is organizational suicide—but rather to give the appearance of preparation, so that the members will continue to believe that the holy war—like the carrot in front of the donkey—is just one step away (less than that when an adherent like Bob Mathews comes along, who takes the rhetoric and the training seriously and tries to carry it to its murderously logical conclusion).

The military training also provokes camaraderie among the trainees, who see themselves as sharing in a great adventure the outside world knows nothing of. Racist literature serves the same isolating function. It, the members are encouraged to believe, is the only repository of the written Truth in a world in which dissemination of information is otherwise filled with lies under the control of the Jewish conspiracy. Bob, for instance, rarely read anything other than racist material, so that it became inevitable he would believe (from his sanctuary in Metaline Falls, where the worst crime anybody ever committed was stealing a chicken) that black men were assaulting white women every second of the day, under the direction of their Jewish masters. Out of the same desire to avoid the enemy's devious propaganda, Bob—and he was not the only one—refused to allow the Jew-controlled television into his house. He was especially worried that his little boy would be exposed to dreadful scenes of black and white children playing together on "Sesame Street."

I had traveled far along that path of belief and of exorcism of the outside world, but never all the way. I never stopped reading the regular newspapers, never stopped watching the news on TV, and the more I read and heard, the more difficult it became for me to believe, as an American, that Israel was our enemy. On the contrary, by the summer of 1983, I was becoming convinced, despite myself, that we needed Israel's alliance in the Middle East. Once I began thinking that way, I was on my way—not all the way, but on the way—to questioning all the anti-Zionist propaganda to which I had been exposed.

It was not, however, by any means, merely my intellectualizing about Israel and the Middle East that made me question the anti-Semitic teaching. Much more important, I found myself no longer able to deny—no matter how much I wanted to—the realities I was exposed to in my daily life.

During that summer I often visited friends in the northeast section of Philadelphia, which has a large Jewish population, and I found myself impressed, as I drove through their neighborhoods, by the nice clean row houses, the small, well-tended lawns—I'm not talking about rich people here—and I was forced to contrast their appearance with that of my own Aryan neighborhood. Was it a Jewish plot that *they* kept their section so nice and somehow made *us* keep ours so littered and filthy, or—and was this ever a revolutionary thought for me—wasn't it just possible it was our own wonderful Aryan fault, at least partly our fault, that we lived in a pigsty?

Then there was my job. For several years now I had been employed as a maintenance man at a public housing project in which three-quarters of the tenants were white. I couldn't close my eyes to what I was seeing there either. The blacks, in my racist literature, were criminals, dopers, welfare bums. But the whites in my project also committed crimes, did drugs, cheated on welfare. Not all of them certainly, but enough of them were involved, as I observed every day, in the same activities I had been taught proved blacks were an inferior race. If they were inferior, what did it say about us?

With that realization, I also began to re-think scenes from my childhood. Mine were different from those of Bob, of rich kids like Billy Soderquist, of protected middle-class types like Dr. Pierce, all those who saw the white people as a superior race. When I was a boy, it was common for me to walk into the living room of a friend's house and see him or his kid brother plunging a needle into his arm; and I thought of the times, hundreds of them, that I'd go by the vacant lots where twelve-year-olds—some even younger—inhaled glue; and all the pills I'd seen passed round (crack, meth, speed); and the fathers beating up the mothers, the booze, the whole besotted scene. That's what I had grown up with, and it had made me want to change the world. I had wanted to find somebody to stand up with me for this poor, uneducated white class, and only the racists seemed interested in doing that. Now, after my years in the KKK and the NA, I was becoming discouraged with the very people I wanted to help. I had banged away and banged away and they were still boozing and doping and beating, and I couldn't see that I had done one bit of good and neither, more to the point, had any of the racists who supposedly were speaking for us. All they brought to us were ideas about how superior we were, and yet how we'd become victims. Not our fault. Not my fault. That was their lie.

As my anti-Semitism began to peel away, and with it my faith in my own people, I remained, however, as much opposed to affirmative action, to busing, to interracial marriages as I had ever been; that is, my feelings about blacks had not changed, which, in part, explains my reaction to the incident in Horsham. However, despite that episode, for the most part, by 1983 my anti-black bias—my sense of what should be done about the advantages given them over us—no longer had the emotionally charged quality that had previously characterized it.

Jesse Jackson provides an example. I used to thrive on that man. I'd hear he was going to be on a televised interview show, and I'd make sure not to miss it, because it would give me the opportunity to scream at the set and at Susan: "Look at that nigger! Look at that agitator.... He's what's wrong with this country!" and on and on. And Susan would quietly watch me, never saying a word, so that even while I was doing it, I'd think: Who is this raving maniac she's married to, who never talked like this when we first knew each other? I was embarrassed, but I was in a feeding frenzy. Came the summer of 1983, however, when I'd hear that Jackson or someone like him was going to be on television, I'd just not watch. Purposely. A similar response extended to my racist papers. No longer did I devour them from front to back as soon as they arrived. Instead, I tossed them on the desk or put them in a drawer, and while I eventually read them, or parts of them, the compulsion to do so was no longer there.

The Horsham incident cannot, however, I think, be dismissed as but a sudden outburst of my anti-black feelings, or, looked at another way, as a moment of relapse during a period in which I was making strides, almost against my will, to free myself from the grip racism had on me. What it told me, rather, was that the grip—or its consequences—was lingering, if not now on the surface then just below it.

That I had threatened to throw the woman in the restaurant through the window horrified me. I hadn't meant, even as I said it, that I'd actually do it, but those words had come into my mind and out of my mouth. Although I might excuse the threat as an aberration brought about by a moment of anger, I could find no way to rationalize my actions toward the woman's daughter at the hearing. I couldn't imagine myself yelling at a teenage girl, calling her a liar, making her cry, much less doing it in a courtroom. Yet I had. I think I understand why now: By saying I was drunk, she was making an excuse for me—only someone who was drunk could possibly say what I had said, could believe what I believed—and her assessment of me so threatened me that I lost control. At the time, however, my reaction to my outbursts against both mother and daughter was in the form of a stunned fear of myself. I saw myself as having a time bomb ticking away in me that wouldn't take much to set off. It hadn't taken much.

After quitting the NA—I simply sent Pierce a letter telling him I was no longer interested; he probably assumed my leaving was due to his refusal to pay the fine—I also began canceling subscriptions to my racist papers, but not all of them. In that, I was like the glue sniffer who decides he is going to give it up while he has half a brain left but keeps just that little cache off to the side to which he can go when he really needs it.

I felt miserable.

I felt more miserable than I could ever remember feeling. I might no longer believe all, or even most, of the dogma I'd been taught, but because I'd done the thinking I had, there was a hole where once I had an existence full of meaning for me. In the NA, for the first time in my life, I had gained respect and with it friends, and the fact that I might not agree with them any longer on all the beliefs we had shared didn't mean I wouldn't miss them as friends. I had left voluntarily, but I felt as if I had been torn away and cast out, had become less than I had been. Adrift, I was afraid I was going to become just another guy sitting in his row house in Kensington, sucking beer and watching the Flyers on TV—and doing nothing. I'd become the kind of person I had fought to save. I wasn't going to be a castaway for very long, however, not with a friend like Bob Mathews.

11 | The Coming of Carlos

When Bob arrived in January, he brought with him into my house the sense of expectation that I had been lacking and that I had come to associate with him. His smile announced it but, perhaps more exactly, it was in the way he carried himself, sinuously, as though at any moment he were poised to leap—a graceful leap to some strange place.

Yet there was also about Bob, when he was at his best as he was during that visit, a sweetness in the sheer delight with which he responded to people, children as much or more than adults, so that two Bobs could always be present simultaneously: the one the big cat springing, the other the loving puppy dog wagging his tail. His long-time friend Ken Loff recognized that duality when, more than a year later, he spoke in bewilderment of how Bob could be so kind, so filled with gentle wonder about life, yet also have within him such hate and carry out the bloodthirsty crimes he did.

To my surprise, Bob did not come alone. The man he brought with him was a good deal older than us, somewhere in his mid-forties. Tall and slender, he walked hunched forward, and had a washed-out look to him, his hair blondish, his eyes a pale blue. His code name was Lone Wolf, his real name was David Lane. He was to play a brief but major role in my life.

Born in San Francisco of Swedish and Danish descent, Lane grew up in the Denver area and was twice married, once to his high school sweetheart, a cheerleader. For a while, he owned his own real estate firm, became a title researcher and then—in an apparent downward turn of fortune—went to work as a security guard for a small newspaper. In 1983, his racist beliefs well formulated, he met Bob and became a founding member of The Order. He brushed his teeth with soda water and salt because he believed that ZOG—which stood in racist shorthand for the Zionist Occupied Government of the United States—was putting chemicals in the drinking water to render Americans docile.

Lane called in to radio talk shows, including the one Alan Berg hosted in Denver, in order to propagandize his beliefs, and he liked to write about them as well. One article he called the "Bruders [sic] Schweigen Manual." ("Bruder Schweigen" is the correct German term for silent brotherhood.) In it, he gave forth with eighteen pages of advice for "Aryan warriors" intent on overthrowing ZOG.

About having children, he wrote: "It is recommended that no kinsman be put in combat situations, i.e., raise their sword against ZOG, until he has planted his seed in the belly of a woman. The same for kinswomen; if possible they should bear at least one warrior before putting their own life on the line." Warriors should also, Lane ordained, be always armed, because they never knew when they might meet the enemy: "That is the reason for your .308 caliber. You must stop and immediately disable any ZOG vehicle. Then, proceed to switch vehicles, safe houses, escape routes, or whatever.... Should a unit be inclined to raid the gold of ZOG, beware of exploding dyes...and radio beeps planted in money...." Aryan stalwarts were warned against drinking: "...booze lubricates the lips and every young warrior wishes to brag to the fair young damsels." The silent brothers were also to avoid: "Porno theatres and bookstores [which] are full of filth showing homosexuals and niggers doing vile acts with White women. A large bomb planted in one of these places not only creates an excellent diversion but it serves the will of our God." Then there was this little homily on ingratiating oneself with the enemy: "Until you can sit at a table or in a bar with a beautiful White woman and her nigger boyfriend or husband and convince them that you are over-flowing with brotherly love and affection, you are not yet a completed agent of the White underground. When with a reassuring smile, es-tablishment patter, and a friendly pat on the back, you are able to convince them to take you into their confidence, perhaps even invite you into their home, then you are in a position to engage in a little affirmative action of your own. Again, let your conscience be your guide."

The character Lane exhibited in his manual was not known to me when I first met him. My impression of him, both then and the two subsequent times we were together, was of a self-important person, humorless and dull. He did, however, appear genuinely to like chil-dren. My nine-year-old, Diane, seemed particularly to delight him: He called her his "little princess."

Lane, however, lacked the naturalness with children that Bob pos-sessed. Bob knew how to talk to them and responded to them unaf-fectedly. His favorite was my boy, three-year-old Tom, Jr., who was about the same age as Bob's own adopted son. In the months ahead, as images of violence increasingly occupied Bob's mind and his words, his references to my children became less frequent—save as symbols in his ideology—though when he expressed them they bespoke the same tenderness as they had during that January visit.

The evening of the first day of his visit, we decided to watch a movie on my VCR. Bob asked if I had a Clint Eastwood one. Racists, I've found, are great fans of Eastwood's vengeful cop stories. But I had another film, *Fighting Back,* which I thought he might like even bet-ter. Its plot concerns a storekeeper who forms a vigilante group that uses baseball bats to battle juvenile gang terrorism. One of the vil-lains is a black pimp, whom the hero kills by dropping a bomb from a roof into the pimp's car. Bob was fascinated by that. He asked me to rewind the movie to show that scene again, and then again. Alto-gether, he must have looked at it ten times, sitting cross-legged on the floor, eyes twinkling. He told me it was the best movie he had ever seen. "Tom, we're doing something about it, too," he went on, referring to the pimp and his white prostitutes. "We're ridding the world of sexual immorality. Seattle! You should see Seattle, Tom. We're hunting them down, this friend and I. White whores!" he added, shivering in distaste. "We're cleaning up Seattle. What the heck, it's a start, Tom."

Bob, I knew, constantly worried about female morals, even though he himself, by his own standards, acted immorally: He kept a mistress as well as a wife, and went to brothels. Women who wore tight clothes (he was constantly noticing them when I drove him around Philadelphia), or acted in other ways that made him lust after them, upset him in much the same way (and provoked the same tone of voice) as he had when he pointed out to me the bag of trash defiling the mountainside over Metaline Falls. I didn't ask him what he meant by hunting down—I think Susan came into the room at that point—and we never got back to the Seattle whores, then or later. I remember I assumed he meant that he and the friend assaulted the women, but it is also conceivable that something more serious was involved. During the period Bob was talking about, I later learned, a series of prostitute murders had occurred in Seattle. No one has ever been arrested for those crimes, and they ceased after Bob was no longer roaming in that area.

The following day Bob mentioned to me that he had gotten to know a shadowy figure named Louis Beam the previous July at an Aryan Nations conclave. From the way he spoke of him then and later—"He's the best leader we have in the right wing today, Tom"—it was apparent to me that Beam had become an influential figure in Bob's life. The extent of that influence was not entirely clear, although a chronology of events is suggestive: At the Aryan Nations meeting, the federal government subsequently charged, a secret planning session took place at which Bob was present, along with Beam, the Aryan Nations' Butler, James Ellison of the Covenant, Sword and Arm of the Lord (CSA), Reverend Robert Miles and possibly others. There a plot was allegedly launched to commit various acts of "war." As part of that scheme, the CSA is supposed to have participated in a synagogue bombing and an attempted sabotage of a natural gas pipeline during the fall of 1983, after which it faded out of activity, leaving the field to The Order. Whether any or all of that happened, I don't know. Bob never mentioned any such planning session to me, only his meeting with Beam. What is clear is that a month after conferring with Beam (and possibly others), he told me in my hotel room that he hadn't long to live, immediately followed by his speech to the National Alliance convention urging revolution and the formation of The Order.

Like Dr. Pierce, Beam is an inconsequential-looking man with dark greasy hair and moustache, his face scarred by acne. At times, he has advocated terrorist murder. In a book he wrote, *Essays of a Klansman*, he developed an assassination point system. Killing a police officer, for instance, was worth one-tenth of a point; a full point could be earned all at once, and with it "Aryan warrior" status, by murdering the President of the United States.

A Vietnam War veteran, Beam held the title of Grand Dragon of the Texas KKK the only time I met him in Louisiana at a Klan rally in the late 1970s. In more recent years, Beam's activities have been largely shrouded in mystery. He has the ability to drop out of sight for protracted periods—according to one report, frequently visiting contacts in Central and South America. In 1984, a year after Bob met him, he showed up as a self-styled "ambassador-at-large" for the Aryan Nations, for which, that same year, he set up a computerized "news" bulletin board, through which two death sentences were issued on the man both he and Bob considered the single most dangerous foe of racism in the United States: attorney Morris Dees.

Dees' life, unlike Beam's, is an American-as-apple-pie success story. A ruggedly handsome, blue-eyed, blond-haired man, now of middle years, with a soft Southern drawl, Dees got his start in business while still a teenager by operating a successful chicken farm. As a student at the University of Alabama, where he got his law degree, he published student directories to pay for his education and subsequently sold cookbooks and encyclopedias by mail order. His sale of the businesses to the *Los Angeles Times* in 1970 made him a millionaire if he wasn't one already. Since then he has been a chief fund-raiser for four Democratic candidates for President (George McGovern in 1972; Jimmy Carter in 1976; Edward Kennedy in 1980; Gary Hart in 1984) and, of great concern to the racists, director of the Southern Poverty Law Center in Montgomery, Alabama, which he founded in 1971, along with Joe Levin, Jr., a Montgomery lawyer, and Julian Bond, then a state senator from Georgia. The Law Center attempts to help poor people obtain their legal rights, but it is best known for its publication, *Klanwatch*, and the series of successful criminal and civil actions it has brought against racists. (Dees' first clash with Beam came in 1981 when Dees obtained a federal court injunction that halted the harassment of Vietnamese shrimp-fishers by Beam and his KKK ruffians.)

Dees' victories in his battles with the racists, however, may not be the only reason for the vehemence of their feelings against him. A psychological factor could also be involved. Their own leaders—the dark-haired Beam, the bookkeeperish Pierce, the flabby Butler—don't in any way fit the Aryan stereotype, any more than did Hitler. Dees, in every particular, does—he could have walked right out of a Nazi training film. Yet he, with his blond hair and blue eyes, advances against them relentlessly, scorning their superiority doctrines. In a reaction to him that may be as revelatory as it is pitiful, racist publications regularly claim that this ideal Aryan is a Jew.

The day following my showing of the movie *Fighting Back*, when we were alone except for the children, Bob took me by the arm and drew me over to a corner of the room. Glancing about as though he feared eavesdroppers, he said, barely above a whisper: "There is a man. There is a man I know named Carlos. I know him well."

"Is he Hispanic?" I asked, thinking Puerto Rican but hoping Spanish like me.

"No, no, he's an Aryan warrior, Tom," as if a Spaniard couldn't be, "and he wants me to do him a favor and I want you to do me a favor."

He paused and then, as though giving me the time of day, added: "This fella Carlos, he held up a bank and got us a lot of money."

I glanced over at my children. I didn't know what to say and finally settled on: "Wow."

Bob nodded soberly. "He's going to support our organizations, Tom," he went on. "You know, buddy, that's the problem we have, we have no money, our people, we're poor. We don't have the money to build. Look at all the leftists, all the Jews, they have all these big conglomerates, own all these big corporations. They support their causes. We need somebody with money, and this Carlos is taking a chance; that's why I'm here."

"He didn't hurt anybody, did he?"

Bob, quickly: "Oh, no, no, no, he wouldn't do that."

He glanced up to see if I was reassured.

"What favor?" I asked.

He smiled. "Well, that's what I came here for." And there was his little-boy-under-the-Christmas-tree smile.

He had brought a valise with him, which he now opened. I saw that it had thousands of dollars in it—tens and twenties, a few fifties, most of it wrapped in rubber bands.

As I learned later, the robbery occurred on December 20, the day Bob called me to say that he was coming to Philadelphia. The take was $25,952. The money had dye marks on it, produced by a time-delay bomb the bank had put in the bag before it was handed to Carlos. He or someone else apparently had tried to remove the dye, and some of the bills were smeary as a result, though others just had speck marks. As we both looked down at this odd-looking cash, Bob said rather wistfully, "Gee, I hope you can help me pass this money."

I backed away from it a little: "I don't know, man."

He considered that a moment. "If you help us, Tom, we'll help you, give you something out of it later."

There was a time that Bob never would have thought to offer me money for my help. He knew I did things for the cause, not for payment. But he had now listened, first during the December phone call and again since the beginning of his visit, to my tales of financial woe. The house, which I had bought shortly before I left the NA, had caused me one expensive problem after another. First the roof leaked, water seeping into the ceiling beams and rotting them. Then the toilet wouldn't flush, the pipes burst and the faucets stopped working. Because of the constant repair costs, our financial situation was becoming desperate, and I couldn't see any way out of it, at least not immediately, because of something else that had occurred: At work, a garage door had fallen on my foot, breaking it. My workmen's compensation check helped, but the injury meant I couldn't hold down a second job as I ordinarily would have, in order to get us over the financial crisis.

Giving me a sad and sympathetic look, he added only, "You *know*, Tom," as in, "You know, Tom, you could use it." Then: "But don't misunderstand me. We don't want you to pass the money, Tom. It's just that you know the city. All we want you to do, if you will, is drive me and Dave around. And, look, it's not as though we were going to be cheating anybody. It's good money." He riffled through a pack of the discolored bills. "You know, we go in a store, we buy a pack of cigarettes, change a ten that way. That's not hurting anybody, is it?"

I nodded. The way he put it, I could see that was true. And if he gave me some of it, well, I could always pay him back, couldn't I? And besides, I'd just be driving them around; if I didn't, they'd pass it anyway, so what I did didn't matter. Except that I knew it did: I knew I would be committing a crime by helping pass money I knew to be stolen, and I also knew I'd be helping Carlos, whoever he was, who went around robbing banks for a cause I was now doubting.

All that went through my mind even as Bob was trying to convince me, but none of it, I think, had more than a marginal bearing on my decision. That had been made, although I hadn't realized it, as soon as he asked me, and was related to the reason I'd not told him I was questioning our supposedly shared beliefs. The closest I'd come was my "kind of" to his keeping-the-faith question in our December 20 conversation, a reply to which he never returned. (Bob always avoided asking questions that might produce answers he didn't want to hear.) As I stood on my wrecked foot in my wrecked house with my life going nowhere, and Bob stood before me bright with life and danger, I felt important again, pleased and proud that he would come all this way because he needed my help.

I had taken a big step away from the corner to which I was heading when I challenged my anti-Semitic beliefs. But I had found nothing to replace them. Now I had: Bob Mathews.

Off we went, the three of us, to pass the money. Soon, I didn't stay in the car. Into the stores I went on my crutches, the one person likely to be remembered if anyone got suspicious and called the police. But nobody did. We were able to pass even the worst-looking bills. We told the few shopkeepers who asked that the money had been left in a pair of wranglers and gotten smeared when they were washed. I was even able to change several hundred dollars in a bank using that story. Apparently putting dye bombs in bags of stolen money isn't as effective as the folks who dreamed it up think it is. I had never done anything so easy as passing that money. For five days we did it. Never did get to those steps Rocky climbed at the art museum.

12 | The New Eden

The Order's second bank robbery (several others had been planned but not carried out) occurred in Spokane on January 30, 1984, three weeks after Bob's visit. The proceeds were a disappointing $3,600. The Order's criminal income, at that point, was still under $30,000.

·Bad news had also arrived from another front. The counterfeit $50 bills that had been churned out at the Aryan Nations printing plant proved to be of such poor quality that the chief of the operation, Bruce Pierce (no relation to Dr. Pierce), had been arrested when he attempted to pass them. Pierce skipped bail and was now a fugitive.

Bob was about to come up with a more immediately profitable way of raising money than bank robberies or counterfeit bills. He conceived the idea during his second visit to me, in February. It was to produce $4 million over the next several months.

He arrived on Valentine's Day evening—no advance notice, just a knock at the door, and there he was, grinning: "Hell's bells, buddy, good to see you. How's your foot?"

While Susan was putting the children to bed, he took me by the arm and led me to the kitchen, sitting me down at the table across from him as though he were the host. Giving the table a single vigorous rap with his fist, he said, "Damn, Tom, but you know I think the world of you." ("Damn" was about as strong as Bob's language ever got.) "You're a man, you're a man who's respected in the movement, and that's because everybody knows you're the kind of guy who can always be relied on to keep confidences." He went on in that flattering vein for another minute or two, informing me of my many other virtues. I think I preened a bit. Leaning back on his chair, he paused as if changing the subject: "And, hey, there's something I want to talk to you about. It may come as a surprise to you, Tom. You remember that man Carlos, the one I told you about?"

"Yeah," I said uneasily, wishing he had chosen another subject. "How's he doing anyway?"

"Oh, fine, Tom. He's doing just fine. By the way, fella, you know who Carlos is?"

I shrugged my shoulders. "No. How would I know?" I asked.

He paused, lips pursed, holding it back for one more delicious moment: "I'm Carlos."

I stared at him. He's Carlos. He robs banks. For the first time, it occurred to me that the name Carlos was familiar. It should have been. Bob had adopted it in emulation of Carlos Sanchez, the terrorist who had murdered the Israelis at the Munich Olympics.

He smiled, pleased as punch at my reaction; I must have looked stupefied. "Weren't you scared?" I was surprised to hear myself ask, as though it were a matter of grave concern, the only one.

He replied airily: "Oh, no. Yahweh was with me," using Reverend Miles' word for God. "Right after I walked out of the bank, the clouds opened, Tom, and the snow came down. My tracks were hidden. Immediately. It was a miracle, Tom!"

He was at his ease now—and why not? I hadn't picked up the phone to call the police, had I?—the charm on full throttle, as he began to weave for me the dream of a future he wanted me to believe in, not the revolutionary slaughter that occupied his dreams. (In all the time I knew him, aside from the night he asked me to call Dale Strange, I never heard him use the word "revolution." When eventually he began to speak more frankly to me about his plans, it was "war" he talked about.) "Look where you live," he began sadly. "Look at the filthy streets, this city, the filth, the graffiti, the corruption; raising kids here? And here you are, Tom, a hard-working white man cleaning streets, a white man cleaning streets, and they don't even care if you get your checks on time."

The tone was sympathetic, the aim unerring. There was much I didn't like about my job at the public housing project where I worked, but the part I hated most was sweeping the sidewalks. I felt demeaned by that, and for exactly the reason he said. But it was his comment about my checks that struck home the sharpest. Since my accident, as I'd told him, my workmen's compensation payments never came regularly, often three weeks between one and the next. At times, that had put me in the humiliating position of having to beg my creditors for extra time to pay. As upsetting as that was, far more galling to me was the attitude of the bureaucrats to whom I complained. Their indifference sent me the same message that living under the roar of the El all my life had: I was too unimportant a person to bother seeing to it that I got my money on time. "It sucks," I said.

"So why don't you do something about it?" he asked mildly. "Why stay? Why stay?" Sing-song, voice rising: "Oh, I'd love you, I'd love you to come out to live where I live." He launched into another of his descriptions of Metaline Falls, how you didn't have to lock your door at night and how, getting up in the morning, you were greeted by the grand mountains, the green trees, the blue lakes, the glance of the shy deer. The softness of his words, the sweet medley of their images, cocooned me. "Yes, yes, I would move out with you," I said. "The city, you're right, this city is no place for a white man to raise his children," I said.

Bob didn't reply. Patiently he waited for me to convince myself. But I didn't need more time; I'd had enough of time and the failures it had brought me. I looked up from my callused hands, folded on my lap, looked over to him. "Oh, I'm sick to my heart of it here," I said.

To that, he nodded somberly. Rising, he went to the window as if to judge for himself the nature of the city I had just so righteously rejected. Then, turning back to me with the most gentle of smiles, he proceeded to weave a bit more of the tapestry he had planned for my enjoyment and in which he intended to enfold me. "What we will do, Tom, this is what we will do, and you can be a part of it—now this is the opportunity of your lifetime, Tom—we are going to build our community there. We'll have our own businesses. Franchises. A Seven Eleven store. Maybe you'll manage it. We'll live off those businesses, yes, but what we'll be doing, Tom, we'll be living in peace amidst people like us, only people like us, who feel like we do. It's as Bob Miles says, we'll be the family of families."

To bring the dream about, however, he explained, was going to require money. A great deal more money, he said regretfully, than could be raised by bank robberies: "Taking ZOG's money is only a means to an end."

He had seated himself again and now was leaning forward, coiled with purpose: "I'm going to lay some heavy stuff on you now, buddy. To raise that money, to buy all the property, what we are going to do is get into counterfeiting. We've been thinking about trying that, my friends and me—you'll like them, Tom—and we're in luck. We have this man in our movement, name of Robert Merki. He's a good printer, an expert, and the money we're getting from the bank robberies, all of that is going in to buying paper and plates. That kind of thing is expensive. But once we get the counterfeiting going..." He held his hands out palms up, inviting me to imagine the cash that would fill them. "And that'll be the end of it, Tom. I promise. Once we get the money we need to buy the businesses, no more crimes after that. We won't have to do anything like that again. We'll be free men. Free from the Jews, from the blacks; we'll have the good clean air of Metaline Falls. Ours!"

That was the design of his tapestry, a New Eden. Thinking of the bureaucrats ignoring me, thinking of all the streets I'd swept, having never swept any dirt away in my whole life, I felt for New Eden a hunger akin to that I'd had in the past for my racist literature. New Eden would be good.

Bob Mathews knew his man.

When our conversation ended that evening, much had been left unclear in my mind about what was expected of me. For the most part, it seemed he wanted to welcome me as a member of New Eden solely because he "respected" me as a friend and for the abilities I had shown as a fund-raiser for the NA. At one point, however, he told me it was just possible a time might come when he might need my "help" on some aspect or the other of the counterfeit operation. He was sure he could count on me for that. I agreed. As I did, I don't believe going to New Eden was the decisive factor in my mind, though it was important. Rather—if anything, less worthily—I couldn't not agree: I wouldn't be a man in Bob's eyes, or my own, if I refused.

But I had my compunctions. I meant them, and I also needed them for my conscience. "Now, look, man," I said, "I can't go with this, Bob, if it means violence. I mean, I don't want anything to do with people getting hurt."

His answer, which I only later realized didn't respond to my objection, was: "Hey, hey, Tom, I respect your beliefs, buddy. You know I wouldn't ask you to hold up a bank or anything like that. You know that. I'd never want anybody to do anything he thinks is wrong."

The next day, however, he did go to the doctor with me and asked him questions about when I'd be able to have normal use of my foot. I put it down, at the time, to his genuine interest in my welfare.

That afternoon we went to an Acme to buy groceries for dinner. He insisted on paying, remarking that he had a $50 bill he wanted to change, left over from the bank robbery. As we were leaving the checkout counter, an armored-car guard came in. From a vault, the manager handed him sacks filled with money. We followed him outside, watching as he rolled a shopping cart loaded with the money to his truck. "Do you know how easy that would be?" Bob whispered to me. "Do you know how *easy* that would be?"

CHAPTER

13 | Mrs. God

The early afternoon of March 16, 1984: A Continental Armored Transport van is parked in front of a store in a Seattle shopping mall. A guard emerges from the store pushing a shopping cart loaded with bags filled with cash. Bob Mathews, who has been standing six feet away pretending to read a magazine, moves to intercept the guard. He gives the man a cheerful smile as he draws his gun and levels it at him.

Crouching by the door of the store is lanky, mustachioed Bruce Pierce, who, drawing his weapon, now comes forward and disarms the guard. A blue Chrysler, followed by a white Ford van, comes speeding into the lot, screeching to a halt by the armored truck. Five men, wearing stocking caps, pile out of the cars, grab the bags full of money and load them into their vehicles. With a farewell wave to the guard, Bob, followed by Pierce, gets into the Chrysler. The two cars drive off. The entire operation has taken less than two minutes. The Order is $43,000 richer.

It was, just as Bob thought it would be at the Acme, as easy as it looked.

*   *   *

When he left in February, Bob gave me $500, my share from the money passing in January, which I used to put a new roof on my house. He also left me $1,200 of the dyed money, and over the next several days I passed it with no more trouble than on the previous occasion. I mailed him the proceeds.

As I hobbled along from store to store, I did not have any sense that I was committing a crime. Not only was I not doing anyone any harm as I saw it from Bob's explanation in January, but, more positively, thanks to the New Eden pep talk in February, I could now perceive my actions as being an investment in my family's future.

That's how I explained it to Susan. She had noticed the proliferation around the house of little bags filled with candy, gum and the like that I had purchased in order to exchange the bills, and when she confronted me, I told her what I was doing and why. She was horrified. "Tom, you mustn't! You mustn't...that man...that man, he's going to ruin you. You must get away from him."

How dare she talk about my friend that way? "He's trying to help us." She stared at me. I pointed my finger at her: "I'm not doing it for me, or for him. I'm doing it for you. And the children." When that failed to mollify her, I reminded her she'd told me that Diane was beginning to have behavioral problems at school; a child who had always been quiet and gentle was now having moments when she screamed at—occasionally hit—other children. "You want her to keep going to these lousy schools? They're the trouble." I was beginning to shout now. "We do what Bob says, and we'll be free of them, free of this lousy life we're leading. Diane'll be fine then."

She looked at me disbelievingly—I knew her looks by now, no matter how mild—as if, for some reason, she thought I was responsible for Diane's problem. She shook her head sadly, gently put her hand on my wrist and murmured, "Oh, Tom." I drew my hand back, really furious now. "It's none of your business anyway!" I stared after her as she walked away. I'll make the decisions around here, I fumed; that's what women have husbands for, isn't it?

*   *   *

Once Bob had succeeded in getting me to accept the necessity of robbery and counterfeiting for the sake of our peaceful future, he felt free to ask me to take the next step. It seemed innocuous enough. During one of his calls, he asked if I'd install a separate phone with a message machine, for which he would pay. I agreed. The machine, it turned out, was rarely used. Virtually every call relating to Bob's affairs came in on my own line, and all but a few of them were from the same person saying the same words: "This is Mr. Closet. Everything's okay," which information I would duly relay to Bob when he phoned. During one of those conversations, he referred, for the first time, to his "friends" as The Order, though he didn't explain the derivation of the term or tell me who belonged, so that the only members I was aware of then were Merki the counterfeiter, David Lane, and, I assumed, the repetitious Mr. Closet.

Mr. Closet, whom I was soon to meet, was a twenty-four-year-old Floridian named Andy Barnhill. His code name was derived from his frequent assertion that the proper way to treat women was to keep them locked in a closet when they weren't needed. Every Order member, Bob later explained to me, received at least one code name, and most also used one or more aliases. The alias record holder was Bob's chief lieutenant, Bruce Pierce, who had preceded Merki as the chief counterfeiter. A saturnine-looking man with cold and empty eyes, Pierce had two code names, "Brigham" and "Logan," and used, at one time or another, seventeen aliases: Brigham Young, William Allen Rogers, Will K. Rogers, Bill Rogers, Scott Adam Walker, Roger Martin, Roger J. Morton, Michael Schmidt, Mike Schmidt, Joseph Shelby, Charles Lee Austin, Lyle Dean Nash, Larry Martin, Mike Williams, Floyd Shaw, Richard Paulson and Patrick Larouche, the last apparently in honor of another right wing leader, Lyndon LaRouche.

For each of their aliases, Order members were provided with false identification papers, printed by Robert Merki, a balding man in his fifties who, like the Aryan Nations' Butler, was an aircraft engineer, but who had been living a life of crime for some years before joining with Bob.

The Order code names could be descriptive of the person's appearance—sometimes cruelly so, as in "Legs" for the bow-legged George

Zaengle, "Beanstalk" for Jackie Lee Norton and "Cripple" for Billy Soderquist, because he walked with a limp following an operation. More rarely they referred to an occupation ("Smith" for a locksmith) or a psychological quirk, as with Barnhill's "Mr. Closet." (His desire to keep women locked up struck even this crew as odd.) Frequently the code names had a Biblical or religious connotation: Richard Scutari, another of Bob's lieutenants, was "Joshua," although, more often, he was simply "Mr. Black." Randy Duey, with his little Hitler moustache, was "Luke," "Calvin" served for Randall Evans, and, as with Joshua, from the Old Testament, "Noah" for Merki. His wife, Sharon, who became as deeply involved as her husband in The Order's crimes, was sometimes known as "Mother Goose" but usually as "Mother God" or "Mrs. God." Noah and Mrs. God had a son whose code name was "Jesus."

Code names and aliases were not the only subterfuges employed by Order members. Bob once said: "You can hide out right in this country. We've got plastic surgeons; they'll re-do your fingers; they'll take your face and change it; you can get a hair transplant, a nose job. We have the finances to do it."

More conventional disguises—wigs, false moustaches—were also used, although Mrs. God's husband was a bit different: He specialized in female impersonation. An informant once recalled: "...Noah was telling us...that he used extensively female disguises, that most of the time when he did something, he regresses to female. He said he has even gotten picked up as a female and let go as a female, and he said it's the best disguise. He told us, he said, 'I'm a master in identification, forgery and disguises.... I teach classes in this.'"

And above them all, above Brigham Young, above Mr. Closet, above Noah, even above Mother God, reigned Carlos. He and his subjects were about to become very rich. Some of them were also about to become murderers.

14 | A Message to Miller

On the evening of April 22, a bomb planted by The Order as a diversionary tactic exploded inside a porno movie house in Seattle. Luckily, no one was killed. The following day, as police squads guarded the cordoned-off area near the theater, in the nearby Northgate shopping mall, two men were peacefully washing windows. Not far from them was parked a Continental armored truck, behind it a car containing two men. While the window washers continued at their task, a white Ford van drew to a halt across the street.

Through the mirror the windows made, the two washermen could see, directly across from them, The Bon, a department store that was one of the principal shops on the mall. When a guard carrying a bag of cash came out of The Bon, the men laid down their brushes and fell into step behind him as he passed. The taller of the two washermen, Bruce Pierce, took a handgun from his waistband. As he did so, a tall athletic-looking young man, probably Richie Kemp, stepped out of the white Ford. He was holding a hand-lettered sign, which he held up for the guard in the truck to see. It read: GET OUT OR YOU DIE.

As the athletic young man made his approach, the door on the driver's side of the Ford opened. Bob Mathews leaped out and ran over to the armored truck, a few feet from where Pierce was relieving the guard of his monetary burden. Bob pointed his rifle at the head of the guard in the truck; by that time, the second window washer, Randy Duey, had arrived at the other side of the truck and was shoving his weapon through its porthole. The guard raised his hands in surrender. Bob demanded the key to the back of the truck; he tossed it to one of the two men who had, until now, been sitting in the car behind the truck. Once inside the truck, they began to toss bags filled with money and checks to their confederates. Their mission completed, they dashed back to their car, as other members of the gang piled the bags into the white Ford van. Both cars roared off. The entire robbery had taken two minutes. The Order had enriched itself by $340,000 in cash; another $160,000 in checks was discarded.

I knew nothing of the Northgate robbery when, the following evening, Bob called to ask if I would do him a favor. He was anxious, he said, to set up a meeting between a North Carolina man named Glenn Miller and several Order members who were presently heading toward Philadelphia. I had heard of Miller but had never met him, and I told Bob that. "I understand, Tom," he said, "but all I want you to do is call Reverend Miles in Michigan—he knows Miller—and ask him to tell Miller it is okay to meet with my men."

The request didn't surprise me. In the far right wing, it is considered prudent to have a trusted person, such as Miles was, act as an intermediary when members of one group are seeking an initial contact with another, so that the party being approached can be confident he is not being set up by the FBI. As I now know, Bob at that time already knew Miles, and could have made the call himself; by asking me to do it, he was seeking to involve me further in his enterprises. I phoned Miles, who said he'd get in touch with Miller.

Glenn Miller had by then become a prominent figure in racist circles. Lean, sallow complected, with narrow-set eyes, a Vietnam War veteran, he had, during the 1970s, headed a tiny band called the North Carolina Nazi Party. In 1980 he transformed it into the North Carolina Knights of the Ku Klux Klan, giving as his reason: "That swastika turns too many people off." Apparently, wearing sheets had the same effect, because just a few years later a second transformation took place; his organization's newest name: the White Patriot Party. The members wore camouflage fatigues, berets and black boots and were expected always to be armed. Miller has claimed 5,000 members. A more likely figure is 200, but even at that, by 1984 his was one of the largest armed racist groups in the country, bigger than the survivalist Covenant, Sword and Arm of the Lord in Arkansas and probably bigger than the Aryan Nations.

Bob's two emissaries to Miller, Andy "Mr. Closet" Barnhill and Denver Daw Parmenter II, arrived a day or two after I had made the arrangements with Miles. They spent the evening at my house.

Barnhill, whose boyish features bore a strong resemblance to Bob's, carried a .45-caliber pistol, which he enjoyed brandishing about. Fearing that it might go off accidentally, I offered him a place where it could be safely locked away, but he refused to let it out of his sight. "No, brother," he informed me, "never. This is for wasting feds." He was, he also advised me, a man of great religious piety, a devout follower of Christian Identity teaching, which meant, among other things, that he kept kosher as strictly as the most Orthodox Jew. When Susan made the dire mistake of serving meat and milk at the barbeque supper she made for us, he was shocked and gave us a stern lecture about the necessity of keeping the sacred temples of our bodies pure by adhering to the dietary laws.

Considerably less obnoxious as a house guest—all he did was drink—was Parmenter, a lean and sad-eyed man in his thirties. I kept him content that evening by letting him watch the 1914 silent movie, *Birth of a Nation*, on my VCR. Probably the single most racist film ever made in this country, *Birth of a Nation* played a major recruiting role for the Ku Klux Klan, helping to swell its ranks—in the early 1920s—to an all-time high of 4 to 5 million members. By the 1980s that number had declined to about 6,000.

While Parmenter was watching the movie, Barnhill regaled me with an account of his heroics in the Northgate robbery. As he discoursed on those joys, he was stretched out on a bed smiling at how handsome he was as he pointed his gun at the self he saw in the mirror across the room.

"I don't want to hear any of that stuff," I told him to no avail. It was one thing to know from Bob that robberies were necessary to make the New Eden possible; hearing about them in bragging detail from this gun-toting kid had a frightening and chilling effect on me. My only wish, at that moment, was to pass on to him and Parmenter the arrangements for meeting Miller that Miles had relayed to me and get them out of the house.

Barnhill had with him a suitcase containing about $19,000 of the $20,000 which, he said, he was given as his share of the Northgate proceeds. As he riffled lovingly through the bills, he expressed contempt for Parmenter: "He's already spent all but a couple thou of his twenty grand," he informed me, in what I guess he assumed was gangster talk. "Drinking and carousing," he added a moment later in a deploring tone, shaking his head over Parmenter's immorality.

The following day they were on their way to North Carolina to meet Miller. Barnhill subsequently told me that the purpose of the meeting was not merely to establish a meeting of minds with Miller but also to hand him a $1,000 donation.

In doing that, Bob would have had in mind that it was possible, perhaps even probable, that Miller, like so many other right-wing fanatics who went around posturing with guns, would be all talk and no action. Nevertheless, considering his current cash flow, investing such a small sum in Miller was worth it in the event he was the genuine article—the genuine article who, if rumors were correct, might also have guns for sale.

A thousand for Miller, $20,000 for Barnhill and Parmenter, $500 for me, these were Bob's investments. I don't know Miller's background, but in the case of Barnhill, Parmenter, and me, they were also investments in men who had never been involved in crime before Bob got hold of them, and to whom the thought would never have occurred to hold up banks or train guns on armored trucks or even pass stolen money. In one way, it was easy for Bob to convince us to follow him. Like him, we were idealists who could, as Lane put it in his "Bruders Schweigen Manual," believe that by taking up arms against ZOG, we were committing an act of patriotism, not one of crime. Bob counted on those beliefs to get us to do his bidding. But he also knew about money and what it would feel like when he put it in our hands. He was a natural leader; he knew how to buy people.

By then, he was also learning how to kill people; he got others to do that, too.

PART II | Cornered

15 | Alan Berg and the Chubby Woman

She arrived in Denver early in June 1984, a nice-looking little woman with a sweet, maternal smile—one could imagine her baking brownies for the church social—a lady who might be just a bit worried about her weight. Pleasingly plump, she'd be reassured, but perhaps worried about her looks, too, now that she had reached her fiftieth year.

Inconspicuously dressed, hardly noticeable among all the other middle-aged women going about their shopping, she did have one peculiar habit. During the several weeks she spent in Denver, she never strayed far from the building that housed the studios of radio station KOA. Her pattern, indeed, varied only when she noticed its star performer leaving. Him she followed. Had anyone thought to ask her, she might have declared, with an embarrassed smile at revealing she was so smitten: "Oh, I just love him! I'm one of his biggest fans!"

The man who was the object of her attentions was also fifty years old, and as memorable in appearance as she was nondescript. Tall, very thin, he wore his gray hair in a mop that flopped down over his forehead, a gray beard to match, and eyes, amazing eyes, that managed to look amused and angry at the same time.

His name was Alan Berg. In the years before he came to Denver, he had been a criminal defense attorney in Chicago, one of his clients the controversial comedian, Lenny Bruce. At one time, he wrote routines for another comic, Jackie Mason.

Despite representing Bruce and a number of organized crime fringe figures in Chicago, Berg found success as a lawyer elusive, perhaps because he was an alcoholic, perhaps because of his violent temper. In 1966, along with his wife, Judee, he left Chicago for Denver, where he had attended law school. Soon after his arrival, he began treatment for his alcoholism—he never took another drink in his life but substituted for that by smoking up to six packs of cigarettes and drinking more than forty cups of coffee a day—and eventually went into the retail business, opening a custom-made shirt shop. Following the breakup of his marriage to Judee, with whom he remained friendly, he entered into a series of relationships with beautiful and expensive-looking women.

The event that changed his life and led to his death occurred in 1971, when a friend who had a radio talk show invited him on as a guest. Berg's rip-roaring sense of humor, his ability to leap into one controversial subject after another, caused the phones at the station to light up. Soon after, he was hired to host his own show, and was on his way to becoming one of those men-you-love-to-hate personalities who turn up all over the country on radio, occasionally on TV. The format is simple: The host has an opinion on anything and everything, never expresses a doubt, is witty, sarcastic, insults callers who disagree with him and hangs up on them. As Berg once put it: "I stick it to 'em. Hopefully, my legal training will prevent me from saying the one thing that will kill me."

After several changes of employers, Berg had taken his "Rant and Rave" show, as the *Denver Post* called it, to KOA, which had been in a ratings decline until he arrived. His targets were many, but he seemed to take especial delight in excoriating anti-Semites.

His attacks could be effective, too. In June 1983 he had as a guest on his show Roderick Elliott, the publisher of the *Primrose and Cattleman's Gazette*, a newspaper of sorts that Berg charged was biased against Jews. Following the broadcast, advertising dropped off at the newspaper to the extent that Elliott had to fire eight of his nine employees, one of whom was his security guard, David Lane. When the paper failed, Elliott sued Berg and KOA for millions; the charges were dismissed.

Much closer to Bob Mathews' rising interest in Berg was a subsequent broadcast in February 1984, in which Berg took on Pete Peters, pastor of an Identity church in Laporte, Colorado, where Bob and Lane both had attended services. Whenever Lane made one of his periodic call-ins to Berg's show, his fellow workers were likely to ridicule him the next day, telling him how stupid Berg had made him look.

The chubby woman's interest in Berg seemed to cease on Monday, June 18. That day, she met with four men, and may have turned over to them notes she had been taking. They took over her watchful duties.

By then Berg was holding down the coveted 9 a.m. to 1 p.m. slot on KOA, ratings ever rising. The previous weekend Pope John Paul II had issued a statement declaring it sinful for people to have sex purely for pleasure. That gave Berg his topic for the day. "Since the Pope has denounced sex for pleasure," he began, "can you figure any way as a man you could have sex without pleasure?" It was a great beginning for a typically hot, if not necessarily informative, Berg show.

When the program was over, he taped a commercial for the American Cancer Society, discussed with his producer the subject of the next day's program—gun control; he favored it—then went on to meetings with several advertisers. The four men followed him.

They were also present at 6 p.m., parked in their car outside the restaurant where Berg had met his ex-wife, Judee, for dinner. Afterward, Berg dropped her off at her car and continued on to his condominium in downtown Denver, stopping along the way to buy food for his Airedale terrier, Freddy. It was 9:30 when he parked in front of his apartment building. Picking up the bag of dog food, he stopped to light one of his Pall Malls, the last action he would take in his life.

As he touched the match to the cigarette, a man stepped out of the shadows carrying a MAC-10 machine gun with a silencer, the kind that fires thirty bullets in a clip. This time, it jammed after the twelfth shot, but those that had fired were sufficient. A single squeeze of the trigger had sent seven bullets tearing into Berg's upper body and arms; the other five blew away his face. When his body was discovered a few minutes later, his right foot was still inside the car, the cigarette smoldering next to him.

The gunman ran past the body, joined on his way by the two men who had been posted as lookouts. The three climbed into their car, at the wheel of which sat the fourth man. "I'm surprised he lived in such a sleazy neighborhood," said one of them in a disapproving tone as they drove off. Shortly after they had reached their destination, a motel on the outskirts of Denver, a phone call was placed to Metaline Falls.

CHAPTER

16 | Earl Turner's World

I made my long-projected trip to visit Bob at Metaline Falls on Wednesday, May 23, three weeks before Berg's death. By the time I returned the following Sunday I had been told that somebody in Colorado "was going to get it" soon, but not who. I had also been present during the planning for another crime which, when I learned of its commission months later, left me in fear for my own life.

My companion during the flight to Spokane, for which Bob had paid the expenses, was a stockily built Kensingtonian named Jimmy Dye, whom I had known from the Klan and the NA. Jimmy, who had a plate in his head from a Vietnam War wound, and his best friend, bandy-legged George Zaengle of Fishtown—like Jimmy a former Marine—both fit Bob's description for the line troops, not the officers, he was seeking for The Order. "Ex-Marines make the best followers," he told me. "They're tough and obedient." And if he sometimes worried about certain of his recruits' drinking habits—when George Zaengle was drunk, he'd put on his camouflage pants, his White Power T-shirt, and wander the bars shouting racist slogans— he felt he could get them to shape up. The troopers for the blood bath ahead were going to be well trained, too. With some of the stolen money, Bob had purchased two isolated sites for boot camps and military maneuvers, one on 160 acres in Missouri (which I don't believe was ever used), and another on 110 acres in Idaho, where Barnhill's friend from Florida, Richard Scutari, was drillmaster.

Bob wasn't there to meet us when we arrived at the unloading gate in Spokane, but David Lane and Richie Kemp, my friend from the National Alliance, were. Kemp, because of his genial disposition and his size, had "Jolly"—as in "Jolly Green Giant"—for his code name, and at the age of twenty-two was, along with his former high school classmate Billy Soderquist, the youngest of The Order troopers.

As we were walking through the airport, I spotted Bob sitting in a phone booth. He glanced at us without recognition, much as he would six months later at the luggage counter in the Portland airport. His reason was the same, too, one he expressed when he joined us outside: "Watching out for Feds, fellas."

He led us to his pickup truck, drove us to a garage where Lane got into his yellow Volkswagen and followed us to a point outside the city limits, where both cars pulled to a halt. Bob and Lane got out to give each other the Nazi salute, after which Lane drove off. Bob explained that Lane was on his way to pick up the first batch of the counterfeit $10 bills that Merki was printing.

Metaline Falls was a two-hour drive east from Spokane, close to the Idaho border and about a hundred miles north of the Aryan Nations compound at Hayden Lake. To get onto Bob's 80-acre property, we drove up a dirt road under a canopy of trees to a clearing where two permanent mobile homes had been set. Chickens tiptoed around, pecking here and there, and in a small meadow I saw two cows. None of the land, however, was under cultivation; the large portion was as forested as it had been when Bob and his father purchased it. Behind it, in the distance, rose the awesome snow-capped Rocky Mountains, the sky high and vaulting and blue.

The only other structure, behind the two mobile homes, was a 35-foot-long, two-story frame building, which reminded me of an army barracks and which Bob and the others called the Bastion. It was on the upper floor of the Bastion that the original Order members had taken their oath seven months before.

One mobile home was occupied by Bob's widowed mother, the other by him, his wife Debbie and their adopted two-year-old boy, chubby, blue-eyed, blond-haired. Debbie, a bit overweight, struck me as a homebody who loved nothing better than to cook and bake for menfolk.

Bob, however, was constantly critical of her, displaying a maliciously petty side to his character which I found disturbing, no doubt because it didn't comport to the hero-worshipping image I still had of him.

The most upsetting episode occurred on the morning of my departure. He placed a little fuzzball on the top of his briefcase—he kept a gun and his family pictures in it—and then went in to take a shower. When he came out, he delightedly pointed out to me that the fuzzball was no longer on the briefcase, proving to him that Debbie had been snooping in it. Grinning, he opened the case to show me the top picture. It wasn't of Debbie but of his girlfriend, a redhead named Zillah who lived in Laramie, Wyoming, and was pregnant by him. "Serves her right," he said, chuckling, as he envisioned Debbie's reaction when she saw that. (Bob had first met Zillah during a trip to the Aryan Nations; her mother was a chubby little woman of fifty named Jean Craig.)

Bob's best friend, Ken Loff, had a farm nearby, where we visited him. A balding, serious-looking man, perhaps a half-dozen years Bob's senior, Loff by that time had a single significant cash crop: cash. Buried on his land and hidden in his barn was more than $200,000. In another two months, the crop would grow into the millions.

Either that day or the one following, after we had finished pitching hay for the cows, Bob took me into a room where I saw that he had piled a hundred or so copies of a paperback book. Pointing to the stack, he said, in his most solemn tone, "Tom, in there is what the future will be. You must read it." He handed me a copy. "You must." I promised I would, though I had no intention of doing so. The book was Dr. William Pierce's *The Turner Diaries*.

Written under a pseudonym and first published in 1978 by Pierce, the lead character in the novel is an engineer named Earl Turner. Except for an introduction and an afterword, the story, as the title suggests, is told in the form of a journal that Turner keeps over a two-year period ending in 1991. The narrative revolves around a racist underground, called The Organization, to which Turner belongs, and its inner circle of leaders, The Order, who are in a battle to the death with ZOG, also called The System.

As part of its tactics, The Order floods the country with counterfeit currency to disrupt the Jew-controlled monetary system. Only then does it begin its course of armed robbery and murder. Later, The Order brings about the destruction of Washington and Baltimore, where millions die, Turner notes with satisfaction. In Los Angeles, where Turner is one of an Order gang in charge, about half the population is hanged. The victims include white women who have slept with black men, although, as Turner explains, "about ninety percent of the corpses...are men...the politicians, the lawyers, the businessmen, the TV newscasters...the judges, the school officials... and all others...who helped promote The System's racial [equality] program." White males who want to join The Organization are required to bring in the head—not the body, just the head—of a black person, and if they fail in that quest, The Order executes them.

Eventually, The Order provokes a nuclear war between the United States and the Soviet Union, leading to widespread devastation of both lands. Gaining control of what is left of North America, The Order has Israel vaporized, and for good measure unleashes chemical warfare in Asia to destroy the inferior, slanty-eyed Chinese. Turner, by then, has died in flames during an assault on the Pentagon, revered as a martyr to the cause.

I first became aware of *The Turner Diaries* shortly before I joined the NA, when Reverend Miles sent me a copy while he was still languishing in prison. Although I knew generally what took place in the book, and at the time should have been enthusiastic about it, as a good racist, after reading the first few chapters and before getting to the counterfeiting and The Order, I stopped. The reason I gave myself—a strangely inadequate one considering the content—was that the book was "in poor taste." Thus, the writing that provided Bob with his detailed plans for the future—that led him to want to cut a swathe of destruction across the United States—I found to be repellent.

Nevertheless, within weeks of laying the book aside in disgust, I joined the National Alliance and accepted the author, Dr. Pierce, as my new and revered leader. I had no qualms in doing that, saw no contradiction; it did not occur to me that there had to be something wrong with any person or organization that could produce and publicize a book like that.

To the contrary, I quickly worked out—and my recollection is that I did this even before I became an NA member—a rationalization that allowed me to accept the "truth" of the NA's program and Dr. Pierce's infallibility as its leader *without having to change my mind about the book*. It was all very simple: Since I didn't want the world to end the way it does in *The Turner Diaries*, I reasoned, that meant Pierce didn't want it either; rather, what he'd done—a proof of his great intelligence—was deliberately write all those violent and melodramatic scenes to appeal to the low-brow, beer-swilling racists who weren't worthy of belonging to our elite corps but who would buy such a book, providing money for our coffers. (To some extent, it has done that. Widely advertised in various gun magazines, in *Soldier of Fortune* magazine, in *USA Today*—briefly: the editors pulled the ad as soon as they realized what the book was about—and in just about every hate sheet in the country, it has sold somewhere between 5,000 and 10,000 copies at $5 each.)

Did I believe in my rationalization? I thought I did. Consciously, I never let myself doubt it. Yet during the three years I was an NA member, I always avoided mentioning *The Turner Diaries* to Pierce for fear I'd inadvertently reveal my opinion of it, and he, as a result, would think less of me. Why, I told myself, he might even drum me out of the cadre for daring to question it. Which, I now think, was a rationalization on top of a rationalization: My real fear, I believe, was that if I discussed the book with him, he'd tell me he meant every bloodthirsty word of it. I didn't dare put myself in a position to hear that. It might destroy my faith.

My need to believe in the infallibility of my leaders extended itself to the way I handled the similar problem I had with the Holocaust theories they peddled. According to neo-Nazis, both in this country and abroad, the Holocaust never occurred. There were no death camps; they were a fiction perpetrated by the Zionists to make people feel sorry for the Jews. That there were concentration camps is admitted—they could hardly be denied—but the deaths that occurred in them were contrary to the humanitarian policies of Hitler; had it not been for typhus epidemics, no one would have died. I, however, had never doubted the Holocaust had taken place, and not for any documentary reasons: When I was fifteen, I visited my beloved brother Lee in Germany, where he had his permanent Army station; he had married a German woman a good deal older than he, and she told me, from her personal knowledge, of what the Nazis had done to the Jews. Books might lie, but I knew she wouldn't.

To solve my Holocaust dilemma, I applied the same avoidance reasoning I had with Pierce and *The Turner Diaries*. Yes, I told myself, there was a Holocaust, but—since my leaders could never lie—the truth had to be that the number of Jewish deaths was vastly exaggerated, perhaps a mere million or so, with the Jews lying about the other 5 million. Therefore, my leaders weren't prevaricating when they called the Holocaust a Zionist plot. (One might wonder why the new Nazis, in their rabid anti-Semitism, did not want to give Hitler credit for slaughtering the Jews. One reason—though there is a second and even more important one, which I will discuss later—is public relations. If the Nazis admitted to the truth of the Holocaust, they would also be admitting that their doctrine led to the single most monstrous act in human history, not the best means of attracting members— and money—from other than certifiable psychopaths.)

By as early as 1980, then, I had gone against (or at least avoided accepting) two major cult "truths": one, the need for armed revolution to overthrow ZOG as depicted in *The Turner Diaries* and other racist literature; the other, the fiction that the Holocaust was a fiction. Still, I managed to keep my faith intact by developing, *on my own*, rationalizations that allowed me to remain within the cult.

What I did, I think, distinguishes someone who has become enmeshed in a cult from the person who really "believes" in something. That person, for example, may recognize that democracy has some weaknesses but, on balance, is better than other forms of government and therefore "believes" in it. The cultist, however, because the cult is "truth," finds it necessary to take those aspects of the cult's teachings he finds unpalatable and fit them into the "truth" the cult teaches.

When he has done that, as happened with me on the Holocaust and *The Turner Diaries*, what had seemed unpalatable becomes just one more proof of the cult's wisdom. Only if the cultist can no longer do the fitting, as eventually I could not, will he leave, though probably with the same terrible sense of regret I felt. His unhappiness does not rise so much from any anger against the cult for having betrayed his faith by proving false to it—though that is a factor—but primarily because he now sees himself as robbed of the sense of superiority that membership in the cult had permitted him to enjoy.

CHAPTER

17 | The Conversation at
the Bastion

Saturday evening, Bob and I walked over to the Bastion after dinner. Bunking out on the second floor—I was a house guest—were Kemp and Dye, returned that day from a trip to the Aryan Nations headquarters in Hayden Lake, Idaho. Earlier that week Bob had purchased a new handgun, and Dye, he told me, had promised to show him how to clean it. Probably for that reason, early talk was about weapons, and when Ken Loff, who had not been on the Aryan Nations trip, arrived fifteen minutes later, he joined in on it.

Not long after, I wandered over to the other end of the room, a good thirty feet from the others, where my attention had been attracted by a pile of *Life* magazine books on World War II. As I began looking through them, I heard Richie Kemp speaking: "Tom says there's a problem." I couldn't hear the next few words; then: "He's running his mouth about Gary's army."

I had no idea who Gary was, but the Tom to whom Richie referred was, I knew from something Kemp said earlier, Tom Bentley, an Order member in his mid-fifties who lived at the Aryan Nations compound and whom I had briefly met several years before. I picked up one of the *Life* books, paging through it, studying the pictures.

"He wants him taken care of," that too from Richie, though only after I heard Bob's voice intervening in a questioning tone; I couldn't hear his words, probably because his back was to me.

Engrossed in the book, I paid no attention to their conversation for the next several minutes, though I was aware that they had lowered their voices. Then Bob's sing-song tenor broke through: "He'll trust Randy Duey," to which Richie said, "His wife's left him." I thought he meant Duey's. Glancing over, I saw that Bob was smiling: "Tell him we're going to take him to his wife. That'll get him out there," and the others laughed in an anticipatory way as though they were about to play a practical joke on someone.

I went back to my reading. When I next picked up their talk, my impression was that the subject had changed, since they were now referring to an "it" rather than a "he." Bob, in a regretful tone: "Geez, I can't do it tomorrow. I got to take Tom"—meaning me, not Bentley—"to the airport."

"I'll take care of it for you, Bob," Richie assured him in a manly and eager way.

I laid my book down. Bob, I saw, was looking at him with uncertainty: "Are you sure, Rich? Are you really sure?"

Richie, drawing back his broad shoulders to a posture of military attention, replied: "Don't you worry about it, Bob. You can count on me. I'll take care of it."

I strolled back to the table at which they were sitting and joined them. Bob gave me a glance and then looked back at Richie. "Well, all right," he said. "You take Jimmy with you, and I'll make a few stops, and now you make sure you take care of it."

Richie frowned. "The only problem is where we should take it," he murmured thoughtfully.

Continuing to use the word "it," they debated the problem for several minutes. Bob, at one point, suggested an old coal mine shaft nearby, the matter apparently settled when one of the others (I can't recall who) mentioned a name I didn't catch, saying, "He'll know what to do about it." At that, the conversation drifted off into silence, and from the way everyone seemed to be deliberately not looking at me, I realized they were waiting for me to leave. Gathering up several of the war books, I did. As I walked back to the trailer, I speculated that the "it" referred to hiding either counterfeit money or weapons. The first part of their conversation was a mystery to me, and I dismissed it from my mind.

When Bob and I left the house the next day after the fuzzball episode, he had his briefcase in one hand, a leather bag filled with clothes in the other. I followed him, carrying the machine gun he had handed me. After packing everything in the trunk of the car, we drove off. We hadn't been on the road long before he pulled off to the side and parked in front of a deserted-looking building, which he told me had housed their printing press before they moved that operation to the Aryan Nations.

Out of its door bounded Randy Duey, brushing at his moustache as he approached us. As he almost always did, he was wearing a cap to hide his baldness; when he had it on, he looked younger than his thirty-five years, but he looked older when he didn't. Until just a month before, he had worked as a post office clerk, attending Eastern Washington University as a part-time student; there he had become friendly with the morose and heavy-drinking Denver Parmenter. I found Duey scary, the way some people can be when your principal sense of them is that they are wound tight with a ferocious fear of their own.

Bob got out and he and Duey walked off a distance where I couldn't hear them talk. When they came back to the car, Duey, brushing faster than ever at his moustache, was saying obsequiously, "You can trust me, Bob. You can trust me. I'll take care of it. Right away, Bob. Right away."

As Bob and I continued toward Spokane, I remembered the previous evening's mention of Duey, whose wife—I thought—had left him, and I asked Bob if there was a problem. "Heck, no," he said. "It's nothing important, but I do have something important I want to ask you, Tom: Do you own a gun?"

I told him I didn't. He shook his head. "Tom, Tom," he said reproachfully. "Every white man should own a gun. How are you going to protect your family if you don't?" Briskly: "And that's what I'm going to do. I'm going to buy you one."

Weapons had never appealed to me, but I didn't think it was manly to say that, so I agreed that a white man should indeed always be armed, making my excuse by pointing out that I could hardly board a plane carrying a gun. "No problem," he said. "Here we are."

He stopped the car in front of a survivalist store. They can be found in surprising numbers in wilderness areas, offering everything from tinned foods to sophisticated weaponry to bows and arrows. I followed him inside, watched as he chose a .45-caliber pistol, twin to the one he carried, and a leather handcase to go with it. The cost came to over $400. After he had peeled off the necessary bills—he always paid for weapons in cash, he told me—we returned to the car.

Again I asked him how I could get on the plane with a gun. "Easy, buddy," he said. "All you have to do is go up to the counter and open the case and show it to them. They'll tag it and when you get to Philadelphia, they'll have a room there where you can pick it up." He was right: It was that simple. Apparently, in the United States, if a person wants to transport a weapon by air from one part of the country to another, regardless of ownership or registration, that is how it is done. The traffic in illegal weapons that way may be quite substantial.

As we were nearing the airport terminal, Bob repeated to me his hope that I'd move with my family to Metaline Falls, and I, having now seen the peaceful beauty of the place for myself, told him truthfully that I wanted it too. "Good," he said and grinned. "There are a heck of a lot of things going down, and they're going to work. Believe me! Just keep your mind positive! Tom, it's going to work for us." He paused. "Of course, there's some problems up and down. We have one coming up real soon."

I asked him what it was. "I can't reveal it, Tom. It's too important." Even so, he couldn't resist giving me a hint: "Somebody's going to be taken care of, buddy. Just keep your eyes and ears open. In the newspapers. It'll be in Colorado."

I don't think I had ever seen him look so happy.

CHAPTER
18 | The Counterfeiters

The morning of June 19, the newspaper headline read: "Talk Show Host Murdered in Denver." Jewish. Controversial. Foe of anti-Semites. By evening, the story was on the national television broadcasts. I heard from Jimmy Dye's friend, George Zaengle: "Hey, they ain't fooling, are they?" he said.

Bob called an hour later. Susan answered. I whispered to her to tell him I wasn't home. He phoned again the following evening. He's not home, said Susan. On the third night, when Susan repeated the same message, he said: "You tell him to be home. Tomorrow night. Tell him, Susan," and he gave her the time.

I was there. "Hey, there, Tom, how ya doin', fella?" he chirped when I answered.

"All right, oh, I'm all right. Bob, listen—" You don't want to ask this, I thought, because right now, at this moment, you still don't know he did it. I breathed in: "Listen," I repeated, "there's a question I have to ask you." I paused; he remained silent. "Because, well, now I'm not mentioning things, but there's a lot of big news about Colorado. I think you know what I'm talking about."

I could almost see him smiling into the phone. "Yeah, I have the feeling I do."

"Was that you?"

He laughed. "Yeah. Yeah." He laughed again good-naturedly. "That was us."

"My God, Bob," I said.

He seemed to be waiting for me to say something else. I glanced over at Susan; she was staring at me. "So what's up?" I asked.

As though our previous words had not been spoken, he replied: "Do you remember the tall guy with the light hair?" That would be David Lane, and I was about to say so when he went on: "I don't know if you recollect his name. Lone Wolf. Well, he's on his way there. He's got the stuff."

In the wake of Berg's murder, the counterfeiting scheme had dropped entirely from my mind and with it my agreement, at first only a half-promise, which had become an assumption on his part during my Metaline Falls visit, that I'd help pass it. "Yeah. Yeah. Why, ah, okay, Bob," I said.

I laid the phone gently back in its cradle. "What's the matter?" Susan asked.

I looked at her blankly for a moment. "Nothing. Why should anything be the matter? Nothing's the matter."

Nothing, I repeated to myself as I stared at the phone. If only I had a friend, I thought, someone I trusted, to ask what to do. I meant a man. I couldn't ask Susan. She was a woman and I was supposed to protect her, not bring her into anything like this. It was only in a realization I quickly buried that it crossed my mind I couldn't tell her because she had warned me of where my friendship with Bob would lead.

As I stared at the phone, I imagined myself picking up the receiver and dialing; I'd be dialing the FBI. That's what my brother—I trusted him—would tell me to do. I had no doubt of that. He was military police. It's your duty, Tom, he'd say; you have no other choice. "I want to report that I know who killed Alan Berg." That's what I'd say.

But I wouldn't. I wouldn't make that call, no matter what my damn brother said. No way, Lee. You're wrong. You want me to be a snitch. That's the worst thing a man can be, an informant, informing on his friends.

I imagined making the call again, but this time there was a reply to it: "Oh," the man who answered would say, the agent would say, the government agent, the agent of the government I'd been taught for the past ten years hated people like me, he'd say, "and how do you know who killed Alan Berg?" I'd say—not right away, but they'd get it out of me; they have their ways—I'd say, "I know, sir, because I'm a criminal, too. Let me tell you the things I've done. I've passed stolen money for him, the murderer. I've kept quiet and not called you guys when he told me about the bank robberies he's committed. Armored car robberies, those too. Oh, and while I'm at it, I let him put a phone in my house for me to take messages for him from his confederates. Oh, yes, and while I'm at it, I forgot to mention, I also had them in my house, his confederates, when they were carrying money I knew was stolen. Oh, yes, and I almost forgot, one of them is coming to my house right now so I can help him pass counterfeit." They'd put me away for a thousand years when they heard that.

Two days later, a Sunday, Lane phoned from a nearby motel asking for instructions to get to my house. I was taken aback at hearing his voice. By then I had almost convinced myself, because I wanted to believe it so badly, that I'd never hear from any of them again. Maybe, I thought, they were on the run, knew they were about to be caught. My wish unfulfilled, I realized, I had no more idea than I had on Friday night of what to do. I had managed to vanquish entirely any thought of going to the authorities when, in my mounting paranoia, it had occurred to me I might even be charged as an accessory in the Berg murder. (Hadn't I known someone was going to be murdered in Colorado three weeks before it happened?) I was lost. I no longer had any leaders to follow, to tell me what to do. About the only certainty was that, until I did figure out how to get away from them (and I used "them" in my mind rather than "Bob"), I didn't want them to think I was trying to avoid them. The certitude was there; I took it no further than that. "Wait there," I said, "and I'll drive over and you can follow me back to my place."

When I arrived at the motel, Lane was standing by his car, keeping busy while waiting for me by handing out copies of Dr. Pierce's "Who Rules America" leaflet.

Once inside my house, he handed over two large packages he had been carrying. They were gift-wrapped, my daughter's name and address on them. I opened the top package. It contained counterfeit $10 bills, four to each uncut sheet. If he had been arrested on the way and the police had seen those bundles with my address on them—I didn't dare finish that thought.

But it was at that moment I got my idea. A plan: I had a plan. It seemed to come to me full-blown. What I'll do, I thought, is seem to go along with my promise to pass this stuff, and then, after a couple of days, I'll call Bob and tell him I've almost been caught. That way, because they'll think I'm hot, they'll stay away from me, so I won't have to act like I'm trying to stay away from them. Hey, Martinez, you're a Goddamn genius.

And perhaps if had I stopped my idea right there, it might have worked. At the very least, it would have given me breathing room. But I studied the paper. The color looked good to me, especially the front side, not quite right on the back. I grasped one of the sheets between my thumb and forefinger. It's the feel, I thought; it doesn't have that crispness. Still...

Lane was watching me. Closely. Seeming even closer than he was because of that hunched-forward stance. "Good, huh?" he asked.

"Yeah." It looked better than the dyed money. We had no trouble passing that. "Good," I agreed.

When I said that, my plan had already taken on a new blossom. I'll not only promise to pass the money, I decided, I will pass it. But only a little bit of it. Only enough to pay my bills. Not a penny more. Then, only then, will I call Bob. Only then will I tell him I was almost caught...that I had to destroy the rest of the counterfeit. Yes, that was excellent. They couldn't question that. That's what I should do if I was almost caught.

I licked my lips. "Yeah, it looks real good," I said.

Besides, I deserved it. From them. Look at what they had put me through. For some reason, I thought of an incident that happened a few days before: I was sweeping the sidewalk and as I did, the top drug dealer in the project strode by me, the poor dumb white man with a broom, without a glance he strode by me, he who lived on taxpayer money, my money, and made $4,000 a week, yes, like I was dirt. A white man like me. And now that I think about it, how about all those crooked politicians? I ran a finger across the top sheet. Yeah, how about them? They were always stealing.

And it wasn't, I informed myself, as if I was going to hurt anybody. I'd never hurt anybody; not me. (I don't think I knew the meaning of the word "countenance" at that time, as in countenancing murder.) The people I'd pass the money to, I thought, they'll just pass it to somebody else and eventually it will all end up in the banks, and banks must have insurance for that kind of thing. "George'll help us," I said.

I'd forgotten all about Alan Berg.

We got to work the next morning, Lane and Zaengle and I. There was a lot to do: 950 sheets at $40 a sheet, $38,000.

We worked in the kitchen, the shades drawn. I'd made sure my little girl was visiting a friend. My wife was at her factory job; the babysitter, as usual, had taken my little boy to her house. We wore surgical gloves as we worked, to avoid leaving fingerprints. On the table we had placed a piece of plate glass, over it, one by one, the money sheets. Using plastic rectangles that were the exact size of a bill, we cut around them carefully with razors.

Lane, by then, had given me Xeroxed instructions on passing the money, which I realized meant I wasn't the only one recruited for this job. (Merki later testified that he had two of his children and a son-in-law among those doing the passing. It is unclear if Jesus was one of them.) The list was in a *do–don't* format. For example, *do* pass the bills in department stores and other large crowded places, *don't* in small stores where men are gathered. (I'm not sure of the reasoning for that last part, but it may have been because Lane, who I think was the author of the list, had it in his mind that men were more likely to recognize counterfeit money than were women.) Another instruction was *don't* pass the bills anywhere near where you live; *do* go out of state to do it, an order Lane repeated to me verbally. He also told me to buy a book, hollow out a hole in its pages, in which I was to place the profits and ship them to an address I was given.

It wasn't until the third day of our cutting that I remembered Alan

Berg. Because Lane was from Denver and seemed to be a confidant
of Bob's, I thought it likely he would know something about the murder, though I assumed he hadn't been involved himself. (I'm not sure
why I assumed that; it may have been that I had not yet fully grasped—
despite my panicky fretting—the thought that anybody I knew could
commit a murder. Even Bob hadn't admitted to the actual shooting;
all he had said was "It was us," which could be any faceless people
I'd not yet met.)

I said: "David, I want to ask you something. What do you know
about this Berg thing, man?"

He looked at me, a smile beginning. "What do I know about it?"
He was skinny enough, but he appeared to be puffing as he said that.
He laughed. "Know about it? Hell, man, I was the Goddamn get-
away driver."

"You were what?" George laughed, too, one of his nervous "heh
heh" coughs of a laugh, and continued slicing with his razor, concentrating on his work. "You were what?"

I felt thirsty.

He made a casual wave of his hand. "He was just a Jew-kike," he
said. "No big loss."

19 | Caught

That was June 27 and on that day—perhaps a day or two later, the exact date has never been pinned down—Bruce Pierce, he of the drooping moustache, of the cold dark eyes, arrived in San Francisco. There he met at least once, probably several times, with a man named Charles Ostrout. Subsequently, Ostrout and Pierce conferred with a third man, Ronald King. Ostrout and King were executives of the Brink's Armored Car Service.

On June 28, the day after David Lane left my house, taking with him $8,000 of the best bills, I began my brief career as a passer of counterfeit.

Despite Lane's instructions to go out of state, I decided I would not even venture far from K&A. In retrospect, that seems to have been a perverse—even stupid—choice. By staying close to home, I increased my chances of getting caught, most likely by someone who would recall me as the passer when I was next in the neighborhood, as I was constantly. A psychologist later told me my choice of crime scene proved that I wanted to be caught. If by that he meant I felt guilty about committing the crime, I don't think he was right. I had passed the stolen money in February with little compunction, and no uneasy conscience that I was later aware of. Any desire to be caught that was lurking inside me, rather, would have been motivated by my inability to untangle myself, by myself, from the situation I was in: In that sense, although my street code forbade me to be an informant *voluntarily*, perhaps if I were arrested and *forced* to talk, I'd both be doing the right thing and not have to feel guilty about it.

If that, or something like it, was what my subconscious was bidding me to do, my conscious motive was simpler and, relatively speaking, far less worthy. As I saw it, I chose K&A to pass the bills because I was positive my nerve wouldn't hold for a trip to Ohio, as Lane had suggested, or some other place where I would be a stranger committing a crime in a strange town. My home turf provided a sense of security and the opportunity to get it over with right away. Speed was important to me, too, because—and this suggests that my conscience was working, but in a quite peculiar way—I felt, illogically but strongly, that I'd be guilty of a *worse* crime, more premeditated somehow, if I spent time traveling to commit it.

The first place I passed a ten was a corner store where I purchased a pack of gum for 40¢, so that I walked out with a $9.60 profit. Wow, I thought, this is a great business to be in! I went to another store, two doors away, a *Daily News* this time; profit, $9.65. At $19.25 for two minutes' work, the hourly wage, I perceived, was going to be astronomical.

I continued on down Kensington Avenue, eventually accumulating thirty newspapers, a dozen or two packs of gum, and a large assortment of other cheap goodies, all of which I periodically stored in my car. Ordinarily I didn't lower my net proceeds by spending more than 50¢ on a purchase: my only splurge that day was buying eight $1 lottery tickets. Who knows, I thought, I might get lucky and hit the jackpot.

I spent the morning and afternoon making my rounds, went home for a bite of supper, then back out in the evening. When my labors were finally completed, I had cleared $1,500. I was exhilarated. I had started out with trepidation, but with each successful purchase my excitement mounted, like a craps player whose dice are hot and stay hot. Time and again during that day, I told myself: Just one more place, and that's it, then home you go. But each time I did, secretly I knew it was a lie. I was at a gambling table I couldn't walk away from, and the only reason I finally quit that night was because I couldn't find any more businesses open.

My original resolve—to stop as soon as I obtained the $4,000 I needed to pay for the repairs on my house—had by mid-day been replaced by another: $4,000 plus enough to pay off my car. That seemed fair to me. But not a penny beyond that. It would be morally wrong, I scrupulously advised myself, if I went beyond getting myself out of debt. I now have absolutely no doubt that, had I had the opportunity, I would have passed the entire $30,000.

My final stop that evening was at a store in a small shopping mall. I'd been in there often in the past, usually to buy lottery tickets. This time I bought the 50¢ kind, the clerk accepting my bill without giving it a glance, just as had happened everywhere else.

In the small mall was a branch office of my bank, and the following morning I drove over there, the children with me, to deposit my previous day's earnings. Hidden under my seat was most of the remainder of the $30,000. I left the bank and started back to the car, waving to the children, having no intention, because of their presence, of continuing my spree right then. I stopped. I glanced at the store where I'd bought the lottery ticket. I felt the adrenaline of the previous day seeping upward through me. Could I? Not that I would— But could I do it a second time in the same store?

A young blond woman was standing behind the counter. She looked at the ten and turned to the owner, Art Gold. (That's not his real name; because his life has been threatened, I have changed his name and certain identifying details about him.) The clerk said to him, "Doesn't this look like the other bill we got?"

He said, "Yeah." He studied me. "You're the SOB who passed one of these the other day."

I said, "You're crazy." My stomach churned. "I didn't give you nothin'," I added sullenly.

"I'm calling the Secret Service," he said.

"You're nuts." I glared at him. "I'm going to get a cop," I shouted, and strode out of the store in all my outraged innocence.

He followed me. Probably I could have run, evaded him that way, and later got back to my children, but instead I walked right to my car and got in, even as he was standing on the curb taking down my license plate number. I thought: Ah, the hell with it; this is it; it's all over; I don't care.

By the time I arrived home, that sense, almost like relief, had been replaced by terror. I only realized that when I was parking the car in front of our house, and my little girl asked me, "What's wrong, Daddy?" Then I saw what she saw, that I was shaking from toe to head.

I told her to take her brother into the house and up to her bedroom. When she was out of the way—I visualized the Feds showing up any minute—I gathered the money from under the car seat, dashed with it into the house, picked up the rest of the money I had secreted, the surgical gloves, the razor cutters, the do–don't list, the piece of paper with the post office box number to which I was to send the proceeds, dumped everything into a green trash bag, ran out into my yard, looked around, saw my neighbor's yard which had high weeds, thought of hiding it there, saw their Doberman pinscher, decided not, dashed back into the house with my bag, collapsed on the couch, saw the phone, picked it up, called Susan at work: "Get home! Get home! It's important, Susan."

I hung up. I called George Zaengle and told him I couldn't talk but he was to meet my wife near my mother's house, that I had got caught. "Man," he said disgustedly, "you were told to go out of state."

I screamed, "I'm not explaining nothing to you. But you got to meet her. You got to destroy the money."

I was hardly off the phone again when Susan, whose factory job was only a block from where we lived, came dashing in. She looked frightened: Had something happened to the children? I told her I had counterfeit money and she was to take it over to my mother's, where George would meet her, and give it to him. She said, "Tom. Why? Why?"

I shouted at her not to lecture me, just do as I said, "or you're not going to have a husband." She looked at me a moment longer, sighed, and picked up the bag. "Now don't walk the main streets...go...go around...don't let anybody see you...." I ordered her, ordered my wife to carry counterfeit money for me in a trash bag on the streets of Kensington in broad daylight.

When she got back—the longest half-hour I'd spent in my life until then, though there'd be longer ones—she told me she had made the delivery with no trouble. By then it had occurred to me that if I went back to Gold's store, perhaps I could smooth things over. When I got there, he looked at me in surprise. I raised my hand in a sign of peace. "Hey, listen," I said as I brought out a real ten, "I'm in deep trouble. I didn't mean to rip you off, man. I didn't mean to hurt anybody. Here."

I put the ten on the counter. "I already called them," he said.

I nodded. "That's all right," I said. "My luck was running out anyway, pal. I'm sorry." And I walked out of the store.

From there, I went to George's house and used his phone to put in a call to David Lane's safe number. Lane got back to me within minutes of my return to my house: "This is Lone Wolf. What's up, Spider?" I told him what had happened, the irony completely escaping me that I had planned to make just such a call pretending I was in danger of being caught. Just as George had, Lane, the self-confessed murderer, berated me for passing the bills in Philadelphia. Furiously, I shouted: "I'm not going to argue with you, you son of a bitch; I'm having George burn it." To which he replied plaintively: "Why the hell didn't you pass it in the black neighborhoods so they'd get blamed?"

As I hung up, Susan was quietly watching me. "I have to explain," I said, but all I found myself able to do was strum the refrain of my previous speech: Everything I'd done was for her and the children. She listened. We waited for the Secret Service to come.

It was a long wait. At one point, as we ate, I mourned: "This may be the last meal we're going to have together. I'm in a lot of trouble."

She asked me how much, but once again I rejected her. "I can't get into it," I said. "I know a lot of things, a lot of things that happened. And I don't know what to do about it."

After dinner we went to the back yard, and sat there by the pine tree waiting for them. Our three-year-old was with us. Diane was out front, riding her bike. The neighbors were sitting outdoors, taking in the last warmth of the day. It was seven-thirty when they came, still light out. I heard one car, didn't pay attention to it, then there were others, screeching sounds, cars jumping up on my lawn, my street blocked by cars at either end. An agent came running over to the back fence, the neighbor's Doberman snarling at him. Somebody was reading me my rights. I was taken by the arms; they were coming from all sides of me, it seemed. I glimpsed Diane wheeling her bike up from the corner toward me. They brought me inside the house, I all the while denying I had done anything wrong, pleading: "Don't put handcuffs on me. My little girl's out there with her friends; don't let them see me like that. Please, please." They put the cuffs on, tight, my arms behind me. I was led out of the house. They walked me down the block. The neighbors watched. My daughter screamed.

I was taken to the federal building and into a small room like those I'd seen in the movies where they question the suspect—bright yellow lights, plain wooden desk and chairs, and darkness. Five of them did the interrogating. They used the nice-cop/mean-cop routine on me. At one point the "mean" cop, who had temporarily left the room, banged back in and slammed his fist on the desk, his face up to mine: "You're going to get fifteen years for this, pal. You know you did it. You think that pretty wife of yours is going to wait fifteen years for you?" I said, "She'll wait fifty years for me," and among all the lies, the ones I'd told and the ones told to me, I knew that was truth.

"I must have been given that money. I didn't know it was counterfeit," I lied, over and over. "How would I know?"

I kept to that, and finally the "mean" cop stormed out and the "nice" cops apologized for his cruel ways. I could get out of this, they told me. All I had to do was help them, just a little. "We're going to see what we can do for you," one of them said. "We want you to go up to K&A for us, and go into bars, and we know who it is, so we just want you to ask some questions. You know K&A, Martinez. You've been on those streets. We know all about you...."

"No way! You want me to die?"

Until that moment, I know now, they had assumed, as their co-operation offer suggested, that I wasn't mixed up in anything more serious than a typical, small-time K&A grifter operation. My blurted fear of dying convinced them they were onto something much bigger, and after that they wouldn't stop digging. I immediately sensed their reaction and felt bewilderment at my own, and I drew it back, deep down into me. I'd said it but I wasn't yet ready to face what I knew: "I said that because you want me to be your little stoolie." I wished I could stop sweating. "I'm not being a snitch. I didn't do wrong. You want to throw me in jail, then give me a trial and I'll get out of this."

I was out of breath, too, but that turned out to be almost the end of the questioning. It was after three in the morning when they drove me to the Philadelphia Police Administration Building, which has holding cells in the basement. I was put in one by myself. I lay on a little metal bed staring at the cold walls.

Ten o'clock Saturday morning the agents took me out of the cell and back to the federal building, where they interrogated me for another hour, but in a more desultory fashion this time, as though they were no longer as convinced as they had been that they had caught a major criminal. I mined a little fool's gold from that.

When they were done with me, they took me to a bail hearing where I was released on my own recognizance, probably because I'd never been arrested before, had a job, owned that white elephant of a house. They let me go and out I walked, without a penny in my pockets, into a pouring rain.

I walked for blocks, my shirt and trousers drenched, not thinking at all anymore. Finally it occurred to me to get a cab and pay him when I got home. I looked ten years older, Susan later told me, in less than twenty-four hours. My little boy looked at me wide-eyed and said, "Daddy!" as he put his arms behind himself.

My daughter ran over to hug me. She was crying: "Daddy, why did they take you out?" "It was a mistake, Diane. They just made a bad mistake. I'm okay." "But, Daddy, they scared me."

"Bob called right after you left." She had told him what had happened and he had asked smoothly, as though it were the most ordinary thing in the world: "How many of them?" She told him, and he said, "Ten? Really? Listen, Susan, everything will be okay. I'll get back to you. Don't worry. It'll be fine."

That evening he called again. His tone was friendly, concerned, supportive, as if visiting a friend in the hospital. "What a bad break, buddy." That was the difference between Bob and lesser men like David Lane and George Zaengle, whose immediate reaction when something goes wrong is to ladle out blame. Bob must have been upset, too, that I had disobeyed orders by passing the money where I had, but to him blame was an irrelevance, a self-defeating concept. Mistakes caused problems, and it was the problems—not their cause—that had to be dealt with, contained, and if possible turned to his advantage. Based on his subsequent actions, he saw my "problem" as creating two possibilities: Either I would become so frightened by my arrest that I'd become a fugitive and join The Order—a good result; or else I'd become so frightened I might be tempted to become an informant—a bad result. Wise management could make the good result probable, the bad result avoidable.

He took the first step to avoid the second (and potentially disastrous) result in that phone call. "Tom," he said, "you're going to need a lawyer, a good lawyer, and they cost money that I know you don't have, but you're not to worry about that. What the heck, fella, I got you into this trouble, and so don't you worry about what a lawyer's going to cost. I'll pay for that. There's going to be plenty of money, Tom. Listen." He paused. "What I'm saying is there'll be a lot more money than you need for a lawyer. For you, buddy."

He was right. There would be plenty of money.

20 | Ukiah

On the morning of July 19, 1984, eleven men met in a motel room in Santa Rosa, California. They knelt in prayer, asking Yahweh to bless their day. Their obeisance completed, they rose and left the motel in twos and threes to board two flat-bed Ford pick-up trucks parked nearby. Each man wore a white T-shirt and carried a bandanna to cover his face; each was armed. They drove off in a northerly direction toward the town of Ukiah, located just off the Pacific coast fifty miles north of Santa Rosa.

Some twenty minutes behind them, as they knew, a Brink's armored car was also heading for Ukiah. Tailing it was a battered Oldsmobile, at its wheel the one-time engineer and current counterfeiter, Robert Merki. He was wearing a wig, makeup, and women's clothing. When the armored car turned off the road onto a ramp leading to Highway 20, just a few miles south of Ukiah, Merki picked up the microphone of his CB radio: "Have a good day," he said.

That was the signal the men in the pick-up trucks had been waiting for. On their arrival at the ramp, they had parked just behind its exit, several of them milling about as though they were members of a highway work crew. Now they got back into their trucks, two to the front of each, the others crouching in the flatbed. When the Brink's truck reached the top of the ramp, its driver brought it to a momentary halt to watch for traffic. As he did, the two trucks started toward the Brink's. As one came directly alongside, the young man in the passenger seat, Billy Soderquist, held up the same sign that had been used in the Northgate robbery: GET OUT OR YOU DIE.

The Brink's driver stepped on the gas in an attempt to escape, but his way was blocked immediately by the other truck, which had now positioned itself at an angle across the highway. From the back of it, a half-dozen men rose simultaneously, faces covered with bandannas, leveled their rifles, sent out a single burst of fire. The Brink's stopped. Two men from the truck containing the shooters jumped out and began dumping nails across the road. From the other truck, Bob Mathews made his gun-wielding appearance. He leaped up on the front bumper of the Brink's and fired into its window over the heads of the two ducking guards. They raised their hands in surrender.

A third guard, locked inside the back of the Brink's with the money it was carrying, was a woman named Lisa King. She refused to surrender. Picking up her walkie-talkie, she cried, "Mayday! Mayday! A robbery—" In mid-word, she was intercepted from his radio by the alert Merki, who had remained parked at the bottom of the ramp. Smoothly, he said: "Don't be joking on this line, lady. It's for emergencies. What are you trying to do, start a riot?"

By then the guards in the cab of the Brink's had been forced out of it and were lying face down on the road. While two of the robbers, their guns pointing at the guards, kept them in order, a third, Randy Duey, stood to one side, waving traffic through. A motorist later said he assumed that what he saw was a movie scene being filmed. It was California, after all, wasn't it?

Even as Lisa King was being cut off by Merki's interruption, she became aware that the rifles were barking again, this time their bullets snapping at the walls on either side of her. She knew it would be only moments before they would locate the key that opened the back of the van. She surrendered.

Bob scrambled by her through the open door. The meetings that Bruce Pierce had with the Brink's officials a few weeks earlier had paid off not only in the timing of the robbery but also equipped Bob with the knowledge of which bags contained checks, which cash. Leaving the check bags alone, he passed the cash ones out to his confederates, who loaded them onto the flat-bed trucks. Leaving the prone guards and the bullet-riddled van behind them, they drove off in different directions. The robbery had taken less than five minutes.

Soon after, they rendezvoused at a motel. Merki, still in his female disguise, was already there. Giving them a lipsticked smile, he greeted them at the door of the cabin for which he was registered as the wife of one of them.

When they finished counting their booty, they stared at one another in awe. Their take was $3.6 million.

They had just pulled off the largest armored car robbery in American history.

Only one mistake had been made. Bob made it. While passing out the satchels of cash, he had laid down his weapon and forgotten to pick it up. The gun was registered in the name of Andy Barnhill.

Including the proceeds of the Ukiah holdup, Bob and his accomplices had stolen more than $4 million within six months. Among the purchases Bob was planning to make with his newly acquired wealth were laser weapons with which he intended to knock out the Los Angeles power supply, just as The Order in *The Turner Diaries* had done. In the book, that achievement had produced widespread vandalism and race riots, paving the way for the great day of the mass hangings, and Bob hoped for the same result now. Another portion of the Ukiah robbery money was set aside to step up the counterfeiting operation. Instead of the mere thousands that Lane was lugging around the country, now it would be possible to print billions, delivering the legal monetary system into chaos, that too exactly as foretold by *The Turner Diaries*.

CHAPTER

21 | "More Money Than I Had Ever Seen"

When I arrived at George Zaengle's house a few nights after the Ukiah holdup, Jimmy Dye was there, having just arrived from the West Coast where he now lived. Jimmy, who had subsisted largely on his Vietnam wound pension, had always dressed as poor as he was. No longer: Flashy but expensive-looking double-knit slacks, shiny new shoes, glittering wristwatch—he bragged he'd paid $200 for it— and toting a cowhide briefcase.

With a swagger I wasn't used to from him, he flipped open the case and stood back with a paternalistic smile as George and I gaped at the contents. It was filled with money, and not counterfeit this time either. Grandly, he hoisted a thick wrapped packet. "There's ten in there," he said and nonchalantly tossed it over to George. He pointed to a second $10,000 trove. "That's to recruit Bill Nash," he explained. Nash, who was from Kensington, had racist connections, and Bob fancied him for The Order because he was a locksmith. (At least Nash said that's what he was; I'd once hired him to change a lock on my front door, and had to finish the job myself.) Remaining in the briefcase was another $20,000. "That," said Jimmy, pointing at me, "is for you."

A regular pay schedule, Jimmy explained, had been set up for members of The Order. Each of the brothers, he said, received $10,000 every three months just for belonging, earning bonuses of $20,000 for each crime in which they participated.

I was never present when the gang was paid by Bob, but an informant attended such a session in Boise, Idaho, at a house he was told belonged to Jean Craig, the chubby little lady who had tracked Alan Berg to his death in Denver. As the informant recalled the session in Craig's house: "So before the evening was over, there was probably between sixteen and twenty people there, including Mike and me." Mike was Mike Norris, whom I'd known since my days in the National Alliance. In 1981 he had been the only one of ten defendants to be acquitted of participating in the aborted invasion of the Caribbean island of Dominica. Six of those involved in this bizarre adventure—it's never been clear whose idea it was—were Klan members, as Norris had once been. "...and everybody," the informant went on, "was fellowshipping and all, and I would see Carlos and Black [Richard Scutari] go back in these rooms, and people would come out and they'd give them a paper bag. It looked like when one of them was coming out, there was a wad of money in there. I mean more money than I had ever seen in my life."

Jimmy handed me my $20,000. It was all in hundred dollar bills, ten packs of them, each pack held together by a rubber band. I stuffed several packs into the pocket of my shirt, turned to my trousers next, but still had packs left over, broke them open to make it easier to distribute them around my person. As I did, for the first time I appreciated the problem faced by that Abscam congressman, just pushing money into himself, bills popping out here, popping out there. "Bob told me to tell you," Jimmy said, "that $10,000 is for a lawyer, and $10,000 is for services rendered."

Who my lawyer should be had become a sensitive subject between Bob and me. In the June 30 call, after promising to pay my legal counsel, he'd gone on: "I know a couple of attorneys who are sympathetic to our cause, Tom." That didn't surprise me; I had met several myself in the National Alliance and was aware that the KKK never seemed to have any difficulty hiring a lawyer when actions were brought against its members. "I can get a good one, buddy," he said. "That's the way you ought to go, you know."

I didn't think so. Any lawyer he'd engage for me, I had no doubt, would have his first loyalty to Bob, who was paying the bill, and to the racist movement. He might be representing me but he'd also be there to keep tabs on me. With that in mind, I told Bob I'd rather hire a Philadelphia lawyer. He didn't try to force the issue. Neither then, nor later, did he indicate by so much as a hint that he might refuse to pay unless I agreed to his attorney. If he had decided to lay down that condition and I refused, he would have lost the hold on me that paying for my lawyer provided him.

He was, nevertheless, volubly unhappy about the attorney I did hire, a member of the firm that had done legal work for me in connection with my house. He knew by the name: "Tom! A Jew lawyer? A Jew?"

As it happened, I didn't want to keep that lawyer either, though not because he was a Jew. By that point, in fact, I rather liked the idea of Bob paying for a Jewish lawyer. My thinking now was to hire a major downtown criminal defense firm. Hard hitters, I'd been told. Win all the time, I was told.

My upcoming trial had become an all-consuming interest to me. The night I'd spent locked in a cell had made me terrified of going to prison, pushing to the back of my mind any concerns I had about The Order and its crimes. I was constantly dreaming up new defenses. Although I recognized that it could use some refining, one of my favorites was this: I would say that I had sold a couple of hunting rifles to a man I didn't know at K&A and he had paid me all in tens, which innocently I had spent; why, I was as much a victim as the shopkeepers I had given them to! I recognized that such a story might not hold up terribly well if the Secret Service learned I had passed 150 of those tens all in one day, buying newspapers and chewing gum, but from their questioning of me, they didn't seem to know about anything beyond the lottery tickets I'd bought at Gold's. I held onto the hope they wouldn't find out.

Winning my trial—and hence the need for the heavy-hitters—might also, I began to realize, provide a way of separating myself from Bob and The Order. Once I had won, he would have no reason, as I saw it, to worry about my talking, as he might if I lost. All I would have to do was gradually stop returning his calls or, at some point, simply tell him I wanted nothing more to do with his war against the System, and he, so busy with his plans, would decide I wasn't worth bothering with anymore.

And that, I told myself, as I felt it in my pockets, is the only reason you have taken this money. Now you can afford the heavy-hitters. Now you will win. Man oh man, I thought, you might get out of this yet! I felt a surge of happiness. I dismissed, even as it treaded its way across my mind, my realization that Bob's division of the money, half for legal fees, half for services rendered, could be interpreted by law enforcement authorities, if they learned of it, to mean that I was now on Bob's payroll, a member of The Order and responsible as a conspirator for all its crimes. I even dismissed my realization that I had again accepted money I knew was stolen. Finally, and most important, in that moment I dismissed an annoying little truth-teller who was still within me and who was saying to me: This is more money than you have ever seen in your life, and that's why you are taking it—because you lack the character not to.

I told the truth-teller, because I knew that's what the truth-teller was getting at: Let somebody else catch them; that's not my job.

22 | The Death of Walter West

By the time Jimmy handed me the money, both he and George had begun their evening's drinking. I sat down with them and opened a bottle of beer, which I nursed along. I had no doubt that the money, to say nothing of Jimmy's sporty new clothes, came from the Ukiah robbery. I already knew that The Order had committed it. In one of his phone calls, Bob—in an offhand, proudful way—had said to me: "Of course, that was us; the ZOG papers are full of headlines about it, aren't they?" They were.

I asked Jimmy about Ukiah. As I had suspected, he had been there, and he was also eager to talk about it. By the time he had wended his way through the details, his tongue had become well loosened by drink. "You remember that night at the Bastion?" he asked me.

"What about it?"

"We talked about that guy what was blabbing about Gary's army?"

"I didn't pay much attention."

"We took care of him." He nodded wisely. "Sure did."

"You took care of him?" I asked, not knowing what I was asking.

"We murdered him, man."

The killing had been carried out within hours after Bob's conference with Randy Duey on our way to the Spokane airport. I had misunderstood the reference to the wife. It was not Duey's who had left him but the wife of Walter West, a forty-five-year-old alcoholic member of the Aryan Nations. According to Jimmy, Duey's job, as West's friend, was to convince West that his wife wanted to see him and that he would take him to her. We'll take a shortcut through the woods, Duey told him.

Waiting for Duey and West were Jimmy, Richie Kemp, and a third person whose name Jimmy didn't tell me but whom he later identified as twenty-two-year-old David Tate, another Aryan Nations recruit who either by then was or subsequently became a member of The Order. While Richie and Tate stood watch, Jimmy dug a hole.

When Duey and West arrived, Jimmy said, West seemed surprised to see the three of them there in the middle of a forest, looking at him, not saying a word. As West's gaze went beyond them and saw the hole they were going to put him in, Richie Kemp moved behind him and bashed him over the back of the head with a sledgehammer, in honor of which his code name was soon after changed from "Jolly" to "Hammer."

"So this guy fell," Jimmy told me, "and he's kind of on his hands and knees, bleeding and looking up real scared, you know, an' he says, 'What are you doing?' and as he's saying that, his pal Randy is picking up the guy's own weapon and he points it at him and shoots him right between the eyes. Then I got the dirty job, man. I had to clean the remains up, drag it over and dump it in the hole." But that wasn't his only job. Because of the bullet wound, he explained, West's brains came seeping out of the back of his head, and "I went and got a shovel and picked up his brains and put them in the grave, along with the body," he said, laughing nostalgically.

Alan Berg, I knew, had been murdered because they saw him as an enemy to their cause. In a way, I could understand that. Walter West, one of their own, was murdered because they thought he might be talking: because they *thought* he *might* be talking. I laid my emphasis word for word, just like that, in my mind. Leaning back on my chair a bit, I said, I think smiling: "Hey, Jimmy, if you were told to kill me, man, would you?"

"Yep."

"George? You were told to kill me, would you kill me?"

"Had to be. Yeah."

"Man, I couldn't kill you guys," I said. "I just couldn't kill you guys. What is it...what is it?"

Jimmy said, "You're you and I'm me."

They both laughed at that and they sucked on more beer, and Jimmy said, "So...so let's go out somewhere."

23 | Interlude Alone

I was lying on my bed, my pillows propped up, hands behind my head. Through the window, I could look out into the night, the vacant lot below, and catty-corner to the stretch of wall where the factory had been. I had music on low. My body wasn't quite as big anymore. Since that night with Jimmy, I had lost twenty pounds. Gone to the doctor. Said I had stress at work. Valium. Took them. Stopped taking them. Didn't do a bit of good.

I was like this most nights now. I spent them alone in my room. I had cut Susan out entirely. Not because I wanted to exactly; it was more that I couldn't talk to her because of what I might let out.

The night monster—the monster that hides in your closet when you're a child and is so horrible you close the door on it before you fully look at it, for fear you will let it out and it will turn out to be real: That was the monster I had now freed—or perhaps that had forced its way out of me—and as I lay on my bed it sometimes surprised me, in a strangely objective way, how well I had managed to keep it locked in until the night with Jimmy. Actually, it had leaped out only the one time—"Do you think I want to die?" I had asked the Secret Service man—yet I realized that in some ways I had acted as though I knew about it even before then, knew about it when I shut it out by concentrating on my trial. I have to get away from them, I'd said; I don't want to be mixed up in murder. But it wasn't until Jimmy told me about dragging that body and dumping it in a hole in those lonely woods that I admitted I knew whose murder.

Jimmy was scared too by now, and that frightened me almost as much as what he had told me. Fear had hit him later that same evening. As he had suggested, he and George and I had gone out. We ended up at a bar near Kensington Avenue where an aging corner boy came shuffling over to Jimmy and said, "Hey, Jim, where you been? You look great, pal. Last time I saw you, you said you was makin' a lot of money and things was happenin' for you. Looks like they have, man."

The corner boy wandered off and Jimmy looked over at me, eyes wide, hand across his mouth. "I ain't tellin' nothin'. I ain't tellin' nothin'," starting in a whisper and rising shrill. Might I not say to Bob—it was in the eyes, the shrill—might I not tell him that Jimmy Dye, he's a problem, running off his mouth, got to do something about Jimmy, Bob. I said quietly, "I didn't say you did, Jimmy."

The way I said it made the sweat start on his forehead. In a tight, snarling tone, like a cornered animal: "You're nothin' but a coward!" referring to my statement that I wouldn't get involved in murder. Tit for tat: He could tell Bob that about me.

George laughed one of his "heh-heh" laughs, and I studied Jimmy while I slowly sipped my beer. "Jim, you got a complex problem," I said and I got up and walked out of the bar. "I didn't say nothin'. I didn't say nothin' to nobody," his voice rode after me.

The following evening I saw Jimmy again, and I asked him if he remembered what he'd said to me the night before. He said he didn't, he was drunk, and I reminded him, and I told him I'd rearrange his face for him if he ever called me a coward again. I had done that purposely; I wasn't sure of much, but I knew I couldn't let them think for one second that I was scared of them with their machine guns and their .45s.

I was terrified of them. I got up and walked over to the window, pushed the curtain aside. I looked down at the street. It was a side street. Cars hardly ever came down it. At night, you could watch for hours and not see another soul. I thought about the man coming down that street—after they thought I might talk—and it was never Bob, it was never one of the ones I knew. Not Jimmy Dye. Not Randy Duey. Never Richie Kemp carrying a sledgehammer. I usually thought it would be Bruce Pierce. I'd never met him, but I had heard about him, the ice man. (One of the most unbearable things to me about Walter West's death was that he knew, that the last thing he knew in his life, was that it was his friend, Randy Duey, who was pulling the trigger.) So it would be Bruce Pierce. At times, he was holding a gun as he walked down my sidewalk, a glistening gun, swinging easily at his side with the motion of his arm, and he knocked at my door and I answered and I saw his eyes. But other times, most often, it happened this way: The man without a face came down the street on a night when I wasn't home, and he pulled back his arm and threw high in the air—the way we threw a ball on the playground when I was a kid: "I got it! I got it!"—and through the window it went, the bomb. Susan was dead. Diane was dead. Tom, Jr., was dead. That's how I'd find them.

That's what would happen if I didn't talk and they thought I did. That's what would happen if I did talk and they learned I did. I had never felt so alone in my life, save for the one time when that black boy in my class said he and his pals were going to put a homicide on me. Then I'd been able to run, run from my black enemies. I didn't know how I could run from my white friends.

CHAPTER

24 | Interludes with Bob

Bob smiled up at me, a mischievous smile. Surprised you, didn't I? it said. "Hi, Tom," he said.

I stopped in the doorway of the kitchen. George had invited me over to his house, and when I got there, Jimmy was on hand, too. Bob was sitting in a chair and Maggie, George's wife, who was a beautician, was dying his hair blond.

Genially, as though we were one big happy family, we chatted about this and that, and I was relieved to observe that Jimmy was obviously still worried about me. It was to him that Bob turned and said: "Jim, I want Tom to meet Zillah. You go get her."

Jimmy answered, "Yes, Bob; right away, Bob," and off he went to the motor inn nearby where Zillah and Bob were staying. That left only George to fawn over Bob, which he did. Bob, I thought, is getting like a godfather, although, I supposed, when you pay your men $40,000 a year plus $20,000 per crime, you buy a lot of fawning.

Zillah turned out to be a redhead, heavy with child, and I could see Bob was proud of her pregnancy—his wife couldn't have a child—and while Maggie continued to work on his hair, he told Zillah to

119

come over and stand in front of him. She did so, stood quietly while he patted her belly over and over again. I thought about the baby inside whose father was a murderer and a robber; a hero, Bob would say, long to be remembered for overthrowing ZOG.

When his hair was done, now an eerie platinum color, Bob suggested I pick up Susan so that the two of us could join him and Zillah for dinner at a restaurant. Jimmy and George were invited, too, but when we arrived there, Bob ordered them to sit at a table away from us. Throughout the meal, Susan was the object of Bob's attention, boyish Bob, charming Bob, reassuring Bob. "No chance anything bad's going to happen to Tom, Susan; I guarantee it." He said that one way after another. Mostly she listened. Now and again, she'd nod or say a few words that he seemed to take as agreement. She knew him—perhaps better than I did, certainly sooner than I did—for the dangerous man he was. He was to be placated, she knew, not crossed.

By the time we left Bob that night, I had come to the conclusion that the only reason for his long trip, bringing his pregnant girlfriend with him, was the event that had just taken place, the dinner with Susan and me. No alternative reasons seemed feasible. Jimmy was living on Bob's place or nearby, so Bob hardly had to come to Philadelphia to discuss crimes with him; and for that matter, I couldn't imagine him confiding in Jimmy, much less in the likes of George Zaengle and Bill Nash. All three were troopers, not officer material. That left only me, me and Susan. He wanted to ascertain for himself, I guessed, how well I was standing up under my ordeal and—perhaps more important—Susan's state of mind. He had to assume she blamed him for the trouble he had gotten me into, so the possibility existed that she might talk me into going to the authorities. Hence the dinner with the others excluded; hence the charm; hence the message of hope; hence Zillah as part of the presentation package. If Susan perceived them as a happy and loving pair of expectant parents, that might take the edge off any animosity she felt toward him. Bob thought things out that way. But I think he also had another motive. I believe he genuinely liked Susan, was hurt to think she might no longer approve of him, would want to win her back for that reason alone. That was Bob's way, too.

Susan's way was different. She never reminded me, either before that dinner or after, as she could have, how she had warned me of the trouble Bob was leading me into. Of him, in the days following the dinner, she spoke little, of Zillah not at all. Her response, rather, was to cling to me, arms around me, telling me over and over again of her love for me, and that made me sad and uncomfortable, helped drive me farther from her, because I sensed in her love the keening note of a widow, wailing her love in mourning. She never had any doubt, I know now, what the result of my trial would be.

August 28: Thanks to Bob's money, I had been able to switch lawyers. The expensive hard-hitters of the downtown firm were now on my side. A $5,000 down payment had secured them, with the attorney assigned to me a young fellow named Perry DeMarco. (Bob, as a result, was somewhat mollified; he still would have rather I had accepted his offer to provide me one of his attorneys—at one point, he offered to send in three of them—but since somebody named DeMarco couldn't possibly be a Jew, he remarked, that was a step in the right direction.) In changing lawyers, I had not asked the previous firm to refund to me part of the $1,500 down payment I had made them, which had depleted my counterfeit-passing savings account. Perhaps I saw it as play money; in any event, with a peculiar fastidiousness, I didn't want any of it back.

On the phone: "Hi, Tom. Just flew in." By private plane, he later told me: They could afford that now. "How are you doing, buddy? Holding up okay? How's Susan? The kids? Gee, I hope everybody's fine. Listen, Tom, I want you to meet me over to George's. Got this guy with me. He's a real expert. You'll like him. Voice stress analyzers."

I asked, uneasily, what they were.

Airily: "Oh, they tell when people are telling the truth. It's fascinating. We're going to give the test to George and Bill Nash." He barely skipped a beat. "Like you to take it, too, Tom. You don't mind?"

That was his first sign, the hint that he could be suspicious of his good pal. For once in my life, I thought fast. In a previous conversation I had told him, quite truthfully, that I had spotted strangers who looked like Secret Service agents—you don't see many men wearing suits around K&A—and now I reminded him of that. "If they're following me, that could be dangerous. Going to George's," I said.

He immediately agreed and asked me to name a safe place. I did, a very public one. From there, we went into a nearby luncheonette, where he ordered a steak sandwich and an extra-thick chocolate milkshake. As he stuck his straw in it, he reminded me of one of those kids on the old *Saturday Evening Post* covers, freckled and with a cowlick, but now all grown up and evil. I told him I wasn't going to take a lie detector test, not from somebody I didn't know. "He might be an informant, Bob," I warned in a solemn and worried tone, hoping that would give him something to think about. I don't know whether it did; he did, however, wave away the idea that I should have to take such a test, and he never mentioned it again.

I have since learned the questions I probably would have been asked by the expert, a middle-aged Texan named Ardie McBrearty, who, like Bob, got his start in racism through membership in a tax resisters' league. His code name was "Learned Professor." According to the informant I quoted earlier, the Professor's subjects were first given a copy of *The Turner Diaries* to look through, and then were taken to a room where "[t]hey had all kinds of equipment set up there...they had like a polygraph, they...[had] a voice stress analyzer, they had all kinds of electronic equipment, they had a tape recorder....Okay, so they asked me some questions...like have I ever been a government informant, have I ever given information to anybody who is a member of the United States government, have I ever infiltrated a group who opposes our views, you know, blah, blah, blah....They... asked me if I used drugs, and I said, yes. They said, 'What kind of drugs do you use?' and I said marijuana and cocaine....He said, 'Are you addicted to them?' I said no. They said, 'Can you walk away from it?' I said yes. He said, 'Are you willing to commit your all for the movement?' I said yes. So then they went to the other side of the room in there like where the bathroom is...and...then came back and said, 'You passed....' They turned on a little tape recorder, you know, like that, and said, 'Now give us all the information you have on Morris Dees.'"

While sipping at his milkshake, Bob shifted from lie detector tests to my future. Until that moment, and all his chatter about lawyers had been part of that strategy, he had sought to give me, as he had Susan, confidence that victory would be mine at trial. Only once or twice, as though an idle passing thought, had he remarked that if I wanted to skip trial a welcome would be waiting for me with him in The Order. Now, apparently, he had decided the time was at hand to push that idea.

He approached it by asking why I didn't get a new car. The one I was driving was rented, since my own, as I had told him, was impounded by the Secret Service as evidence. "You buy it; I'll pay for it," he offered. I answered, "No need, Bob; I'll get mine back after I win." I had said that before, too, and he must have been expecting the repetition because immediately he shifted into a deeply saddened expression. "Tom, Tom," he said, explaining the facts of life, "I haven't wanted to say this before now, but you aren't going to win. There's no way they're going to let you walk out of there. ZOG never lets its enemies get away. I've been thinking about it, Tom, and, hell's bells, I just don't think you have any choice. Come with me, Tom."

He raised a hand to stop any objections. "Hey, now, listen, don't misunderstand me. I'm not asking you to leave your family. I'd never do anything like that! I know how much they mean to you. They'll come, too."

Obtaining new names for us would not be a problem. Whenever the need arose for that, he explained, Jean Craig—who had performed such yeoman service trailing Alan Berg around Denver—would visit her favorite cemetery to find names of dead people who had been born around the same time as those for whom the identifications were required. Their birth certificates were sent for, and from them Robert Merki produced the false IDs. Bob shook his head as if in wonderment at himself: "If you'd only see what we have, the people, the money, the places, the contacts I have, Tom. If you go underground with me, I can show you."

As a proof of his contacts and the glorious future they foretold, he informed me that Ukiah had been made possible through two Order members who worked for Brink's. They had revealed the details of the route that would be taken, the amount of money aboard, how to distinguish the bags of cash from those containing checks. Having Brink's employees on his team was going to pay off even more handsomely in the near future. The insiders, he confided (though he didn't give names or places), were providing blueprints and access to a vault. The robbery would take place following the scheduled arrival of an exceptionally large amount of cash. The size of that haul would dwarf Ukiah, he added complacently.

I said, "Yeah, that's really something." It was—Bob with his hands on even more millions. "I just got to think about it," I temporized, referring to going underground with him.

"I can understand that," he said. "Just think about it."

He continued to sip his extra-thick milkshake. It was while he was finishing it that he told me for the first time that the Berg murder was not an isolated event but was to initiate a series of assassinations of high-level officials and other enemies of the cause. He smiled at me. The *Saturday Evening Post* boy grown up now had a perfect chocolate moustache on his upper lip.

25 | Art Gold

My trial was scheduled for October 1, postponed from an earlier date to give my new lawyer time to prepare my case. When I next heard from Bob, by phone, early in September, I told him that DeMarco thought the worst result I could expect was probation and a fine. That wasn't true, but I wanted him to think I wasn't worried, so he wouldn't worry. He seemed to accept my word: "Hey, that's good news, buddy."

It was during that same conversation that Bob made a slip. (One of the problems of being a liar is that you sometimes forget to whom you've told which falsehood.) He mentioned that Bruce Pierce had been arrested the previous December on charges of counterfeiting $50 bills. That's how I learned that Bob, when he was weaving New Eden for me in February, had not been telling me the truth when he said the only purpose of the robberies was to get money to buy counterfeiting equipment; they already had it. As I hung up, I recapitulated that conversation to myself: It had all been lies, dreamed up to snare me. Bitterly, I thought of how much he must have laughed to himself about my gullibility. (I now don't think that he did; the New Eden he told me about was tailored to fit his shrewd perception of what I was then ready to accept, but New Eden itself—his New Eden—he believed in passionately.)

I heard from him again three days before my trial. He was calling, he said, from Wyoming; terse, tense, disjointed, no preamble: "What you got to do, Tom," his first words, "is get out of there, and I mean tonight. I'll arrange everything. It can be done right away. Tom, we need you. This is our last leg of battle as Aryans. We have to do it this time. Tom, Tom, I have a million things on my mind."

The words came tumbling out, much as they had in my hotel room at the National Alliance convention: "We're going to get a dam," going on to describe the explosives and technology they had on hand to destroy it. (Later I learned that the site he had in mind was Boundary Dam in Washington, which supplies electricity to Seattle.) "And something else is going down real soon, too. You know *Klanwatch?*"

I said I did.

"That Dees, he's our next target, and Irv Rubin of the Jewish Defense League in L.A., he's next after Dees."

I tried to placate him. "Hey, that's a lot going on, Bob."

He seemed to take that to mean I was impressed, which, in a way, I was. He returned to the primary subject of his call. I backed away, feeling as desperate as he sounded: "Nah, nah, Bob. I'm not going to become a fugitive. Like I told you, it's going to go okay. Believe me."

He obviously didn't but, like a father who is disappointed in his little boy's stubbornness but is going to make everything all right for him anyway, he said, "Well, if that's how you feel, but we can solve your worst problem."

"What do you mean?"

"Art Gold."

For a second I couldn't even remember who he was: "Art Gold?"

"Yeah, you won't have to worry about him." Then I visualized Gold, standing behind the counter of his store; on the sidewalk taking my license plate number as I sped away. "When someone harms one of us, the brothers take care of him," Bob went on.

"Bob, you aren't talking about killing him?"

"We can make it look like a robbery."

"For Christ's sake, Bob!" I was yelling at him now. "You can't do that." I didn't even try to tell him it would be wrong. "They'd never believe it. Killed right before my trial? I'd go to jail for murder, man."

"Okay, okay, if that's how you feel."

He sounded convinced. Even so, I was glad he was nearly 3,000 miles away.

The next day I went over to Maggie Zaengle's house to get my hair cut for the trial. (By now, George had gone underground with Bob, and Maggie was supposed to join them in a location somewhere in the West; the plan, though I don't know if she was told anything of it, was to open a beauty salon for her which would act as a center for taking code messages for Order members.) When I arrived at her house, she asked, "Did you see Bob?"

Unsuspectingly, I answered, "Not since he was here in August."

"No, he was here last night," she said. "He was here to get his hair dyed again. He had a man with him, a man with a brown beard." That could have been Bruce Pierce. "Didn't he reach you?" she asked. "He called you from a phone booth right near your house."

"No, I...I guess he missed me," I mumbled.

When Bob called me Sunday evening, I asked him why he had told me he was calling from Wyoming when he was actually in Philadelphia. His reply: "Ah, I had something to do. Something didn't feel right." That meant he had no intention of telling me, so I didn't pursue it. I am still not certain of his motivation. Most probably, he expected me to agree to go underground with him, and if I had, he would then have revealed that he was in the city and arranged to meet with me; as he had said, it could be done right away. It is also conceivable that he and Pierce, if Pierce was the second man, came to Philadelphia to murder Gold and intended to do that regardless of how I decided about joining them. Still another possibility is that they came prepared to murder me. For three nights prior to Bob's call, I had observed, during the course of my lonely evenings in my bedroom, a car parked in a way so that it faced my house. Each night when I turned off my bedroom light, it drove away. I had assumed the car contained Secret Service agents keeping me under surveillance, and conceivably that is the explanation, but equally likely it was Bob and Pierce, watching, trailing, wondering if I were going out to meet men in suits. That I hadn't may have saved my life and given Bob confidence that he was right to trust me. It was a confidence that would pay a bitter dividend in Portland two months later.

On my way home from Maggie's house, I went by Gold's store, though almost afraid to do so. But there he was, safe and sound, standing behind the counter. I thought of going in to warn him his life might be in danger, but then I realized if I, the person he was going to testify against, did that, he'd be sure to take my warning as a threat, and he'd testify to that, too.

I stood, looking down at my hands. They opened and closed on nothing.

CHAPTER

26 | Cornered

October 1, a bright Monday morning, and Susan and I were standing, close to one another but not speaking, a few feet from the courtroom where my trial was to be held. At the other end of the hall I saw Gold, his blond-haired clerk with him, both of them glancing at us every once in a while. Waiting also, just off to one side from us, briefcase in hand, eyeing me closely, was Perry DeMarco.

Perry had been to my house the day before, even though it was a Sunday, to impart some disturbing news. The prosecutors, he informed me, had just revealed to him that my phone records had been subpoenaed. A call that seemed to interest them was the one I had made to Reverend Miles to set up the meeting between Bob's emissaries and Glenn Miller. Next to the number was a notation that Miles had served seven years in prison on the school bus bombing charge. My link to the racist movement was indicated by that, but was hardly criminal in itself. Much more worrisome were the calls to and from a Robert Jay Mathews, identified on the papers Perry had received as an associate of one Bruce Carroll Pierce, a suspected counterfeiter. That was how—devastatingly if inaccurately (Pierce had nothing to do with printing the money I passed; that was Merki's handiwork)—they were going to prove I was no innocent recipient of the bills I'd foisted on Gold. If they had that much, they might have a great deal more.

Perry had spent most of the afternoon urging me to tell him the truth about my activities. He was positive, probably had been for some time, that I was deeply involved—"in deep trouble," I'd told Gold, who had almost certainly informed the prosecutors I had said that—in matters that went beyond passing the two tens at Gold's. Even so, Perry believed that if I leveled with him and the government, he could still save me from going to prison. I resisted him, truculently, passionlessly, without hope.

I don't want to die, I thought.

Susan's arm brushed against me. I had a sense of her voice traveling up to me from a distance. "Tom?" I didn't want her to die. "Tom, you should." In my mind's eye, I saw Diane wheeling up the sidewalk, rising on the seat of her bike as she saw them taking me away; screaming.

"You know I love you, hon," I said.

"Tom. Talk. For us, please."

I turned to her, and as I did I thought, so that is what you are going to do, after all. Not for the life of Morris Dees, not for Irv Rubin, not for Art Gold a few feet away, gesturing as he talks to his clerk. You're going to do it because that's all that's left that you can do. I had finally gotten there. Step by step, I had backed myself into the corner where I now crouched. I ran my hand across my face as if hoping that when I lowered it, I'd be able to see something. "Please, Tom."

"Perry," I said, "I want to talk to somebody."

PART III | The Road from Portland

CHAPTER 27 | Informant

The room was similar to the one I had been taken to the night I was arrested. A desk. Wooden chairs. Walls bare, paint pale. I waited. A Secret Service agent was sitting at the desk, McDonough, he said his name was; tall, trim, athletic-looking, watching me expressionlessly. The door opened—it seemed I had been there hours already, but probably less than one—and along with Perry came a conservatively dressed man, a man of authority, self-assurance in the clothes, in the way he moved. His name, he told me as he shook my hand, was Bucky Mansuy, Assistant U.S. Attorney, assigned to prosecute the case of the United States of America versus Thomas Allen Martinez. He talked calmly, quietly, and I think Perry threw in some words, too—much of this part is vague in my memory, like the verse of a song when it's only the melody you remember—but I recall nodding as he explained that the government, in return for my cooperation, would drop one of the counterfeiting charges against me and recommend to the judge that I receive no prison sentence. Yes, I would agree to allow my phone to be tapped, I said. Will you agree to wear a body wire? That was in it somewhere, too. No, no, I said—

thinking of Bob's security precautions—and they didn't press that issue. Bob sometimes didn't press issues either; he just got back to them later.

"Now," said Mansuy, only then, as I recall, seating himself, facing me, expectant, friendly, but with none of the "nice"-cop artificiality to him, "what is it that you can tell us, Tom?"

"Yes," I said, "I did pass that money." That was what I was charged with, and it seemed logical to me I should begin with it, but the problem was I couldn't think of that, because what it made me think of was Lane saying, "No great loss." I tried to look at Mansuy but my gaze wavered, went beyond him to a spot on the wall behind him and stayed there as I said in a monotone: "I know things. I know who robbed the Ukiah armored car, and I know about other robberies. And I know of a dam that is going to be blown up. And I know who killed Alan Berg. And I know of another individual who is to be murdered. I know of these things. I know, I know about many things."

Mansuy held up a hand. He glanced at McDonough, over to Perry. "I think," he said, "I think we better get the FBI in here."

Two of them came, looking cool and professional. They had pads; they took notes. I talked. Once I started, I didn't stop and they didn't interrupt me. It wasn't as though—and they may have sensed as much—that I could either start or stop. I was in a rhythm of words as I wandered the landscape of Bob's world.

When I did stop, my head was down. I was bringing my hands up to meet it. "What you did, Tom, is right. It took a lot of courage." That was Mansuy. I looked over at him in surprise, not so much at what he said but that he was there. "You see, I love my family," I said. "I love my kids," and I began to cry. I cannot remember a time before in my life when I cried, although there would be one time later. As I shook my head—that would stop the crying—I sensed them watching me, and for a moment it was as though I were watching me, too, and then I was back inside myself but strangely: as if I had been all separated out, body here, head there, coming back together.

"You're going to be all right." That was one of the FBI agents speaking, and either he or the other one added: "There'll be no harm come to your family, sir. We promise you that."

Susan was sitting on a bench in the hall, waiting for me. As I came out of the room, she half rose. I went over to her, sat beside her. She studied my eyes, the tears tell-tale on my cheeks. "Are you all right, hon?" she asked.

I stared at her. "Why...why, I feel great," I said in amazement.

I had done the right thing. I was in the hands of the right people. Euphoria.

It didn't work out quite that way.

CHAPTER

28 Gary's Army

By October first, investigators were no nearer an arrest in the Berg murder than they had been on the night it occurred more than three months before. Neither, until I became an informant, had a connection been made between Berg's death and the Ukiah holdup, nor between it and any of the previous Order robberies. Now I had given the FBI the keys to these crimes, and I had also given them the names of the perpetrators of a crime they hadn't even known had been committed, the murder of Walter West.

On Ukiah, unlike the Berg murder, some progress had been made prior to my help. The gun Bob had left behind in the back of the armored car had been traced to Barnhill, its serial number leading to a post office box in Missoula, Montana, where FBI agents discovered a batch of Nazi literature. Running a further check on Barnhill, they learned that he had been arrested and released in Oregon a month previous in the company of Randall Evans, following an altercation in which one or both men assaulted a person they alleged was a male prostitute. In Barnhill's possession at the time were documents in the name of Keith Merwin. FBI agents proceeded to the small Idaho town named on the Merwin identification papers. The street address proved to be an empty house, but records showed that Merwin had rented it some months before. In the house the investigators found a newspaper clipping describing the armored car robbery in Seattle, in which a GET OUT OR YOU DIE sign had been used as in Ukiah. Along with the clipping was another paper containing "Rules of Security" for "The Bruders Schweigen," written by someone named Carlos. Among the rules: The brothers should never mention racial matters in public; refer to each other only by their code names; always be armed; always carry $500 wrapped in a sock; only use pay phones when calling one another.

All that was intriguing, but it did not prove the second GET OUT OR YOU DIE robbery was connected to the first—the second robbers might have simply copied the idea from the Seattle holdup—nor had the agents any way of knowing what, if anything—it could be someone's fantasy—the Bruders Schweigen was or who Carlos might be (until I told them).

Other information the investigation had uncovered related directly to the Ukiah holdup. Shortly after making their getaway, the robbers had deserted their pick-up trucks, one of which was traced to a man who had sold it to two strangers who, he gathered, from an overheard comment, probably had been staying at a motel on Cleveland Avenue in Santa Rosa. A number of motels were located along that strip, and phone records of each were checked along with those of nearby pay phones, the latter revealing that, during the three days prior to the robbery, calls were placed to the home of Robert Jay Mathews in Metaline Falls, to that of the ex-wife of Denver Parmenter, to a Gary Yarbrough in Idaho, to the house of a young woman in Salinas, California (subsequently identified as a friend of Billy Soderquist), and finally to an apartment in nearby San Leandro shared by two San Francisco office Brink's employees, Charles Ostrout and Ronald King.

But after that the trail had grown cold, and by the beginning of October no further progress had been made. Barnhill, who was assumed to be Merwin, had disappeared. No one named Mathews, Parmenter, Soderquist, or Yarbrough had been registered at any of the Santa Rosa motels, and—while suspicious—the calls to the apartment in San Leandro could have been made by anyone for perfectly innocent purposes. Mathews, now known to have phoned me and also suspected to be a friend of the suspected counterfeiter Pierce, provided the most promising lead, but even if he could be located, he could hardly be charged with participating in Ukiah or anything else on the basis of a call made to his house by pay phone from an unknown person near a motel where the robbers might have stayed.

My information put the pieces together. I was even able, as soon as I heard his name, to place one of the Brink's employees within the neo-Nazi movement. I had never heard of King, but Ostrout, though I had never met him, was known to me from mentions of him in the National Alliance bulletins as a San Francisco area member. Both he and King were placed under surveillance. When, several months later, they were taken into custody, the fifty-one-year-old Ostrout, who was a money room supervisor, confessed that he and King had plotted with Bruce Pierce on the projected vault robbery, which was to take place as soon as a special shipment of between $30 million and $50 million in cash arrived from Hawaii. Ostrout also admitted that he had provided Pierce with the route of the Ukiah armored car and explained how to distinguish by their tags which bags contained cash and which had checks in them. King, forty-five, an operations manager for Brink's, pleaded guilty to his part in planning the vault robbery but denied knowing anything in advance about Ukiah. It was only a coincidence, he claimed, that his estranged wife, Lisa, was the guard on duty that day who was nearly killed by the robbers.

The whereabouts of the bulk of the $4 million in stolen money, from Ukiah and the other crimes, was a mystery to the FBI and to me. I didn't yet know of the cash crop Ken Loff was raising, although I had given his name as an Order member who probably had knowledge of the Walter West killing. Based on Jimmy Dye's explanation of Bob's payment system, the eleven who participated in the Ukiah holdup would have received, I pointed out, a total of $220,000, with the quarterly "salaries" and other bonuses for various per-crime commissions accounting for perhaps another $500,000; that total was speculative, since it was unclear how many were on the payroll at any given time. I also reported that Bob had told me he was making contributions to paramilitary racist organizations so that they could arm themselves as allies in his revolution, although the $1,000 that Barnhill said he gave Glenn Miller was the only specific sum of which I had knowledge. I believed, I said (correctly as it turned out) that a sizable portion of the remainder was set aside for purchase of arms for The Order itself, including laser weaponry for the projected assaults on the Seattle and Los Angeles power supplies.

In FBI parlance, a person like me is known as a "CS," which means "confidential source," and each CS is given a number—mine was "1"—and that is how we appear, rather than by name, in all files concerning the matters in which we are involved. We are also assigned our own case agent, who supervises our cooperation, reports on it, forwards to us "suggestions" and orders from on high, and is the sole individual we are supposed to contact when we have problems.

The agent assigned to me was Elizabeth Pierciey, a six-year veteran and a member of the FBI's terrorist squad. I was introduced to her on the same day I made my confession, and over the next seven weeks, culminating in the events in Portland, I saw her or at least spoke to her an average of every other day. Libby, as she preferred to be called, was a slender, attractive woman with dark brown hair, probably somewhere in her late thirties. Despite our constant contact, I never felt I got to know her as a person. She had an aloof quality, arising perhaps from her awareness that, as a woman, she had to be constantly on her guard, extra impersonal, extra professional, in ways that the more relaxed male agents didn't feel they had to be. Every once in a while, however, cracks of warmth would show through, of friendliness, and then I could see how, in the days when she was an elementary school teacher, her students would have loved her, found her fun as they learned from her.

Early in our relationship, probably still in the first week of October, Libby had me meet Lou Vizi, another member of the FBI's terrorist squad, who had been stationed in California investigating the Ukiah holdup and who flew to Philadelphia when he learned of the information I had provided. A big, muscular sort who always wore cowboy boots—he called me "pardner"—to me Vizi's most remarkable characteristic was his eyes: They were never at rest, darting here and there as though he constantly expected a figure to emerge from the shadows, shooting. In the course of going over my story, I said that I'd heard from Jimmy, as well as during the conversation at the Bastion, that the reason for killing West was that he was "blabbing about Gary's army." I said I knew nothing else about Gary, not even his last name, except that I was under the impression he lived either at the Aryan Nations compound in Idaho or near it. That interested Vizi, who was aware, through his investigation of Ukiah, of the call made from the Santa Rosa pay phone to a Gary Yarbrough in Idaho.

The reason for the reference to "Gary's army" has never become clear. I never otherwise heard The Order described either as "Gary's" or an "army." (At its height it had only 23 members.) Yarbrough, at the time, was security chief of the Aryan Nations, where the counterfeiting was taking place, and that may have been why the term was used. Whatever the reason, that Gary supposedly had an army interested the FBI and led to its decision to move against him without further ado.

Skinny, with reddish hair and a dead-eyed sullen look, Yarbrough differed from most Order members in that he had a criminal record before joining. Because he did, he was attractive to Reverend Butler and the Aryan Nations, which, in the late 1970s, initiated a "ministry" program to white inmates in several prisons, including the one in Arizona where Yarbrough was incarcerated following a burglary and marijuana conviction. White supremacy pamphlets, brochures, and even taped sermons were distributed, leading to the formation in that and other prisons of white racist gangs calling themselves the Aryan Brotherhood. In recent years, these gangs have fostered incidents of violence; in the California prison system members have led white riots against minority inmates, while in Wisconsin a guard was killed by Aryan Brotherhood thugs.

According to an informant, the Aryan Nations has operated a halfway house for Brotherhood members who had been released, the purpose being to help them go straight—straight to the Aryan Nations, that is. It is not known if Yarbrough passed through this halfway house when he was released in 1979, after serving three of the eight years of his sentence; not long after, however, he did show up in Idaho on Butler's doorstep. Soon he had himself a spiffy Nazi uniform, a 9-mm Browning pistol to carry in a shiny leather holster, and the title of

Security Chief. The title and the perks no doubt stroked his ego, but they didn't provide him with cash. His only known paying job during that period was as a dishwasher at a nearby truck stop called Schoony's Cafe. While employed there, he lived with his wife and a brood of children in a three-room shack renting for $50 a month. By September 1984, life had obviously improved for Yarbrough. That month he leased a luxury home on ten acres near Sandpoint, Idaho, paying for its rent, as he did most of his other bills, in cash.

On October 18 the FBI decided to have a look at him and his army. Dressed as forest rangers, three agents approached the house. Yarbrough opened fire on them. Following an exchange of gunshots, he fled into the woods, leaving his wife and children behind in the house. His pursuers soon lost his trail. He would not resurface until November 23, when I met him as "Reds."

Yarbrough's attack on the agents gave them probable cause to enter his house. There, in a leather briefcase, they found a .45-caliber MAC-10 machine pistol, which ballistics experts determined was the weapon used to murder Alan Berg.

That wasn't all they uncovered. Present in the house along with his family, who could easily have been blown up by some of the contents, was: one hundred sticks of dynamite; blasting caps; fuses; a $1\frac{1}{2}$-pound block of plastic explosive; a hand grenade; smoke grenades; a 12-gauge shotgun; a .38-caliber MAC-10 with a silencer; thousands of rounds of ammunition; a crossbow; an assortment of rifles, gas masks, automatic pistols, knives, thousands of dollars in cash, a list of names, and...several Bibles.

Anyone who shoots at FBI agents—Yarbrough would later claim he merely fired warning shots in the air—becomes an immediate object of intense interest to the Bureau. Agents don't take kindly to being shot at, and because they don't, Yarbrough's presence at Portland would have a direct effect on my future and on Bob's as well.

CHAPTER

29 | Zillah's Baby

I next heard from Bob when he called me on the third of October. By then I had attached to my phone the recorder I had been given, though I didn't expect it to produce much. As the manual of instructions found in the Merwin house indicated, pay phones were to be used exclusively when criminal plans were to be discussed. On those occasions, Bob would either give me a coded number to reach him via a pay phone or else he'd not give me a code but tell me to go to a pay phone for which I'd given him the number and wait for his call there. When I explained his system to the FBI, I was given a taping device for the pay phone calls, too.

The reason for Bob's October 3 call was to learn the result of my trial. There'd been no trial, I told him; acting on DeMarco's advice, I said, I had pleaded guilty to passing the two tens at Gold's. Because it was my first offense, DeMarco expected I would get off with probation, but I could face a fine of as much as $10,000. That was no problem, Bob said; he'd send me the money. He sounded relieved, as I had hoped, but then I made the mistake of telling him that my sentencing wouldn't take place until December 14. (It had been put off until then to encourage my continuing cooperation and, I assume, to give the government the opportunity to assess my truthfulness and the value of the information I was providing.) "Oh, my God!" said Bob when I told him that, and I had no doubt of the genuineness of his concern, since it was extraordinary for him to use God's name as an expletive. "Well, that's a long time." Though he chose his words cautiously because we were on a home phone, he made clear to me that he believed the reason for the delay was to give ZOG additional time to investigate my relationship with him.

He called again the following night, and either the next or the one after. Obviously, he had no specific message for me; if he had, we would have gone the pay phone route. However, from the course of his seemingly idle chatter, it was apparent to me that he was attempting to learn, just as the FBI was, if there was anything I knew that I was holding back. I don't know if I satisfied him on that score or not. But after those calls, days went by and the days became weeks and there was no further word from him.

His silence frustrated the Bureau, which had hoped that in one of his contacts, he'd either tell me he was coming to Philadelphia or else I'd find some way to encourage him to do so. If that happened, the plan, or so I was told, was not to arrest him but rather to place him under surveillance so that he would lead his pursuers to his confederates.

The Bureau made preparations for that possibility. One evening an electronics expert showed up at my house, along with Libby, and placed two microphones inside my living room couch that I could activate if Bob showed up—I'd told them it was possible he'd arrive unannounced, as he had in the past. They also wanted to replace my television with one that had a camera inside it. I pointed out that Bob, who was nothing if not observant, would notice the new set and might, because of his own growing knowledge of bugging gadgetry, become suspicious. They agreed, and decided that a lamp containing a camera, activated when it was lit, would do the same trick and be less obvious. I was far from sure of that, and eventually nothing was done.

*   *   *

October 28: "Zillah's baby is due!" Those were his first words, chipper and proud. He gave no reason for his long silence, nor did I ask him—nor was there reason to because he seemed about to give us what we wanted: "Hey, listen, Tom, I'm going to be in your area in five days. Remember where I had the chocolate milkshake?" I told him I did. "We'll hook up there," he said.

After he hung up, I called Libby, pointing out that we might not have to wait until he got to Philadelphia. His mention of Zillah's baby reminded me that in one of the calls early in October, he had explained that delivery was to be by midwives in a house in Laramie that belonged to Zillah's mother, Jean Craig. "And I'm going to be there, buddy," he said proudly.

The Wyoming FBI was notified, the Craig house surrounded. While agents watched from a wooded area some distance off, a baby girl was born. Hours had passed and darkness descended when a man, with a furtive look about, hat pulled down, left the house. Assuming that he was Bob, the agents followed to see where he might lead them; but after about twenty minutes, it became clear that the man was going nowhere in particular. Only then, as they approached closer, did the agents realize that the person they were trailing was not a "he" but Zillah sent out, dressed in Bob's clothes, as a decoy. Bob's constant carefulness—no doubt at a new height of awareness following the raid on Yarbrough's property two weeks earlier—had paid off for him. By the time the agents got back to the house, he was long gone.

30 | Interlude Alone

The euphoria I had felt on the day I became an informant had during October gradually been replaced by a deepening depression. Again I had begun to hide in my room after dinner, hands clasped behind my head, music on low, staring at the ceiling. Again I had started taking Valium. Again they had done no good, maybe the opposite, and again I had stopped taking them.

My state of mind, I now believe, was triggered by the removal of my greatest cause of stress: By becoming an informant, I no longer had to fear for my own life or that of my family. I had no doubt of the government's ability to protect us, and probably I was not equipped psychologically to cope with the upward turn in my fortune. The elation and the depression that succeeded it, therefore, were like two faces that are identical except that one is smiling and the other frowning.

The euphoria had proven treacherous in another regard. The relief I had felt when I finally bared my soul of my crime knowledge had led me to assume that the end to my problems was at last in sight. I'd talked; they'd act; arrests; trials scheduled. But that had not happened. As each day of October went by, bringing neither a call from Bob nor any indication that the government was closing in on The Order, I began to have an almost physical sense of the dragging time. I was in a limbo from which the night monster may have been vanquished, but the night itself remained.

Even though I was disappointed by the lack of action following my confession, my pervasive sense of dejection did not have as one of its ingredients any regret that I had done what I did. Surprisingly to me, the reaction I had feared most in prospect—a sense of betrayal of my friend by informing on him—had not come to pass, save, at one moment, in one of the early October calls, when Bob had concluded by saying, "Give my love to Susan and the children."

Perspective—and in that sense the passage of time had helped me—added to my confidence in the correctness of my decision. The pre-confession concerns I'd had about Bob's past and prospective victims, while not insincere, had existed as if seen off in a distance through the prism of my own fears. They had been, as it were, a luxury I could not afford, but now I could, and in that new framework the evil of The Order was becoming objectively and increasingly clear to me. Indeed, the only time during October when my spirits were high was when I was meeting with Libby and the other agents. At those moments I had a sense of participation in undoing the wrongs I had committed and permitted.

Yet it was precisely those meetings that, as soon as they were over, propelled me into my deepest states of gloom. While they were happening I could avoid my awareness of why they were happening. Afterward, I could not.

I replayed my life, as I lay there on my bed, night after night, in no necessary order—I might start here, might start there—but wherever I did, I came to the same conclusion. After having lived for nearly thirty years, the only accomplishment I could name was that I had succeeded in endangering the lives of those I loved and the lives of others I did not know. I could, I told myself, excuse some of my mistakes as a consequence of sincere if misguided zeal to save the world, that my ignorance of that same world might explain others, but most of them had only one cause: I was a weak person. I had once fancied myself as a leader; I had proven only that I'd follow anyone or any cult that flattered me.

My sentencing date of December 14 had become increasingly a focal point for the self-evaluation I was going through. My response to it had begun as simple fear. The horror of incarceration I'd felt that one night I spent locked in a cell remained with me, and I dreaded the prospect of being torn from my family, not seeing my children grow up. Yet the longer I stayed in my room, the more there seeped through me the belief that I should go to prison.

I should be punished. That would make things right.

Did I believe that as I lay in my room? At moments, I did. At others, however, I sensed it was no solution, that after my release I'd be every bit as weak as when I went in. With that thought, guilt and self-pity met in me in a state of perfect union.

31 | The Road to Portland

Bob's announced arrival in Philadelphia five days hence had sent the FBI into a flurry of activity. Stakeout orders were issued. A listening device was placed on my car. Dry runs. What I was to say. What I was to do. It all came to naught.

"I just can't come to Philadelphia. Something's come up." It was the evening of November 1, and he gave me a number to reach him through a pay phone. Under the dial-back system he employed, whenever he gave a number, the exchange and digits were correct but the area code was off by one. Thus, in this instance, his 808 code meant that I should dial 919.

Before going to a pay phone, I rang information and learned that 919 covered the Greensboro, North Carolina, area. That scared me. I had read in one of the racist publications I still received—and this may be the only time one of those sheets has ever served a good purpose—that Morris Dees was in and out of Greensboro, pursuing a case against Glenn Miller, involving arms Miller had allegedly bought from soldiers who had smuggled them out of Fort Bragg. I alerted

Libby, telling her that Bob might be there to carry out his announced intention to assassinate Dees.

While I went out to call him—and I have no recollection of the conversation that followed, except that no mention was made of Dees—she contacted the FBI in North Carolina. Agents immediately located Dees at a motel and placed him under guard.

If my quick action and that of the North Carolina agents had saved Dees, at least temporarily, the success did not go beyond that. By the following day it was apparent that Bob had avoided the intensive search for him that had been mounted. It is possible, even so, that he did not leave the state immediately. From an account provided more than a year later by an informant, Bob and Scutari—who would be identified as one of the murderers of Berg—were in and out of North Carolina during early November, apparently in an attempt to recruit new members for The Order. During that period—the exact dates aren't known—the same source says that Jean Craig spent time in Montgomery, Alabama, where Dees' headquarters was located, in order to carry out the same surveillance on him as she had on Berg.

Between the fifth and ninth of November, with the Bureau's permission, I took my family to Disneyland in Orlando, Florida. I hoped that the vacation—if only by forcing me out of my room—would break my depression. On my return, however, not only had my mood not improved, it now seemed well matched to that emanating from the FBI. Bob had proven as elusive to the Bureau as the will-o'-the-wisp lights outside the town of Marfa where he was born. Agents had come within yards of him in Laramie, but he had danced away; they probably were within minutes of capturing him in Greensboro, but he had danced away; the best remaining hope, that he could be picked up when he came to visit me in Philadelphia, had proven another chimera. The situation was becoming embarrassing: He was one man and the FBI—with its thousands of agents, its contacts with every police force in the country, its bugging equipment, the informants it had within the racist movement—was no nearer to capturing him than on the day I informed its agents about him. The land was huge and he was alone in it, somewhere, and FBI officials must have been having nightmares of a dam blowing up or machine guns blasting in the night, and the torrent of criticism that would come their way because they hadn't found him when they knew who he was and what he was planning.

On either the evening of my return from Florida or the night after, I heard from Bob once more, his conversation just long enough to tell me to get to the pay phone we regularly used. I asked him to give me twenty minutes. Immediately I called Libby to tell her he was back in contact. She said she'd meet me across the street from the booth. When I arrived there, the phone was ringing. As I answered, I attached the recording device. "How are you doin' anyway, Tom?" he asked. "Your spirits holding up?"

I said: "Man, I wish you could come to Philadelphia. I could use some morale, you know."

To that he replied: "Geez, I'm afraid I can't right now, buddy." He hesitated a moment. "Things are, they're hot right now. What the heck, they even have a plane following Zillah." (This wasn't paranoia on his part: The FBI plane hovered over Zillah's house and trailed her wherever she went on the lonely Wyoming roads; about a month later it crashed into a mountain and the pilot was killed.)

An edge of desperation, for the first time, was in his voice as he said that, but it was replaced almost immediately by a boyishly enticing tone: "Hey, listen, Tom, buddy, we're really on to something big this time. It's going down real soon." I asked him what it was, but he said abruptly, no, he had to ring off, he'd get back to me on the eighteenth. I didn't know whether he meant that the "something big" would be accomplished by the eighteenth or whether he'd tell me more about it then.

Discouraged, I hung up and walked over to where Libby was waiting for me. As I got into her car, I handed her the tape from the call. "No way he's coming to Philadelphia, no way," I said.

"You have no idea at all where he is." It was more a statement than a question.

I pointed to the tape. "I don't even know where he called me from." Without thinking, I added: "Only way I'd know is if I went to meet him."

"Oh?" A pause. "You think he'd meet with you?"

She sounded doubtful. I looked over at her, surprised. Her hands were on the steering wheel; she was staring out into the night. "Why, sure," I said. "That's all he's ever wanted, me to go underground with him."

"Yes, I see." She nodded. "Would you?"

Now, I thought, this feels right. It was as if there'd been a piece missing all along—my frustration and depression a part of it—a piece I recognized as soon as I saw it, but not before: What I saw was Bob and me alone together. At the end of the world. I should have known, I thought, that's where we would have to end.

"Yes," I said, both to her question and my realization. In retrospect, I'm surprised I didn't feel excited. Or frightened. Rather, I remember I was almost eerily calm, a click-click thinking calmness. "On two conditions," I said, click-click. "Two. One is you got to promise me, you won't arrest him when I take you to him; okay?" If they took him into custody then, he'd know who was responsible and in a matter of days so would all the gun-toting lunatics in the racist movement, coming after me. "The second is you—" I liked him; I still liked him. "You got to promise me you won't hurt the man. You don't promise that, I'm not doing it."

She said she'd run it by her superiors. The next day she got back to me. They had agreed to both conditions. Guarantee. Absolute guarantee.

Bob's November 18 call came through on time, as his calls almost always did. In thinking about it beforehand, I realized he might become suspicious if, after all the times I had put him off about joining him, I now simply said I'd changed my mind. In considering my approach, I recalled the phone records Perry had shown me the day before my trial. I had never mentioned them to Bob; now I did, about to weave a fantasy for him just as he had once woven one for me. I told him I was scheduled to go to FBI headquarters the following week to undergo interrogation about his calls to me and the ones I had placed to Bob Miles; and, I went on, what might be even worse, the Feds had also somehow found out about Carlos and wanted to question me about that, too. In a despairing tone, I concluded: "Like the last time they picked me up, they had me under for five or six hours and the next time it might be twelve. I don't want to go through it. I'm like, I'm all ready to get out of here."

"Okay. Now that's good." He did sound pleased, but hardly surprised by my decision. Perhaps that was because I had woven my fantasy as well as he had his, but I think mostly it was because Bob was never surprised when he got what he wanted. Neither did he spend time discussing my decision—that wasn't his way any more than recriminations over mistakes were—but instead briskly proceeded to the next step. (He would have made, I think, a fine executive.) He'd call me again the following evening, he said, to discuss arrangements. I sensed he had more than that on his mind.

I was right. When the call came through, he was ready to take me to the next step: "It can't be just you, Tom. You've got to bring Susan with you, and the kids. You can't leave them behind, buddy."

I let him go along in that way, every once in a while interjecting an "I don't know" or an "I don't think so," trying to judge if that was a condition for my meeting him, and when I sensed it wasn't, I said, "No, no, Bob. She's been through enough with me. I'm going to be on the run for the rest of my life and I just can't ask her to go through that."

I knew I hadn't convinced him, but he also decided, for the moment, to back off: "Well, then, then...I'll tell you what, bring along pictures, Tom, okay? Because that's what boosts my morale, having pictures of my loved ones with me when I'm on the road."

I promised I would, adding, "Now, look, what I want to do, Bob, first is to meet with you but not to stay. Not right away. What I mean is, man, I have to have money to give my wife to live on. You understand that. My family, I got to take care of them. So, first of all, what I want to do is meet up with you, so we can figure how we're going to hook up and you can give me money for my family. Okay, Bob?"

"Well..." He managed to get all his unhappiness about my insistence on returning to Philadelphia in that one word. "Well, if that's the way you want it. All right. Okay. Now, listen, where we'll meet? Portland. Portland, Oregon. It's a safe place for us right now. You got enough for airline tickets?"

I said I did. "Right. I'll meet you in the baggage department. I can't go into the terminal," not through those metal detectors that would reveal whatever weapon or weapons he was carrying. (He almost always had at least two with him; a favorite—he liked to show it off as a child would a beloved toy—was a fancily tooled Derringer that he could fit right into the palm of his hand.)

After telling me he'd call me back on the twenty-second for me to give him the flight number, he signed off in the way he almost always did. "Eighty-eight," he said. "Eighty-eight," I repeated. The eighth letter of the alphabet is "H," so two eights meant HH, which meant Heil Hitler.

He did ring me the next day. "I'll be on the American flight that gets in at 5:50 p.m., West Coast time," I said, adding that the airline had made a reservation for me at a Holiday Inn.

The plan was this: Libby would fly to Portland ahead of me, there joining agents from San Francisco who were members of a specialized surveillance team. Her presence was needed to identify me to them and because only she knew all the details of the arrangement with me. The San Francisco agents, in turn, were to coordinate their activities with the Portland FBI. When I met with Bob, I was to take him with me to the Holiday Inn, where the room set aside for me would be both bugged and equipped with a hidden camera, operated by agents in the room next door. There was, however, to be no direct contact between them and me. Should I learn a vital piece of information out of their hearing, such as plans for a crime that was about to be committed, I was to dial a special number, at which the person answering says only "Hello," not identifying himself or herself as FBI even if asked that by the caller. I was also to ring the "Hello" number, not the agents' room, if I believed I was in danger.

That much was their plan. Returning to Philadelphia on the excuse that I needed to give the money to Susan was my idea. By doing it that way, I reasoned that the Bureau would have several days to set up a full-scale surveillance at the designated meeting site. If, on the contrary, I simply left the motel with Bob to go underground, he—with his fetish for secrecy—would almost certainly refuse to tell me where we were heading, which meant the FBI wouldn't know either, and we risked the possibility that the agents following us might lose us in traffic. It didn't occur to me to worry that the Bureau people hadn't thought of that safeguard themselves. Instead, I agreed with Susan on the eve of my departure when she said, "They know what they are doing."

We were fifteen minutes from Portland airport when the storm hit. As the plane rocked back and forth in the turbulence, I gave up on the *Time* magazine article I had been reading, over and over again, without understanding a word of it. I looked out the window into the rain, visualized myself walking up to Bob. All it took was one look from him. He saw it in my face. "You've betrayed me, buddy," he said with that Donny Osmond smile of his. I turned away from the window, the storm, and his face.

32 | The Man in Room 14

Bob reached over and patted me on the leg. "Glad to see you, Tom," he said.

The pat meant more to me than the words. Bob, I knew, liked to touch people he trusted, avoided physical contact with those he didn't.

Until he spoke, we had been sitting silently in the car for nearly fifteen minutes, the three of us—Bob and me in the front, Reds in the back playing with his machine gun and hand grenades—while we continued to watch the entrance to the dead-end street in which we were parked, waiting for the Volvo that Bob had spotted following us from the Portland airport.

Although Bob continued to stare intently through the rain-splattered windshield, he was no longer hunched forward; instead, inch by inch, he was leaning back, beginning to relax. So was I. The Volvo should have appeared long before now if it were still on our trail. That we had apparently lost it meant there'd be no shoot-out in which I might be killed, that is, assuming Reds wouldn't have decided I was an informant and put a bullet through the back of my head before he turned his lethal attentions on the agents. That I was also out of contact with the FBI didn't bother me; that situation would be rectified as soon as we registered at the Holiday Inn.

A few minutes later, I learned I had been too confident too soon. As Bob turned the ignition on and drove us out of the dead end, back on the highway, the lights ahead of us blurry in the rain, I asked, "Is the Holiday Inn this way? I'd like to get registered there, and we can talk in my room. Okay?"

"Nah, forget about that place, Tom. I got us rooms at another motel. We're already booked in there."

"We are?" I licked my lips, trying to think. "But what if Susan tries to reach me, and I'm not registered there; she'll worry, man."

He laughed. "Hell's bells, Tom, you can call her from where we're going. No problem."

Even as he was speaking, I saw ahead of us the familiar Holiday Inn sign. I visualized the agents sitting in the room next to the one that was supposed to be mine, all that equipment, no use for it. We drove by. I sat back, stiffly, my hip up against the steel barrel of Bob's machine gun, the tips of my fingers just touching the cover of his Bible.

A mile or so farther on, Bob swung the steering wheel abruptly and pulled in alongside a gas station. He had spotted a phone booth next to it, and he left the car to make a call from it. As he was doing that, I turned to Reds and asked him how Bob was doing. His assurance— "He's doing fucking fine"—didn't convince me. To me, Bob looked as if he'd put on clown's makeup in reverse, cheeks white, eyes red with black circles. As Reds happily juggled his hand grenade, he started to tell me of the "great fucking gun battle" he'd had with the FBI when they invaded his property in Idaho in October. That's how I realized who he was.

Just as Reds was completing his triumphant tale, Bob was getting back into the car. Catching the tail end, he said patronizingly, "Yeah, Reds is a good warrior," and Yarbrough, at that, stopped speaking as if chastised. As we continued on our way, I gave a departing glance at the phone booth, thinking about the "Hello" number. The rain was coming down heavier now.

A few minutes later we stopped again, this time at a diner where we seated ourselves at a booth. Bob ordered us hot pies and milk.

The clock on the wall was nearing eight before we left, and aside from Bob urging me, once again, to bring Susan and the children underground with me, I don't recall the content of the conversation, though I do remember the strange feeling about him I received from our talk, a feeling that was to grow as the evening progressed. During the three years I'd known Bob, I had seen him in a variety of states ranging from the most exuberant self-confidence to suicidal depression, but always an interval had separated each mood. Now I had the sense of him slipping pell-mell from one to another, as though his mind had become a film projector cranked the wrong way, so that the people on the screen walk unnaturally fast.

From the diner we drove to the Capri Motel, neon and plastic like thousands of others like it over the country. He parked the car in front of a room bearing the number 14. Yarbrough, following us inside, looked puzzled. He pointed at the single bed. "Hey, Bob, this room ain't big enough for us," he said.

Bob sighed. Giving me a glance that said "See what I have to put up with?" he patiently explained: "I rented two rooms, Reds. This one is Tom's. Ours is over there." He pointed to a balconied second-floor room from which, I realized, he could look down into my room.

"I want to talk to you," he added to me. Thinking he meant now, I sat in a chair next to the bed. As I did, Yarbrough removed a small electronic device from a paper bag he had been carrying. While we watched, he began running it along the walls. Beep, beep, it went. I thought: My God, suppose we'd gone to the Holiday Inn and he'd done that, the damn room would be exploding with beeps and bullets right now. As it was, Yarbrough was yipping and jumping around at his discovery. I said, "Come off it, man. It's just an air freshener." I pointed to the tiny box on the wall just a few inches from his scanner. "They got little batteries in them," I said to Bob, who nodded in agreement. Undeterred, Yarbrough had come up behind me, pretending he was doing a sweep of the lamp and my chair, his purpose, I had no doubt, to learn if I was wearing a body wire. When I passed that test, Bob motioned me to follow him. Yarbrough nodded toward a newspaper Bob had brought in with him, saying he'd stay there to read it. I assumed he intended to go through my luggage.

As we started up the outside stairs to Bob's room, I looked over to the highway. I saw no sign there or on the parking lot of either the Volvo or the Lincoln Continental with the aerial in the back which had aroused Bob's suspicions at the airport. I knew, in one way, that this was good—if I had been able to spot something, Bob would have, too, probably faster than I would—but the absence of familiar cars on the lot and road also enforced my awareness of my isolation, increased my jittery desire to get to a phone. I realized, however, that I'd have to be careful. The juxtaposition of Bob's room to mine made it too risky to call the "Hello" number from there, and I also suspected his second-floor location (and probably the reason he had chosen it) made it possible for him to see through the window of the Capri office across the way where there'd likely be a pay phone. My only safe bet was to get out of the motel and make the call elsewhere, but at the moment, I couldn't think of any excuse to get away from him to do that.

We entered his room—its number was 42—and after we seated ourselves facing one another, he ran his hand across his brow, as if in an effort to concentrate. "Tom, let me tell you," he said, "what I've arranged. You're to meet David Lane next Tuesday in Pennsylvania"— that would be the day before my supposed interrogation by the FBI— "but it can't be in Philadelphia. That's not safe. Make it, make it someplace you can get to easily, because you'll have to leave your car behind. They could have bugged it, you know."

I said, "How about Allentown?" It was only two hours from Philadelphia by bus, and near it was the small city of Easton, where Lane, I knew, had family. "Good, good, that'll work fine." He sounded a little distracted as he explained that from there Lane and I would drive to a safe house where he would meet us. He didn't say where the safe house was.

In another moment the reason for his distraction became clear: "Now then!" he declared, the boring details out of the way. "Now! I'm going to tell you about your first assignment. Tom, it's a big one! You're going to be part of a cell on the Morris Dees thing." He wasn't looking at me. "We've gathered good intelligence on him, and what we're going to do, two weeks from now, we're going to kidnap him and then we'll torture him and get as much information out of him as we can, and when we have that, we'll kill him, and bury him and pour lye over him."

He smiled dreamily up at the ceiling.

"Fine, Bob," I said. "That sounds fine."

I was bewildered, not by the content of his words—violence was his standard by now, that I knew—but that he should hand me a murder so blithely, me whose compunctions against violence he had always seemed to understand, had even catered to. As I tried to sort it out, it occurred to me he believed—now that he had gotten me to agree to go underground with him—that he no longer had to pay lip service to my qualms or, more likely, saw that by putting blood on my hands immediately, his hold on me would be strengthened. Yet if that was his reasoning, why not, I wondered, wait until I had actually joined him, rather than telling me now when I was going back to Philadelphia the next day and could still change my mind? That doesn't make any sense, I thought, but as I gazed at him, I began to realize that its very senselessness might be the explanation. I could be anyone. The very telling of the murderous plan excited him. He couldn't not tell it.

That was one moment, and in the next, the askew projector still cranking, he was my old Bob again and I was his good pal, the one good pal he could always confide in. "Tom, Tom, I have problems," he said, the lips of that desperate clown's face turning down. For a moment, I thought he was still referring to Dees, but he wasn't. It was as if the Dees murder plans had never been mentioned. Instead, we were now onto personnel problems. One concerned Bill Nash, the supposed locksmith, whose limitations Bob now realized and who had been relegated to the job of cook and general go-fer at The Order's military camp in Idaho. It wasn't, however, as I might have expected, Nash's incompetence that was the problem; it was: "Tom, the man's got poor hygiene. Why, we had to throw out his sleeping bag because it stank so much. Tom, that man never bathes!"

He spoke in the same tone and level of intensity as he had about burying Dees in lye. I didn't, however, get the impression he intended to kill Nash immediately as he did Dees. There would, he said, be no need "to terminate him" until the revolution succeeded, or, in any event, until other and more pressing matters were resolved.

One of them concerned his second personnel problem, Bill Soderquist. Billy, Bob told me, was in California, in disgrace. "Gee, I don't know what the heck I'm going to do about Billy, Tom," he declared. "He's turned out to be a real difficulty. He's drinking." He shook his head. "He's drinking a lot and, well, I just don't think he wants to be involved anymore. He wants out." He pursed his lips, staring down at his hands; he had always said he liked Billy. "We're going to have to do something. We're going to have to do something about Billy, Tom."

Soderquist, it turned out, had good reason to want to get out. What Bob didn't tell me was that a month earlier, Billy had undergone "trial" by The Order. At this affair, which took place in a California motel room, Bob charged Billy with excessive drinking, use of cocaine, and revealing to his girlfriend his participation in the Ukiah robbery. Acting as judges were Bob, Ardie ("The Learned Professor") McBrearty, and Richard Scutari. At a legal trial that took place a year later, Soderquist would recall being told by Scutari that "technically, by the book, I should be killed, but he felt I should go on trial in front of the other members of The Order and if found guilty, a suicide mission would result for me."

The "book" Scutari was talking about was *The Turner Diaries*. In one section of it, Earl Turner, under torture, gives information to ZOG, is similarly tried by The Order of that book, and is sent on the suicide mission in which he dies.

The day following his "trial," according to Soderquist, he was informed he was to be put on probation instead. Under its terms, he was fined $16,000 and prohibited from using drugs and liquor. "Yes, I think we're going to have to solve the problem of Billy," Bob concluded.

Just as abruptly as he'd moved from Dees to Nash and Soderquist, Bob hopped back to his wish that I bring Susan and my children underground with me: "Everybody will have new identities, beautiful new homes, plenty of money, Tom, and the best thing is you don't have to leave them. You never should leave your loved ones behind, Tom. You'll miss them if they aren't with you. You will be lonely."

He seemed to have no recollection that he had just said the same thing to me in almost the same words a half-hour or so before at the diner. This was perhaps the dozenth time he'd broached the subject, beginning with his New Eden description in February, and never once did he give me what must have been his real and quite sensible reason: He feared that if I didn't bring Susan and the children with me, soon I would miss them so much that I would have to contact them, and when I did my phone would be tapped, leading the FBI to me and to him. I have never completely understood why he didn't use that argument—it would have been difficult to counter—and relied instead on the constantly reiterated appeals to my emotional ties to my family. Possibly it was because he was vulnerable on that score himself; after all, he had left Debbie at home and Zillah, too, for that matter.

When—"No, they're better off if I'm out of their lives"—I again refused him, he nodded: "Well, I've got to tell you something you won't like, Tom. I've given some money to Dr. Pierce." Again the switch of subject was so sudden that for a moment I didn't realize why I shouldn't like it. "I know he treated you badly," he explained, "but he helps with our causes; we need him, Tom." He peered at me uncertainly, as if worried I'd be angry, and from that it occurred to me a part of him still sought my approval, as he had when he first knew me. Perhaps, no matter how much they change, we never completely outlive our first relationships with people, and his with me, no matter how well he had learned to manipulate me since, continued to guide him in ways he didn't understand, making him less suspicious of me than he would have been of almost anyone else.

Just then, Yarbrough entered the room, carrying his machine gun. Removing his shirt, he stretched out on one of the beds. His chest was covered with tattoos. "Had 'em done different times I was in prison," he said to my stare, as he scratched at one of them. Around his throat he was wearing a medallion on a chain. All warriors in the sacred silent brotherhood wore them, Bob explained. I'd get mine after I had taken the oath.

As he was showing me his medallion, Yarbrough was also idly playing with his weapon. I asked, thinking it might be good information for the FBI to have, where he had gotten the silencer for it. Bob sloughed off the question: "We have our ways, Tom; we have our ways." Based on testimony at a subsequent trial, the silencers, in fact, were manufactured and sold to The Order by the Covenant, Sword and Arm of the Lord survivalists in Arkansas.

All this while I had continued to ponder what means I could use to get away from them and call the "Hello" number. Now, the combination of Yarbrough's recumbent position and Bob's haggard appearance gave me an idea. Slapping myself on the knees and rising, with as much vigor in my voice as I could muster, I said, "Hey, man, why hang around here? Let's go out, Bob. Go to a bar, get a beer, man. I know you're not much of a drinker, but, hell, maybe get us some ladies, too, huh?"

He considered that. "There are a lot of whores in this town," and he gave me the name of a motel and even the room number where I'd find some. I was afraid that meant he was going to take me up on my suggestion, but: "No, no, I'm beat," he said.

"Yeah, you look rough, man," I agreed. I started to the door, turning around to say, "I'll just go down to my room to wash up and I'll be back in a couple of hours, okay? You know, I slept on the plane and—what's the matter?"

He was looking at my feet, which was how I learned of another crime they had committed, a small but revealing one. Both Bob and Yarbrough were wearing mountaineer boots with thick red laces; my shoes were a pair of gray loafers. "They're going to have to go," Bob said, pointing to them. "What you need is warrior boots like these. Got them, me and Reds, we walked into this store up in Washington State, held a gun against the head of the nigger clerk. That's how we got them."

"Man, that nigger was real shook up," said Yarbrough.

I thought, here they have millions of dollars and they hold up some little store for a couple of pairs of boots. It was with that thought that it finally fully dawned on me that one reason Bob committed crimes was because he had gotten to like doing them, just as I'd gotten a high from passing the counterfeit bills.

While I was thinking that, Bob was saying, "Look, Tom, no need for you hanging around here in Portland all day tomorrow." I had told him I was scheduled to take the midnight flight back Saturday. "Besides, Reds and I, we have some business to attend to," and without asking my opinion about what I wanted to do, he picked up the phone and changed my reservation to the 9 a.m. flight. That turned out to be meaningless; what he did next wasn't. He dialed the operator and put in a wake-up call for us at seven o'clock. "That way we can have breakfast first and then I'll drive you to the airport," finally giving me his Donny Osmond smile.

Reaching into his pocket, he took out his keys. "It's a lousy night out; why don't you take my car?" to which Yarbrough interjected, "No, Bob," perhaps thinking about the guns that were still in it and what would happen if I were stopped, but possibly also still suspicious of me. Sensing that, I broke in over him, "No, that's not a good idea."

"Yeah, you're probably right, Tom." Another smile. Good buddy.

But I hadn't been back in my room five minutes when there was a banging at my door. When I opened it, facing me was Bob, wild-eyed. "Who were you on the phone with? Huh? Huh? I called! Your room was busy!"

Me, offended: "Goddamn it, Bob, I wasn't on the phone with anybody."

He gave a little whimpering sound, hurt like a child that's been talked to mean by his big brother. "Well, maybe I misdialed," he mumbled. "May I come in?"

He slumped on the chair. "I've been thinking, Tom," he said and just as if we hadn't been through it twice in the past three hours—same reasons, same words—he explained why I should bring Susan and the children with me when I met Lane on Tuesday. It was as though we were partners in some strange, compulsive dance and I played my role—same reasons, same words—leading to the inevitable final chorus: I should bring pictures with me, then, "for inspiration in the great war ahead." When I promised faithfully I would do that, he stood up, his expression gloomy: "Well. Well, I'm going to turn in."

Standing at the door to my room, I watched him cross to the stairs. I wanted to call him back. "Hey, Bob, give me your gun," I wanted to say. "Give it up, Bob. They're on to you. It's over, Bob. It's all over." I could imagine him doing it, beginning to sob, head against my chest.

But, of course, I knew that wasn't what would happen if I said that.

In the lobby of the motel I got change, saying I wanted it for the candy machine—I don't know why I thought I should explain that—started for the phone booth, remembered Bob might be able to see it from his room, left the building, headed for the road. By now, it was close to ten o'clock, the rain finally slackening to a drizzle with fog settling in, a feeling of it swishing around me as I walked along the sidewalk. I couldn't spot a phone booth, and the stores along the way were all closed. I saw no other pedestrians, but I did have one companion, a big black automobile.

I had spotted it leaving the motel parking lot right after I did. At first I assumed it was being driven by a guest who had checked out. But within a block or two I had no doubt it was following me; conceivably it was the Lincoln I'd seen at the airport but also conceivably an Order member was at the wheel, sent by Bob to trail me.

I turned a corner. I glanced back over my shoulder. The black car had stopped just as I did, the driver, whose features I couldn't make out through the fog, blinking his headlights at me. I walked on, not looking back anymore. I had spotted the lights of a diner. I picked up my pace. Once inside, I ordered a hamburger and soda, stationing myself at the end of the counter where I could see the road. I tried to judge whether anyone parked outside would be able to see the diner's pay phone. A swarthy-skinned man entered. He sat down next to me. Looking directly ahead at the menu on the wall, he whispered, "Libby says hi."

I laid my hands on the top of the counter. Only then did I realize they were trembling. "Go around the corner," I said. "I'll meet you there."

He was waiting for me in front of a car I hadn't previously noticed. The big black one had vanished. He motioned for me to get in and when I did, he joined me, reaching forward to pick up a phone. "I have our source," he said.

He pulled away from the diner. After Bob had given them the slip at the airport, he explained, they had driven to every motel in Portland looking for his car, spotting it just moments before seeing me leave the Capri office. "Jesus," I said, "while you guys were looking for me, I could have been killed."

He was one of the expressionless agents of whom the Bureau has quite a number, expressionless in face and word. "Well, we've got you now, sir."

Our destination turned out to be the rear of a darkened car wash.

The Lincoln was there waiting for us. Opening its rear door, one of the two agents in it told me to get out in a crouch and jump into their car, lay myself flat on the back seat. I did as I was told. They switched on a tape recorder. I recounted the threat to Dees, the logistics of my projected meeting with Lane, and that our wake-up call was scheduled for seven. "And he has another individual with him," I said, "who I believe is Gary Yarbrough."

"Yarbrough?"

The agent in the passenger seat fished for something, found it, turned around and showed it to me. It was an 8 x 10 glossy photo. "That him?"

I said it was. The agent called his headquarters: "Yarbrough's with Mathews," he said. I couldn't make out the words of the person on the other end, but I had no doubt of the excitement going both ways. It made me uneasy. "Hey, look, there's nothing going to go on, is there?" I asked. "I was promised there wouldn't be shooting."

"No, no, there's no change in plan," said one agent.

"Don't worry. Everything's going to be all right," another assured me.

They dropped me off a safe distance from the Capri, and I walked the rest of the way back. The fog was coming in balloonlike waves now, but I was still able to make out when I arrived at the door to my room that the lights were off in Bob's.

I rested well that night. Perhaps it was exhaustion, but I think it was mostly relief. The rendezvous in the back of the car wash (I had no idea the FBI actually had such places for secret meetings) had given me the confidence I badly needed. Everything was set. Bob, I knew, would be kept under surveillance from the time he drove me to the airport in the morning, and should he be lost sight of—something I now knew was a real possibility—he could be picked up again when I met him (and others: the Dees murder "cell" he mentioned) the following week. With any luck, just a few days more and The Order would be a danger of the past. On that hope, long deferred, I could sleep.

On awaking, I glanced at my watch. It was ten minutes before seven. I dialed the operator and told her to cancel my wake-up call. From where I stood, I could see the office in which she'd be sitting. Things appeared normal both there and in the parking lot—no unusual cars to arouse Bob's suspicions. My gaze turned to the right and upward to the room he and Yarbrough shared. No sign of life. All was peaceful.

While I waited for their call to get together for breakfast, I decided to take a shower. When I emerged, I was drying my hair and figuring that when I finished, I'd go up to Bob's room. The phone rang just as I was about to leave. Assuming it must be Bob, I answered, starting to say, "I'm on my way." I didn't get past the first word. It was a woman's voice; her tone was edgy, desperate: "Tom," she said, "this is Libby. Don't come out of your room. It's going down."

From some distant part of me, I considered the prints that my suddenly sweating fingers were making along the green plastic of the receiver. I heard myself and I was surprised to hear I was shouting: "It can't! They got a hand grenade. Libby!"

"Don't come out of your room," she repeated. "It's out of my hands. I'm sorry."

She hung up.

It's going down, I thought, sickened, and they're up there with their machine guns and their grenades. The phone rang again. This time it was Yarbrough. "We'll be down. You ready?"

"Yeah. Yeah, I'm ready."

Within seconds, Libby was back on the phone. "What'd they say?" she asked.

"They're on their way down here," I answered. "Look, Lib, you can't keep me in here. Put me in the lobby. Just get me out of here."

I didn't know it then, but the lobby was already crowded. While I was sleeping, an FBI squad had gone around to the rooms on either side of those in which we were staying, and the guests, most still in their nightclothes, were now crouching on the office floor; interspersed among them were gun-toting agents in red flak jackets.

Libby's voice now had its distancing tone. "No, you stay there. Whatever you do, don't leave that room," and then she was gone.

And if Bob and Yarbrough reached my room before the FBI could intercept them? I ran into the bathroom. I pushed aside a curtain, expecting to find a window behind it that I could escape through. I found a wall.

After splashing water on my face, I came back into the bedroom and inched my way out of sight of the window until I reached the peephole in the door. Looking upward through it, I saw Bob. He was standing on the balcony in front of his room, looking down toward the office. Then he glanced around the parking lot, stretching, as though he were just a casual kind of guy, limbering up for the day's work, taking in a good breath of fresh morning air. Very slowly, he walked back to the door, stopped there a moment, turned around. I sensed he'd seen something. He went back inside.

And he stayed inside. And I watched and he stayed and there wasn't a movement anywhere.

I stepped back from the door. A long time had gone by, at least a half-hour since I'd seen him on the balcony. I looked over to my luggage, thinking maybe I should take a chance and just leave.

I heard a sound. A commotion. I stopped, my hand above my suitcase. A man's voice: "Mathews. Stop. Halt." Three little words, all separated out.

I heard a shot. I heard footsteps. I turned to the window; just as I looked out, Bob ran by it. He shouted to me. I couldn't make out his words.

I wasn't able to see the direction he had taken, but now, as I turned to the right, into my vision came three of the red-jacketed FBI men, armed to the teeth. They seemed to have sprung right out of the ground, and were running up the stairs, pointing their machine guns at the door of Bob's room. Just as in a movie—the thought crossed my mind—one of them shouted: "Come out, Yarbrough. We know you're in there."

They pushed and slammed at the door with their guns, and as they were doing that, my attention was distracted by the wails of police sirens. I saw squad cars arriving, followed by TV trucks. It was Action News time.

Trapped in my room, I had no way of seeing everything, but from others who were also there, I have been able to put part of the story together.

When Bob, aware of the ambush, made his break, he leaped over the balcony railing and came down on his feet just a few yards from my room. As he did, a female agent hiding under the stairs shot at him but missed, the bullet slicing through the window of the motel office and grazing the manager in the shoulder.

As two agents chased Bob and others ineffectually pounded at his room door, a third group emerged from a van parked behind the motel. By then, Yarbrough, clasping a list of The Order members with their aliases and phone numbers, had found a rear window to his room. He climbed out and was hanging from the sill ten feet above the ground as the agents from the van, joined by Libby, ran toward him.

Seeing her with the men, he screamed down at her: "You fucking slut." She trained her gun on him. "You white whore, you fuck niggers. I'll remember your face, bitch, I'll remember you."

As they advanced, he fell to the ground, still snarling. A black agent, by unspoken agreement—a nod—came forward and handcuffed him.

As he was being taken off in a car, I was watching the agents, dozens of them it seemed, marching in and out of Bob's room. Below, the Portland cops were wandering about, trying to look as though they had something to do, even as, a little farther off, a smiling young man and a pretty young woman, each with elegantly coiffed hair, talked into their microphones. Behind them, I saw the guests, by ones and twos, leaving the Capri office.

And I didn't know if Bob were alive or dead, if Yarbrough were alive or dead, didn't know what Bob had shouted to me: Were they words to warn me of ambush, or were they a curse?

It turned out that Bob was alive. After running by my room, aware that there was no possible way to reach his car, he circled behind the Capri and dashed down a street, two agents following him. At the end of the street was an apartment complex. He entered its yard and hid behind a wall. "I drew my gun," he later wrote, "and waited...for the agents to draw near. When I aimed my gun at the head of the closest agent, I saw the handsome face of a young white man and lowered my aim to his knee and foot," and fired.

That's not quite what happened. Aware that Bob was hiding in the yard, one of the agents, Arthur Hensel, drawing his pistol, cautiously stepped into it. His partner, Kenneth Lovin, covered him with his shotgun. "Look out, Art," Lovin yelled as he glimpsed Bob with his pistol trained at Hensel's head. Hensel fell on his back, lifting his legs in the air to protect himself. Bob's first bullet ricocheted off his shin, the second lodged in his foot. Lovin let loose a burst of gunshot fire, the pellets hitting Bob's hand, causing his gun to spin out of his grasp.

By the time the weapon hit the ground, Bob was already running out of the yard, back onto the street. It is unclear if Lovin tried to pursue him immediately—he may have stopped to look to his fallen comrade—but, in any event, by the time he resumed the chase, Bob was out of sight.

A few blocks farther on, Bob broke into a house, grabbed a towel, and wrapped it around his bleeding hand. Outside again, he hailed a passing car. "I've been in an auto accident; take me to the hospital," he pleaded.

The driver let him in. When they stopped for a light, Bob leaped from the car. As approaching sirens filled the air, he disappeared.

Back at the Capri, I tried the "Hello" number. No answer. It was almost ten now. The police had gone. The TV people had gone. A couple of agents were still trooping in and out of Bob's room, but that was all. Last night's rain was gone. The day was growing bright. Maybe it's good nobody's come for me yet, I told myself. Maybe it's all part of a plan.

I heard a noise. I peered out through the side of the window. But it was just two middle-aged women in maids' uniforms, one of them pushing a white basket on wheels. As one turned to my door, the other said to her, "No, don't go in there. The man in Room 14 is with the FBI."

Even the maid knew. I walked very slowly back into the bathroom. I studied my features. You know, you're a dead man, I said to myself.

CHAPTER

33 | The Word Was Out

Perhaps a person can live with fear and self-recrimination for only so long. Whether for that reason or another, after that paralyzing moment in front of the mirror, I became angry. The bastards, I thought (and I wasn't thinking of Bob and his gang), the incompetent, lying bastards. I'd put my trust in them and they had given me their word— "guarantee" was the exact word—no shooting, just surveillance.

And I would be protected.

Well, I sure had been protected, I fumed: Not only didn't their Goddamn great "Hello" number work when I used it just now, it probably wouldn't have worked last night either if I had to use it then. Why, they even let the maids know I'm working with them! It felt cleansing to be that angry.

I opened the door to my room and walked out. Several of the handful of remaining agents were standing guard over Bob's car. I went by them. None paid attention to me. A maid might know who I was, but they didn't.

I crossed the highway to a restaurant. The people sitting at the counter were talking about the shooting excitedly, just as I would have,

I thought, if I'd been one of them. I found a phone book, located the FBI's regular number, stepped into the booth and dialed. A woman answered. I said, "I want to talk to somebody in authority." She replied: "I will have to know to whom it is you wish to speak, sir."

I asked: "How do I know? Somebody in authority."

"May I ask what this is in reference to, sir? I can't put you through to anybody unless I know what this is in reference to, sir."

I said, "Look, lady, I'm the guy stuck in a room because of you people."

A pause. A click. A man got on the line. In a smooth-as-butter murmur, he inquired as to whether he could help me, sir; I took a deep breath—keep calm; aw, the hell with it; don't keep calm—and I said. "I'm Tom Martinez from Philadelphia, and you sons of bitches get me out of here now," and I hung up.

They did. Quickly.

In the weeks immediately following the shoot-out at the Capri, I attempted to learn why the FBI had broken its word to me. It appeared, from the official silence I met, that they felt no explanation was due me. I have, nevertheless, from various sources and from conversations I managed to overhear, been able to put together a chronology that is probably largely accurate.

In a sense, it was all my fault. Had I not made the innocent mistake of telling the agents at the car wash that Yarbrough was with Bob, it is likely the original plan would have remained in effect. As it was, Yarbrough's presence caused a midnight conference to be held. For reasons I don't know, but which appear to defy all common sense, Libby Pierciey was excluded—the single person who knew all the details of the plan and its purpose. Attending the meeting were Portland agents and members of the San Francisco surveillance squad who, at least, did know that arrests at the Capri were not contemplated and informed the Portlanders of that. The meeting, however, as I understand it, quickly degenerated into a turf battle of the kind I used to participate in at K&A when I was a teenager, with the Portlanders maintaining that since the action was taking place in their town, they were in charge, and that San Francisco (and Philadelphia, too, for that matter) in effect, could go pound sand. Portland won. The head of its contingent—I assume the SAC (Special Agent in Charge), though I'm not certain; he was described to me only as an "older man"—apparently determined that the capture of Yarbrough, the man who had fired at Bureau agents in October, would mean a major feather in the Portland office's cap, and any plans anyone else had were irrelevant. Had Portland not won the turf battle, one more death and one more murder would most likely have been prevented.

Confidential Source 1, who was responsible for bringing Bob and Yarbrough into their sights, was deemed expendable. That may have been a conscious decision on their part, or they may never even have bothered to discuss me. Whichever, the result was the same. Once the decision was made to try to take Yarbrough (and, by way of afterthought, Bob), had they had any concern for my safety, they could have come for me when they rounded up the guests or else, much more wisely, arrested me as part of the raid. By doing that, my cover would have been protected, quite probably until it was time for me to testify at trial.

The FBI agents I worked with daily I had learned to both like and trust as individuals, and one I didn't know, Wayne Manis, would subsequently lead an investigation that resulted in saving my life. But from that morning on, when I was sitting alone and terrified and deserted in my room, I knew exactly what the word of the FBI, as an organization, is worth when it is given to a person they believe to be a nobody like me.

A half-dozen agents, including Lou Vizi, met me at the Philadelphia airport when I arrived ten o'clock Sunday morning. Vizi suggested that I hide out at a motel, but initially I refused. My only thought at that moment was to see my family. By that evening, able to think rationally again, I realized their idea made sense both for me and for the safety of my wife and children. If, as Vizi had pointed out, there was any way for me to maintain my cover, I could hardly be answering my phone or door at home, or continue to have my car parked out front. By the following morning I was registered at what would be the first of a series of Philadelphia-area motels. Despite grumbling from the Bureau, I continued, however, to show up at work. I might be scared for my life, but I still had to earn a living.

Monday evening, in an attempt to get my new cover story out, with a tape recorder attached to my phone, I called George Zaengle in Spokane, but only Maggie was home. Speaking with an urgency that was as genuine as the content of what I said was false, I told her that, when the raid started, I grabbed my luggage and ran out of the room, escaping in the confusion: "I'm tapped out, Maggie. I need money real bad, and I'm scared the Feds will figure out who I am," not from my room registration—I knew Bob had signed in all three of us under aliases, so I couldn't say that—but because: "When I tried to wipe off the fingerprints, I probably didn't get all of them. And I'm worried about that other guy, Reds, too. He might be spilling his guts, Maggie." She was evasive. She and George were low on funds themselves, she said, and they didn't know where Bob was, hadn't heard from him. She told me to call George again, that he'd be home either the following night or the one after.

On the evening of Wednesday, November 28, I reached George. I started to tell him the same lies I had told Maggie. He didn't let me get far: "Listen, man, the, uh, word's out," he said. "The word's out, heh heh, that you're an informant."

34 | The Last of Earl Turner

In all the corners of the earth, the blood will flow
That of the spawn of Yahweh's foe.

—*from "Aryan Genesis,"*
a poem by Robert Jay Mathews

Waving a farewell to the puzzled driver who had promised to take him to the hospital, Bob, shoving his wounded hand into his pocket, crossed over to a filling station where he had spotted a car with ski equipment strapped to its roof. He asked the destination of the two occupants, a man and woman. As he had hoped, they said they were on their way to the popular winter resort of Mt. Hood, some fifty miles away. He asked if he could go with them. He had injured his hand, he explained, in an automobile accident and wanted to get home to his family. In a way, he was telling the truth. Members of The Order family were spread out around the Mt. Hood area in five safe houses he had rented with proceeds from the robberies. The couple agreed to take him, and throughout the trip, he kept the damaged hand out of their view for fear they would recognize a bullet wound when they saw one. Upon reaching a Mt. Hood motel outside Everett,

Washington, Bob left the skiers. He was within walking distance of the nearest safe house.

The FBI got its first lead to where he might be heading only hours later. His car, still parked at the motel, couldn't be searched until a court order was issued, and one wasn't obtained until early in the afternoon. In the car, along with blueprints for Boundary Dam in Seattle, was a list of the addresses of the Mt. Hood safe houses. A team of agents, including Libby and Wayne Manis (who was stationed in Idaho but was present because of his knowledge of the workings of the Aryan Nations), headed toward Everett. When they arrived they tramped through snow up to their knees as they went from one empty house to the next. A few pieces of bloody gauze were discovered, but that was all.

By then, a caravan of cars and pick-up trucks, containing Order members and their families, was headed north, its goal Whidbey Island, a fifty-mile-long crooked finger of land set in Puget Sound. There Bob had three rented houses, and on the caravan's arrival he took up residence in a wooden structure at the farthest tip, right off Smugglers Cove Road. Among the house's contents were machine guns, a large supply of ammunition, explosives, and gas masks.

The site had been chosen for its utter isolation, but because it was an island, if their pursuers could trace the fugitives there, escape would not be easy. The only ready exit was a single bridge that connected the island to the mainland. Over the course of the next two weeks, at least two-thirds of the brothers were on hand at one time or another, some with their wives and children, though, as far as is known, neither Zillah and her baby nor Debbie and her little boy were ever present.

On Sunday, Bob and eleven of his followers met at his house, the lone woman among them Mrs. God, Sharon Merki. By the time the twelve had completed their conclave, they had written—Bob no doubt was the principal author—a document of some 3,000 words. In it, they declared war on the United States.

Large patches of the content seem to have been lifted virtually verbatim from the tons of racist literature that Bob had imbibed over the years and which he could and did quote endlessly to me and others. The declaration's beginning is typical of that type of doomsday prose:

"It is now a dark and dismal time in the history of our race," it says. "All about us lie the green graves of our sires, yet, in a land once ours, we have become a people dispossessed."

The declaration goes on to describe how "a certain, vile, alien people"—the word "Jew," oddly enough, is never used—"have taken control over our country" with the result that "our cities swarm with dusky hordes...our farms are being seized by usurious leeches....The Capitalists and the Communists pick gleefully at our bones while the vile hook-nosed masters of usury orchestrate our destruction." But it's "our" fault, too, the paper points out. We don't seem to care about having our bones picked: "...still, still our people sleep!" is the mournful and repeated dirge.

But, no matter: "We hereby declare ourselves to be a free and sovereign people. We claim a territorial imperative which will consist of the entire North American Continent north of Mexico....This is War!"

After having said that, the twelve signers go on to assure the 250 million Americans who had not yet awakened to join them that the war would be conducted by the rules of the Geneva Convention and those of chivalry. Chivalry, as Bob and his friends interpreted it, included not just shooting it out with soldiers, but killing any civilians—judges, public officials, reporters, businessmen of any sort—who cooperate with ZOG. As for members of Congress who don't come along on the great crusade: "...when the day comes, we will not ask whether you swung to the right or whether you swung to the left; we will simply swing you by the neck."

The declaration ends: "Therefore, for blood, soil, and honor, for the future of our children, and for our King, Jesus Christ, we commit ourselves to battle. Amen."

The first name signed is Robert Jay Mathews. The others are Bruce Pierce, Richard Scutari, the two Merkis, Randy Duey, Randall Evans, Frank Silva, Andrew Stewart, Paul Anderson, Steve Brant, and Fred Jhonson (*sic*). (I don't know who the last four signers were; the names may be aliases.)

Playing around with his Declaration of War was, no doubt, of considerable satisfaction to Bob. Wounded, run to earth as he was, not even any longer on the mainland of the United States but at the far tip of an island off its far end, awaiting his enemies, the childish bravado of the writing ceremony would have been appealing to the Bob I knew. Although others were with him, in a way, I believe, he saw himself back at the beginning when he had been all alone in his room at night in Metaline Falls reading his books of hate.

Ever since escaping from Portland, Bob's concern about the role I might have played had been growing. By Sunday, at the latest, he would have known that none of the news reports mentioned me by name or even indicated a third person had been registered at the Capri along with him and Yarbrough. It was certainly conceivable—as I had claimed in my story to Maggie—that I had succeeded in escaping and that the Bureau, for its own reasons, was keeping quiet about me. I think that's what he wanted to believe, just as I think now he still wanted to believe in me as he ran by my window, that what he shouted to me was a warning and not a curse. However, by Sunday, he also knew he had been correct in his suspicion that he was under observation at the Portland airport. I could have been responsible for that, although it was certainly equally possible the Bureau could have gotten on his or Yarbrough's trail without my being involved. The Capri was the key. Unless his car had been spotted in its parking lot by luck, the FBI could only have known he was registered there from Yarbrough or me. To try to learn the truth, he came up with an idea. It shouldn't have worked, but it did.

Possibly as early as Sunday—though that day was largely given over to writing the Declaration of War—and almost certainly no later than Tuesday, he ordered Sharon Merki to call the Capri. She was put through to Jerry Riedl, the manager whose shoulder had been nicked by the errant FBI bullet. Turning on her tape recorder, she told him she was a reporter. ("What paper are you with?" Riedl asked at one point. Sharon: "With *People*." "You're with what?" "*People. People* magazine." "Oh, you're with *People* magazine!" "Right." "Oh, I see. Oh, okay.") Sharon explained that she hoped he might be able to help her straighten out conflicts in the information the FBI and the Portland police were releasing. Riedl, who, as the subsequent conversation indicates, had not been told by anyone not to talk about me to the press, proved agreeable. After leading him through the events prior to the shooting, Sharon reached her crucial questions:

MERKI: Okay. Now, another thing...about the man in Room 14, because he's turning into a...sort of a shadow character, here.

RIEDL: Yeah.

MERKI: And our source in the Portland Police Department...he feels that the man in Room 14 was actually, possibly, a third party in with the fugitives.

RIEDL: Huh-uh!

MERKI: No?

RIEDL: No, there may...that's my guess, and I'll tell ya why we base that on...is because the person that came in [to the motel office at 6:30 a.m.] and identified himself as an FBI man...at that time he said that people in number 42 are the people we are after, and we know that they have a wake-up call at seven o'clock. Now there is no way in God's green earth could they know already that they had a wake-up call at seven o'clock, if they weren't notified by 14, 'cause he's the only other person on this property that knew there was a seven o'clock wake-up call for 42.

MERKI: Oh, I see.

RIEDL: 'Cause this is the way we know. We know! I mean, there's n—there can't be no other way! There just can't be.

MERKI: I see.

RIEDL: And all the time they were on this property, they weren't even concerned with 14. Not in the least!

MERKI: Okay...It's like they didn't even think about Room 14?

RIEDL: No, they weren't even concerned with anyone that was in 14...that they weren't concerned with 14, at all, and, then because of they knew the seven o'clock wake-up call was...was, uh, the two things that we put together that, ya know, that had to be an agent.

I remain curious to know why the FBI agent felt impelled to brag, "We have our ways," when he could have protected me simply by asking the clerk *when* Room 42 was to be called.

Apparently, Riedl's all-too-accurate analysis was made known not only to Bob and all the brothers on the island, but those elsewhere, too, as evidenced by George Zaengle's statement to me on the 28th that "the word's out" that I was an informant.

A strategy meeting was held by the brothers to decide what to do about me. Exactly when that session took place has never been revealed by the government, which, despite the passage of time, still considers it "part of an ongoing investigation." It could have taken place the day Sharon made the tape, but it might also have been several days later, since, at that point, the brothers' most immediate concern was not me but what to do about the government forces they knew were in hot pursuit of them. A split—perhaps an angry one—developed on that issue. Some of the brothers urged immediate flight from Whidbey Island because of the difficulty of escaping from it if they were cornered. Others—including Bob—wanted to take a stand there against their enemies, engaging in the first great battle of the war they had just declared.

Whenever the meeting about me took place, present at it was an Order member who had, by then, become an informant. (This may explain why the government doesn't want to reveal the date; doing so might help identify that man and put his life in danger as mine was.) After the conference broke up, the informant called his contact. The decision, he reported, was to have Martinez murdered, but added that no one had as yet been assigned to do the deed. (A reminder list in Bob's handwriting was later discovered; on it, Ardie McBrearty is noted as the brother who is to "check on Tom.")

The presence of the informant means that possibly as early as November 26, the FBI knew where Bob was, who was with him, and what plans were being made. The Bureau certainly knew by no later than December 2, because by the following morning, according to the government's own partial recounting of events, agents arrived on Whidbey Island. Even so, for reasons that have never been explained, no action was taken to make arrests until four days later. During that interval, a number of Order members were permitted to go out over the bridge to freedom, with most of the escapes occurring on December 6. Among those known to have left then, or possibly a day or two before, were Bruce Pierce and Richard Scutari.

At that time Pierce had not yet been identified as the gunman who shot down Alan Berg, but he was known to be a fugitive on counterfeiting charges and he had been named by me as someone I was told had been a participant in the Ukiah holdup and probably in other robberies as well. An even better reason existed then to try to detain Scutari. Bob had told me, and I had advised the FBI, that "Mr. Black" was in Denver at the time of the Berg murder, and "Mr. Black" had now been identified as Scutari from the list of aliases found on Yarbrough when he was apprehended. Yet Scutari was allowed to get away, too.

David Lane, whom I had identified as the driver of the getaway car in the Berg case, was also almost certainly on Whidbey Island, and he escaped, too, though when is not known. Another person on the island and who apparently left December 6 was David Tate. The twenty-two-year-old Tate had not only allegedly participated in the Walter West murder but also in the counterfeiting operations at the Aryan Nations, of which organization his father was also a member. Had Tate been stopped, another murder would not have taken place five months later.

Of those who fled, I think Pierce was the most dangerous. As diabolic of aspect as Bob was cherubic, Pierce was the only Order member other than Bob who had the combination of brains, competence, and leadership qualities to keep The Order functioning. (Sharon Merki, described as "extremely intelligent" by a federal prosecutor, may have been brighter than any of them, but because she was a woman, she wasn't even considered a full-fledged member.) In recent months, the two men had not gotten along, and by November Pierce apparently was making moves to challenge Bob for control of the organization. He had begun to complain about Bob to the others, deriding him for leaving Barnhill's gun in the Brink's van at Ukiah; Bob, in turn, was critical of Pierce for endangering The Order's security by recklessly setting off a bomb in a synagogue. (Worse yet, from Bob's view, was that no one had even been injured.)

On December 6, as the exodus from Whidbey progressed, Bob was busy on another literary effort, which he mailed that same day to the Newport *Miner*, a small newspaper in Washington to which he had previously sent numerous "Letters to the Editor" upholding his racist positions. Within days after appearing there, the letter would be republished by the Aryan Nations. In it Bob describes how he had been persecuted by the FBI ever since he was a teenage member of the Arizona tax resister league, and how upon reading "volume upon volume on subjects dealing with history, politics and economics" he became aware of the great ZOG conspiracy. Now, he declared, rather than fleeing—an apparently contemptuous reference to his rapidly departing comrades—he was going to become the "hunter" of the enemy. Because of that decision, he says: "...it is only logical to assume that my days on this planet are rapidly drawing to a close." The letter concludes: "As for the traitor in Room 14, we will eventually find him. If it takes ten years and we have to travel to the far ends of the Earth we will find him. And true to our oath when we do find him, we will remove his head from his body."

The government made its move the day after Bob wrote that letter, December 7, a Friday. Before dawn, the Federal Aviation Administration had diverted all commercial aircraft from flying over the Whidbey Island area, and the Coast Guard had similarly banned civilian watercraft from Puget Sound. By 7 a.m., the people living near Bob's three safe houses had been evacuated by the FBI and the local sheriff's office.

About three hundred agents, accompanied by Gene Wilson, chief of the criminal division of the Seattle U.S. Attorney's Office, then moved in, led by an elite SWAT squad. Fifty agents were deployed to the house at 1749 North Bluff Road, where they ordered those inside to come out with their hands raised. Just before 8 a.m., the single occupant, Randy Duey, the former letter carrier, burst out the back door. He was wielding an Uzi (Israeli-made) machine gun in one hand, a 9-mm pistol in the other. He was immediately surrounded by agents pointing rifles and M-16s at him; he stared at them and in a tone of amazement cried: "You're all white men!" With that, he threw down his weapons. He was taken into custody. The initial charge against him was harboring a fugitive. It was in Duey's house that the Declaration of War was found.

Next in line for arrest were the occupants of 2359 South Hidden Beach Road, Robert and Sharon Merki, who burned some documents before surrendering, though not the tape of the interview with the Capri manager.

The agents then proceeded to a house on Smugglers Cove Road that gave them a view of Bob's two-story frame waterfront dwelling, behind which was heavily forested land. There the SWAT team set up its siege. Wilson, the only civilian on the raid, stayed behind at an inner-island command post.

Not long after the agents arrived, Sharon Merki's sixteen-year-old son came running out of the house, carrying a bag containing $40,000, which he claimed belonged to him. As the agents took him into custody, he told them that women and children were in the house with Bob. A negotiating team thereupon set up contact with Bob through a field telephone; at other times a bullhorn was used. Whichever the instrument, the goal was to talk him into releasing the women and children, then surrendering himself. Joining in the effort were Duey and Robert Merki, both of whom pleaded with Bob to give himself up.

He refused. At one point, possibly several times, he told the FBI's chief negotiator that he'd kill himself rather than surrender. He also taunted the agents by warning them that his rifles had night vision scopes and that he had an arsenal stashed in the building, along with food and water supplies that would allow him to hold out against them for weeks if necessary.

There was, however, no firing from either side. The standoff continued into Saturday, December 8.

At some point, possibly on Friday evening, more likely on Saturday—many of the details of what occurred remain cloaked in official secrecy—the Merki boy admitted he had lied, on Bob's instructions, when he said that Bob had women and children with him. Since hurting innocent people was no longer a danger, the decision was made to take Bob before night set in again. The agents worried that, in the dark, he might be able to escape through the woods behind the house.

They never were able to carry out whatever plans they had made. Around two o'clock Saturday afternoon, a single rifle shot was heard from the house; it seemed to have been fired inside it, not out at the attackers. From that, the agents surmised Bob had made good on his threat to kill himself. To ascertain if this were so, tear gas grenades were lobbed into the house in the expectation that they would drive him out if he were still alive. (Bob had not bothered to tell them that he also had gas masks on hand.) From the house, silence.

At 2:30 p.m., James Jay, the head of the FBI's Seattle SWAT team, accompanied by four of his men, entered the house, fully expecting to find a body. Even so, fortunately for them, they proceeded carefully, inching along the walls of the downstairs room, across from them a closed door that led to an ascending flight of stairs. Just as one of them started toward the door, Bob—who had apparently fired the single shot earlier for the purpose of luring agents into the house—commenced to shoot from the second floor. Through the ceiling his bullets came, splattering the floor and wall in a lethal Z pattern that came within inches of the members of the SWAT team. Jay ordered his men to fire back up into the ceiling. By then, however, Bob had run over to the head of the stairs, now armed with a machine gun, and was firing down it, through the closed door at them. The agents made good their escape.

The siege went on. As dusk approached, a helicopter appeared, turning a spotlight on the house. Bob shot at it from an upstairs window.

At that time, or very shortly thereafter, Agent Jay, acting on the orders of his superiors, used a grenade launcher to fire three illumination flares into the house. Jay later testified: "I was told, sir, they [the flares] would...force him outside the building....I don't think anybody in law enforcement has had much experience in this type of thing before." The result was catastrophic.

The flares that were employed burn white phosphorous and produce not only a brilliant light but are of such potency that they can cause fabric or wood anywhere near where they land to burst into flames. The house began to burn. Bob continued to shoot. The agents shot back. The house exploded.

He died in flames as Earl Turner had died.

35 | Interlude in a Bathroom

By December 8 I was no longer living by myself in the motel. Susan and the children were with me. That change had come about four days earlier when, just upon my return home from my job, the phone rang. It was Libby: "Tom, listen, there's going to be no more work for you."

I didn't like the content of that and even less the tense undercurrent in her voice. When I asked her why, I learned its reason: "We've just learned there's a threat on your life. We can't have you going to your job. It's too dangerous."

Also too dangerous, they decided, for my family. Within an hour, Libby and Lou Vizi, accompanied by a handful of other agents, had arrived at my house. Susan had only a few minutes' notice to grab some items of clothing before she and the children—Diane in tears but three-year-old Tommy seeming to find it a lot of fun—were ushered from the house, through the protective cordon the agents formed, into Libby's car and on to my motel.

I wasn't the only one who had to quit work. Susan was forced to give up her job, too, one she had held for nine years. Diane's life was also changed. She was told she could no longer go to school, could no longer visit any of her friends. She became a bewildered and terrified little girl.

Susan and I were bewildered and terrified as well. Because Libby and Lou said they had no information they could give us beyond the fact of the threat, we had no idea how serious it was, how imminent, or even whether or not the Bureau had the would-be killer or killers in its sights.

Since they also didn't leave any guards to protect us, I found myself again imagining the faceless man with the gun, the faceless man with the bomb. We were strangers in a strange place, hemmed in by the impersonal furnishings of our new quarters, our outer world circumscribed by the motel lobby, and we were alone.

On the evening news of December 7, I heard that a siege of a terrorist group was taking place on Whidbey Island, that there had been arrests, but that one man was holding out. I had no doubt who he was.

Sunday morning, while Susan was downstairs getting the newspaper, I called my father. He said, "It's in the *Inquirer*. They believe Mathews is dead." I listened while he read the article to me. I thanked him politely and hung up.

My daughter was in the room with me. She looked over at me, her hand going to her mouth, her eyes filling with tears. Only then did I realize what she was responding to: I myself was crying. To get away from her pain at my pain, I went into the bathroom.

I couldn't catch my breath. I hit my fist against the tile. "Why?" I said that aloud. I hit the tile again. "Why did you have to kill him?" I said that aloud, too, and wasn't sure who I was accusing. I hit the tile, which I could hardly see anymore through my tears, a third time. I remembered Metaline Falls, playing with Bob's little boy; he sat on my knee. Then Bob took the child from me, lifted him high in the air, the child's tousled blond hair glinting in the sunlight. I lowered my hand, rubbed my sore knuckles.

For weeks afterward, I would dream about him, always the same dream. He was sitting on my couch, coiled and smiling, eyes bright, the voice in its chirruping sing-song, "Hell's bells, buddy," but I could never remember when I awakened what else he was saying.

CHAPTER

36 | How I Found a Friend

The defendant's cooperation has been outstanding. From the morning of the plea, the defendant has provided complete and apparently truthful answers to all questions asked of him by law enforcement agents. His efforts on behalf of the government have... confirmed the existence of an organized, fanatic group of terrorists...known as The Order... [and] have more than fulfilled the terms of the plea agreement, have proven to be extremely valuable to the government, and have entailed great sacrifice, risk, and cost to the defendant....The members of The Order are murderers. Their deceased leader ordered the execution of the defendant. At this time it must be assumed the death of Mathews will only increase the resolve of the members to carry out his final order.

—*Bucky P. Mansuy, Assistant U.S. Attorney, in a letter dated December 11, 1984, to the Honorable Donald W. Van Artsdalen, Judge, U.S. District Court for the Eastern District of Pennsylvania.*

The first time was a false alarm, or at least I think it was. The day was December 14. Regardless of where the FBI had me hidden the rest of the time, Bob knew that on that date I would be in Philadelphia at the federal courthouse to be sentenced, and he might have forwarded that knowledge to whomever he had engaged to kill me. It wasn't safe to assume he hadn't done so, and the result was one of the FBI's bigger production numbers.

It began with Susan and me riding to court in the back of an unmarked van, four agents armed with machine guns with us, two more agents in a car ahead of us, another two in the one behind us. When we arrived at the courthouse a squad of federal marshals, weapons in hands, were standing in front of it, holding back traffic. An amazed group of spectators gawked as I passed through the marshals' gauntlet into an underground tunnel, up a special elevator, and into an unlocked cell behind the judge's chambers. I counted twenty-five protectors in all for this occasion.

After Perry DeMarco arrived, I was taken in front of Judge Van Artsdalen, who looked stern as I thought a judge should look. I had heard he gave out harsh sentences and that he had been considering giving me time in prison, but when he learned the details of what had happened to me in Portland, he had become so appalled that he changed his mind. He placed me on probation for three years.

Following the sentencing, which required no more than two or three minutes, I was led out of the courthouse the same way I had entered, once more past the gun-toting marshals into the van, and was driven back to the shopping mall parking lot where we had met with Libby earlier that morning. Susan and I got in our car. We waved goodbye to our protectors and drove off in the opposite direction from them. After that, any gunman who had been following us from the courthouse could have picked us off at his leisure.

A few days later, I had to report for my first meeting with my probation officer, Don Miller. I was not looking forward to that. The melodramatics of my sentencing had largely hidden from me the reality that I was now the kind of person who has a probation officer, a convicted felon, something I would be for the rest of my life; that realization added a new element to the sense of worthlessness that I had been nursing since October.

The depression it produced had been interrupted—put on hold, as it were—when I volunteered to go underground with Bob. I had seen that as an opportunity to redeem myself, but that possibility had been shattered by the events at the Capri, causing my depression to return. The sense of frustration I felt did much, I am certain, to prompt the furious quality of the anger I'd felt toward the FBI. In a similar vein, Bob's death, apart from my initial response to it, seemed just one more proof to me that anything I turned my hand to was doomed to fail.

Now, having to see a probation officer added one more smearing of gray paint over my life; for three long years it would be a constant reminder of my new and permanently lowered status. Not that I had any idea of what to expect from a probation officer, not in any precise way, but I had the vague expectation of being ordered about by him, having to grovel to him because he had the power to revoke my probation and put me in prison if I disobeyed him. It was an ugly feeling.

Whatever I was expecting, Don Miller, a tall, introspective-looking man in his late thirties, wasn't it. I have never understood how he did it—maybe by not trying to do it—but he had the capacity to calm (that's the word that always comes first to my mind when I think about Don). Within minutes after my arrival, from the first time onward, he had that effect on me, as if he were saying (though he never used these words): You're a fellow who has gotten into some trouble, so now let's just take a little time and see what we can do about it.

Some people talk and have good ideas. You think: Hey, that makes sense; I should really take what this guy says seriously. That's good; people like that are good. And then there are a few people who listen to you even when they are talking to you, so that no matter which one of you happens to be speaking, a mutual listening, not just hearing, is going on. Don was that kind of person, and at times when I was with him, he could bring forth that capability from me.

The first problem we tackled was my sense that I had proven myself to be a weak person. Through the listening and talking, he knew, in a way I didn't know yet, that if there were a secret to bringing me around, it had its core there. My awareness of my weakness had focused on the specific examples of it I had shown, but I hadn't, until my meetings with Don, admitted to my deeper feeling that weakness was unmanly. I had been brought up to believe men were strong—it was never defined, it was just that men had to be strong—and if you weren't, your wife wouldn't look up to you anymore. That, I began slowly to realize, was the real reason I had never shared my fears and uncertainties with Susan; I was afraid she wouldn't love me anymore if she thought I was weak.

Yes—Don wouldn't disagree with that—I had been weak. Yes, I had made mistakes because of that. It had been my weak sense of self that had sent me to those who would tell me I was superior, superior not because of my own qualities but because I happened to be white. It was weakness, too, that later sent me hurtling after Bob, whom I saw as strong, even after I no longer believed in his beliefs. Yes, I was weak. Yes, I had made mistakes.

The problem—the problem we had to solve, he and I—was what to do about that weakness. My choices, I began to see, were starkly differentiated ones. One was to wallow in the weakness and become a virtual monster of self-pity—the direction in which I was heading. The second was to attempt to bury my past mistakes, as I had sometimes hoped to do by going to prison, and resolve to make a fresh start, which would mean to learn nothing from what I had been through. That led to the third choice, the difficult one, to grasp my knowledge of my weakness and from it seek to fashion strength.

In this way, from Don's questions to me which led to mine to me, through speaking and listening, I learned that weakness wasn't a disgrace, but failing to learn from it was. When I not only understood that but, more important, believed it, we were then able to begin to deal with the guilt I felt about Bob's death. Part of that, certainly, still had to do with my sense of betrayal of a friend, no matter how evil a one, but the enormously burdening part of it, the one that led to my dreams, was new: I believed that if I hadn't gone to Portland, Bob would still be alive.

I pounded that idea of my guilt at Don, session after listening session, much as I had pounded it at the unfeeling tiles of my bathroom wall. They had judged me guilty, but Don wouldn't. He kept refusing to do that, no matter how much I wanted him to. Instead, he let me pound it out and pound it out, surrounding it by his calm, and that way, slowly and seepingly, he got across to me the next message I had to accept: Sometimes, I learned, your good actions—the actions you take to save lives, which was why I was at Portland—can have bad consequences, just as your bad ones do, but they aren't *your* consequences. People make choices from your actions. Bob could have chosen one way. He chose another.

So we were left with a question, the one he could take me to the threshold of but not answer for me: What was I to do?

I wasn't certain, from our sessions, of the answer to that yet. I still had a way to go before I'd be completely out of my corner.

CHAPTER

37 | The Federal Witness Protection Program

Shortly after Bob's death, Libby had asked me if I could name any Order members who might be willing to cooperate with the FBI. Remembering what Bob had told me of Soderquist's apparent growing disenchantment—I still knew nothing of the "trial" he'd undergone or his punishment—I suggested he might be the ideal person to go after. The FBI soon located him, probably through his parents, who had always disapproved of his racist ideas. They provided him a lawyer who struck a deal for Billy with the government by which, in return for his testimony against Order members, no criminal charges would be brought, despite his participation in armed robberies, a major felony. Billy's desire to leave his brothers apparently arose from his realization that his life was in danger from them; he continued, however, to believe in the philosophy The Order represented, and subsequently exploited his position as a government witness to launch anti-Semitic diatribes.

A month later, the Merkis came over to the government's side, too. It was a wise decision on their part. The charges facing them, considering their ages—Robert Merki was in his fifties, his wife in her

191

late forties—could well have landed them behind bars for the rest of their lives. For himself, Merki negotiated a thirty-year sentence, for Sharon twenty-five, which meant, if they were released after serving the minimum time, he would be out in ten years, she in eight. It was Robert Merki, I believe, who was the first person to name Bruce Pierce as the gunman in the Berg murder. In an odd kind of defense, Merki maintained to his interrogators that, unlike Billy, he had never believed in the racist tenets of The Order, and had joined its activities solely to make money from stealing and counterfeiting. This, presumably, made his crimes less reprehensible.

On December 18, ten days after Bob's death, Denver Parmenter was arrested and charged with participation in the Ukiah and the Seattle robberies. He also struck a deal with the prosecutors to testify against his erstwhile comrades in return for a twenty-year sentence. Parmenter had rather fascinated me the time I had met him at my house in the company of Barnhill. Unlike Barnhill, who had struck me as an immature braggart in love with his own idea of himself as a desperado, Parmenter seemed more intelligent and sensitive to people's feelings, but a tortured person, drowning some terror of himself and his world in drink.

As the year ended, all the other Order members were still on the loose, most of them armed, most of them dangerous.

By then, the government had still another informant, twenty-two-year-old Eugene Kinerk. An Aryan Nations member, he had known Walter West, and when he learned that West was murdered at Bob's direction, he swore revenge. To carry it out, he broke into the Aryan Nations office in October 1984, stole the mailing list and sent a letter to every name on it in which he attacked Bob and Reverend Miles, who, he believed, was Bob's mentor. The letter was signed by Kinerk as Leader and a man named Kelly Carner as Secretary of something they called the American Nationalist Party, of which they apparently were the only members.

Although written before Kinerk became an informant, the letter reads as though it could be the work of a government agent seeking to cause dissension within the racist movement. In that sense, it falls into the "rat" category, as we called it in my National Alliance days. Such broadsides typically are the work of an ambitious follower who wants to take over a leader's organization or attract members to a rival group he is forming. Whichever, a leader is accused of being a traitor to the cause, often by identifying him as an undercover agent for the FBI, the CIA, the Anti-Defamation League (ADL), or ZOG generally. Attacks of this kind are hard to defend against, since the accused, by responding to them, gives them further currency. To me, however, Kinerk's letter is most interesting as a textbook example of the kind of denial of reality that is prevalent in right-wing thinking.

Very often, racist reasoning starts out from a sound basis. A grasp of a serious problem is in evidence—for example, the burden drugs cause society, the flight of American business abroad, bank foreclosures on farmers. Or, alternatively, the counterproductiveness of a particular racist action is correctly exposed. It is only after the premise is stated that the thinking begins to go awry. Kinerk's letter was of the second variety. He pointed out that if Bob succeeded in his "great plan" of cutting off "the electrical supply of the city of Los Angeles," that act would "hardly disturb the System (remember New York in 1965?), [but] it would cause enough urban violence and looting to arouse great animosity against" the racist cause. Nothing could make more sense; if Bob had managed to carry out that plan—or any of the others like it on his agenda, including the assassinations—the result would have been just as Kinerk foresaw. But from that point on in Kinerk's letter, reason flees as conspiracy enters. To Kinerk, Bob's plans were not well-intentioned errors in strategy but rather were proof of a plot in which Bob was acting on behalf of the "CIA, under orders and funding of the ADL," to involve "innocent people" and force them to commit crimes that would bring about the discredit of the Aryan movement. Miles, who supposedly gave the orders Bob was carrying out, became, in Kinerk's fantasy, a "self-confessed CIA field operative."

Kinerk's efforts to gain adherents for his new party failed; eventually he didn't even keep Carner on his side. Following his arrest on a bank robbery charge, he turned to the FBI for protection, and with good cause: In Portland, Bob had told me quite casually that he planned to have Kinerk "removed." Kinerk's cooperation proved valuable for the government. He turned over to the FBI the Aryan Nations membership list he had stolen, providing the Bureau with a

significant surveillance tool it is still using. For Kinerk, who also promised to testify concerning the West murder, the deal did not work out.
In January, he hanged himself in his jail cell, leaving behind notes in
which he expressed his fears of his former friends.

On the day Kinerk killed himself, I was telling a grand jury in Seattle what I knew of the Bruder Schweigen, the majority of whom
still remained free. There had, however, been a few additional arrests
by then. Jimmy Dye had been taken in Spokane on January 3. Like
the Merkis, he copped a plea to a twenty-year sentence. Four days
later, when police in Klaispell, Montana, raided a poker game, they
found they had on their hands my best friend from the National Alliance, Richie Kemp, and along with him, Andy Barnhill. The charges
against Kemp were the most serious: the murder of Walter West; participation in the armored car robberies; and as a suspect, along with
Bruce Pierce, in the bombing of the Ahavath Israel Synagogue in Boise, Idaho. On January 17, the day after I completed my testimony,
Jean Craig was arrested, accused, among other crimes, of murder,
because of her surveillance role in the Berg killing. It was in this period that Ostrout and King, the two Brink's supervisors, were picked
up and began to talk.

Still uncaptured by the end of January, among others, were Mc-
Brearty (whom Bob may have assigned to arrange for my murder) and
the three alleged Berg killers, Bruce Pierce, Lane, and Scutari. It wasn't
a comfortable feeling for me to know they were still roaming about.

Apparently it wasn't to the government either. It wanted to keep
me alive, at least until I could testify at the trial of The Order members, for which no date had yet been set. As a result of their fears for
my safety, they urged Susan and me to enter the Federal Witness
Protection Program.

That suggestion had come up twice previously, first in October right
after I became an informant and again in December on my return to
Philadelphia from Portland. In each instance, taken up by the events
I was living through, almost reflexively—I just sensed I didn't want to
do it then—I had refused.

On January 30, following my return from giving my grand jury
testimony, Susan and I, though we had not yet given our final approval, took the first step toward entering the Program. In order to

determine if we were emotionally stable enough to be good candidates, we were separately given psychological tests—inkblots, square pegs in round holes, that kind of thing—and then interviewed by a psychiatrist. Apparently we passed these examinations, because we were next brought into a conference room where Libby was present along with several representatives of the Federal Marshal's Office in charge of the Witness Program.

The marshals informed us that, if we joined, we would be given new identities—which had a familiar ring to me; Bob had promised to do the same—after which we would go underground—just as Bob would have done for us—at a location selected by the Marshal's Office. Once we were settled, I'd be given an allowance of $1,200 a month, or about $300 less a month than Susan and I had been making between us before I got us into our problem. Out of that, we'd pay all our expenses until I got a job, at which time the money would be cut off. I asked where we'd be sent. They refused to say.

I didn't like that thought much   it didn't seem to me I was cut out to be a coal miner in West Virginia or a farmer in Nebraska—but far more troubling to both of us was the separation Susan and I and the children would have to undergo from our families. In answer to my question, I was told that perhaps in three years—I have no idea why that date was chosen—my parents would be allowed to meet with us at some halfway point for a single meeting, "but they will never be allowed to come to your new home." If we wanted to write them, or they us, the correspondence would have to go through the Marshal's Office (and I suspected ours would be censored there, lest we reveal our hiding place)

But it was not only being cut off from my parents that concerned me. My daughter's emotional health did, too. Life had already been much more difficult for her—thanks to me—than it should have been. Just two days previous, for the first time since December 4, she had been permitted to go to school, a new one, but under restrictions that were hard for any nine-year-old to understand: she was told she wasn't allowed to tell her new classmates the name of her previous school or even the city she came from. Perhaps more important, Diane, unlike my little boy, was old enough to have some understanding of what had happened in our lives. She knew that Mr. Mathews, who had always been nice to her, was dead, and I had something to do with it. She knew I'd been present in a gun battle in Portland, and she had since become fearful every time I left the house that I might not ever come back. Children are resilient, and so she has proven to be, but at that point she was becoming withdrawn, yet with outbursts of aggression toward other children that were more frequent and more serious than they had been when they first manifested themselves the previous year. To move her to some entirely new place, cut her off from her grandparents and everyone she had ever known, seemed to both Susan and me a new and possibly dangerous psychological burden to put on her.

Despite the many aspects of the Witness Program I didn't like, the argument for joining was a powerful one. Although I no longer lived under moment-to-moment fear of death for myself and my family as I had the previous summer, I was not taking Bob's threat against my life lightly, any more than the FBI was. Rationally speaking, the fugitives from Whidbey Island should be concerned with saving themselves and not in harming me, but rationality was not a valid criterion to use about them. They were fanatics who blamed me for the death of their fallen leader, and one or more of them may have vowed to get me before being caught.

They also had allies who couldn't be discounted. My experiences in the racist movement had proven to me that most of the threats I heard against people were idle boasts, but Bob had proven that wasn't always the case. The Aryan Nations had published a description of me which, fortunately, wasn't particularly accurate; it said, for instance, that I had "swarthy" skin, which, no doubt, satisfied their sense of bigotry but wouldn't help anybody recognize me. More dangerous to my security was a photo of me published by the Klan paper, the *Thunderbolt*, under the heading: "Watch for this Arch-Traitor." The accompanying article said, "Tom Martinez would turn in anyone for money, even his own mother!" Reading that, I remembered how Bob, now the *Thunderbolt*'s martyred hero, had several times described its publisher to me as an "untrustworthy, money-grubbing parasite."

It was this paper's campaign against me that brought me to the decision I reached about joining the Witness Protection Program.

I had come to see from my conversations with Don Miller that if I were ever to do anything positive with my life, I must neither flee from it nor brood about it. Rather, I had to keep my past in front of me at all times. Only that way could I find the means to reclaim myself from it. Becoming a witness against The Order would be a step in that direction, but I had originally promised to do so to gain lenient sentencing, and for that reason, if for no other, testifying was not a sufficient means of making amends. What more I had to accomplish remained vague in my mind, save that I knew it entailed warning people of the dangers that could come to them and their children by following the path in life that I had.

As I listened to the marshals explain their protection program, one that seemed so similar to that Bob promised me, the loss of identity it would force upon me struck me as a new form of weakness I'd be exhibiting if I accepted it. By doing that, I would be giving my enemies the satisfaction of sending me cowering away. If I were to stand up to them, it could not be just from a witness stand; it must be publicly and continuingly. In that sense, I wanted to become, as Bob had said of himself, the hunter rather than the hunted. The risk in that was that I might be killed because I'd be visible to them, but I was going to die some day anyway, and I'd rather it be that way, having finally attached some worthwhile meaning to my name, not what it had meant and would mean if I spent the rest of my life in hiding. (This recountal of my reasoning may make me sound braver than I felt. I was, in fact, scared, but I was used to that by now and, as I figured it, it was better to be scared standing up than lying down.)

Susan agreed with me. We rejected joining the Federal Witness Protection Program.

38 | David Tate, Murderer

During the late winter and early spring months of 1985, to my relief, the round-up of The Order members escalated. Randall Rader, who had headed Bob's paramilitary training program, was arrested in Spokane on March 1 and pleaded guilty in return for his promise to cooperate. The government recommended at sentencing that he be given ten years, but the judge, to the prosecutor's fury, gave him probation. Jackie Lee Norton, arrested two weeks after Rader, was equally fortunate.

Next came Bruce Pierce. After Bob's death, he had proclaimed himself the leader of what was left of The Order. While on the move from state to state, often only hours ahead of his pursuers, he kept in touch with several of the brothers who were taping his calls and turning them over to the FBI. In these contacts, Pierce asked for maps of communications and transportation facilities he intended to sabotage. Although heavily armed when the FBI finally caught up with him on March 26 at Rossville, Georgia, he surrendered without a fight.

Four days later, David Lane was taken into custody in Winston-

Salem, North Carolina, following a tip from Ken Loff, the money farmer who by then was also cooperating with the government.

George Zaengle was arrested on April 3 in Pennsylvania, and he also became an informant, like Rader eventually serving less than a year. The Learned Professor, Ardie McBrearty, was taken in Florida the next day. About two weeks later it was the endangered locksmith Bill Nash, who also talked and, as with several of the others, spent only a few months in prison.

On Monday, April 15, two Missouri state troopers, thirty-one-year-old Jimmie Linegar and thirty-five-year-old Allen Hines, were manning a roadblock a few miles from the Covenant, Sword and Arm of the Lord encampment on the Arkansas border. The final stop they made was of a 1975 Chevrolet bearing Nevada license plates. Its youthful driver, who had a straggly moustache, beard, and dirty blond hair sweeping down over his forehead, showed them an Oregon driver's license in the name of Matthew Mark Samuels. Checking it through their computer, the troopers learned that Samuels was an alias for David Tate, who had left Whidbey Island unmolested on December 6. Learning that he was wanted in Oregon on a weapons violation, the two officers reapproached the vehicle. Tate, wielding an automatic pistol, fired point-blank at Linegar, who crumpled to the ground, struck three times. Jumping from the van, Tate continued to fire, three of his shots ripping into Hines' body. Unwounded himself, Tate, who had trained as a sharpshooter at the Aryan Nations, escaped into the brush.

Tate left behind in the van two more .45-caliber automatic pistols, two MAC machine pistols similar to the one used to kill Berg, a sniper rifle with a telescopic sight, eight assault rifles and forty-four hand grenades. That evening, a state police dragnet of the area didn't capture Tate but did come upon original Order member Frank Silva, whose cross burning in December 1983 had led to Bob's "the revolution has begun" phone call to me. Silva was arrested without incident.

Officer Hines survived his wounds. Officer Linegar died of his. The Order had committed its final murder. Tate was captured in a park not far away on April 20.

The day before, eighty police officers, joined by agents from the

FBI and the Alcohol, Tobacco and Firearms Division of the Treasury Department, laid siege to the heavily armed Covenant, Sword and Arm of the Lord (CSA) site to which Tate had been heading. On April 22, the CSA leaders gave up without a shot being fired. They proved to be better at threatening an Armageddon than participating in one. Among those arrested were Order members Randall Evans and Thomas Bentley, the man who allegedly had said that Walter West was "blabbing about Gary's army."

After Evans and Bentley were taken into custody, Richard Scutari was the one significant Order member still at large. He was rumored to have fled to Costa Rica, where he once had worked as a guard in a silver mine.

CHAPTER

39 | Bring Me Tom Martinez's Head

It was June 28, 1985, when two men arrived at a room in the Red Lion Motor Inn in Spokane. The elder of the two, tall and balding and doughy-looking, was fifty-nine-year-old Elden "Bud" Cutler, who had succeeded Gary Yarbrough as security chief for the Aryan Nations. His companion, also an Aryan Nations member, was more muscular than Cutler, perhaps not as dull in appearance but basically cut from the same mold. His name was Robert Bowyer.

Meeting them at the door, turning off his television as he escorted them inside, was a squat, menacing-looking man, probably in his forties; his face was scarred; one of his eyes looked to be made of glass. Bowyer introduced him to Cutler as Dave Smith.

The conversation that followed can be seen on film, secretly recorded from the room next door. During it, Bowyer rarely speaks, his eyes shifting rapidly from one man to the other. Cutler plays the hick role, Smith the city slicker. Cutler occasionally smiles, laughs, though whether from pleasure or nervousness is not always clear. From Smith, on the contrary, the smile is rare and thin, the laughter never. Unlike the bumptious Cutler, he exudes an aura of menace. At no point does anyone seem surprised at what they are discussing; the tone, for the most part, is phlegmatic. The day is warm, and the men refresh themselves by drinking iced tea as ladies might at a church social. The conversation is a long one, frequently repetitive as Cutler and Smith feel each other out. The significant parts go like this:

SMITH: Bob, um, Bob [Bowyer] called me and told me about this, ah, problem you was having and, ah, he asked me if, if I could do a favor for a friend of his. Um, of course, Bob I owe and, ah, he's a friend of mine...and he said, ah, well it's for a friend of his...but, ah, I'm a little unclear exactly what it is that you want or, or exactly what your ideas are.

CUTLER: (Laughs) Well, the guy is just a, ah, a, ah, bad thorn in the side of the movement, and, ah, we just, he's, he's, ah, ratted to the FBI and he's put the finger on a lot of guys and put 'em in the big house and they're friends of mine....Listen, I'm just a damn old farmer from around the area here... [but] ...I, uh, you know, I've heard of, uh, uh, this over the years ever since, oh way back in the fifties, that these things could happen....

SMITH: Well, well, I understand that...from what, what Bob had told me there was, ya know, some of those had been a pain in the neck to you and caused you a lot of heartache...and he said that you'd had, had asked him if he knew any way to dis—

CUTLER: Oh, we talked it over, you know, but, uh, I had no idea what, uh, the price was or anything else, you know.

SMITH: Price is usually an unusual thing. This one's more of a favor to him and the brothers....Ah, but, ah, when you get into something like this, you don't want to go doing it unless you have an absolute good reason why. For me, I mean, I don't wanna....

CUTLER: Well, it's mainly because of what he's done, right....He's caused us a lot of trouble [and] there'd be different methods of doing it but, ah, we all took an oath that, ah, when something like he did happens that they would do their best to sever their head from the body and do it that way and it was a blood oath and so.

SMITH: ...Okay, well, um, I've got no problems with which you want done. Um, I just want a little bit more understanding of, ah, in fact, with who it is I'm dealing with, an' what your motivations are.

CUTLER: Well, it's gonna upset a lot of federal authorities. He's gonna be their star witness.

SMITH: ...Okay. You go popping somebody, you know.

CUTLER: Yeah, I know.

SMITH: ...I want to mention something about, ah, you wanted his head, thinking about having his head sent to the FBI....

CUTLER: Well....

SMITH: ...Was that what you initially wanted to do or...what do you want done?

CUTLER: This is an idea I toyed with, see. I, ah, that's one reason that, ah, we thought we ought to discuss. I don't know, ah, you know, I don't want to do any, I don't want to hold you to anything that's gonna...(Laughs).

SMITH: You're not gonna damage it.

CUTLER: Oh, well, I realize that. Ah, to me that'd be the ideal situation. Either to them or to a newspaper. There is the idea that if [the head] was sent to the FBI, they'd hush it up and nobody'd ever know.

SMITH: Um, okay. Um, I've got a problem with the hit....You want the head removed at the time, fine. [But] I'm not mailing a head anywhere.

CUTLER: Okay.

SMITH: ...Now, ah, if that's the case, what'd you, what would you like done as an alternative?

CUTLER: Just leave it lay right there. Wherever it happens.

SMITH: Okay.

CUTLER: As long as it's severed, I'm sure it'll hit the newspapers.

SMITH: I'm sure it will, once it's found.

BOWYER: I know it will, and I'm sure it will.

SMITH: Now, as proof to you that this has been done other than the fact that it's gonna hit the newspapers, do you want, ah, I can take a photo of it. You can send that to whoever you want to at the time.

CUTLER: ...If you can get a picture and bring it, that's fine, without, you know, so we don't get jammed up on it somewhere.

From that, Smith and Cutler turn to the question of price. Smith repeats that he owes Bowyer and the brothers a favor and, therefore, is willing to chop off the head for a bargain price of $1,800, plus travel expenses. Cutler pleads poverty—crops bad this year—but he tells Smith he does have $600 with him and he'll be able to get the rest by the time Smith returns with proof of his handiwork. Smith says he wants half, plus the expense money, before he'll do the job. After poor-mouthing a bit more, Cutler agrees.

SMITH: Okay, uh, Martinez was the name I was given on—

CUTLER: Tom Martinez.

SMITH: Martinez, and we've got an address on him and know where he is?

CUTLER: Oh, I don't, other than last known was Philly somewhere.

SMITH: ...This guy might, must mean a lot to you. This Martinez character.

CUTLER: Well, I hope it changes a little of the history of the near future.

SMITH: It might ring some bells.

CUTLER: Rattle a few cages...this Martinez was a fink to start with the Feds. He's the one they planted the ideas and got everything all hyped to go. You know, just, ah, deliberately led them, like these other guys, into a lot of trouble...and...they thought they was pretty hot stuff but they wasn't. Bunch of good guys and, ah, [after Bob Mathews was killed] the rest of 'em didn't have it, you know, no organization or anything else to, ah, stand up. They all folded...and swapping their heads off, but, ah, I think once it hits the news about Martinez, why they'll all get a little lockjaw....

SMITH: Oh, it'll tighten jaws up. It'll tighten jaws right up. [But] who turned up the idea of Martinez? Was that was, ah, for hitting him?

CUTLER: That was me. I just got...

SMITH: I'm surprised you guys didn't do something about him a long time ago.

CUTLER: Hey, believe me, I wanted to so bad I could taste it. But then I'd sit down and say, well, you know, there's, where's the rest of my life in jail just, ah, to do it....I have no idea how to do something like that and get away with it....You will, you'll get the man?

SMITH: Yeah.

The conversation ends with that promise. Immediately before, Cutler indicates to Smith that if he does a good job of taking care of me, two other murders might come his way, one of Peter Lake, a journalist who infiltrated the Aryan Nations and wrote a magazine article about it, the other of Larry Broadbent, the deputy sheriff in Coeur d'Alene near Hayden Lake, who, Cutler indicates aggrievedly, persists in treating Aryan Nations patriots like him as though they were common criminals.

To me, the most revelatory aspect of Cutler's conversation with Smith was his explanation of why The Order failed. Despite the fact that Bob Mathews—by the time Cutler met with Smith—was enshrined as the Aryan Nations' martyred hero, Cutler, the Aryan Nations security chief, throughout refuses to give Bob any credit for his deeds.

Instead, he treats him as a dupe, *my* dupe. It was not Mathews but I, he says, who set up all the Order crimes for the FBI: "...he's the one they planted the ideas." I was the one who "deliberately led" The Order members "into a whole lot of trouble." Cutler's rationale is identical to that found in Kinerk's letter, save that, to Kinerk, it was Bob himself who was the secret agent tricking a "bunch of good guys" who "thought they was pretty hot stuff but they wasn't." Either way, the theory that is being expressed is that the enemies of the racist movement are so diabolically clever that they can force otherwise law-abiding white supremacists into committing crimes to carry out the goals that they, the supremacists, say they want to accomplish.

Much the same kind of self-deprecating logic is displayed when the Neo-Nazis and their allies claim that the Holocaust never occurred. In order to do that, they have to deny that their hero Hitler, with whose anti-Semitism they are in agreement, ever intended to harm the Jews. Instead, the Jews wanted to harm Hitler and bring the entire sacred Aryan supremacy movement into disrepute, which they did—with diabolical cleverness—by fabricating the Holocaust. Just as with Cutler's analysis of The Order's failure, in denying the Holocaust, the Aryan racists are admitting they aren't capable of carrying out their own aims. Each time they appear to have tried to do so—as with the Jews in Germany or The Order—they are actually under the control of their enemy. In this way, claims of Aryan superiority become riddled with admissions of Aryan inferiority, which admissions—because they are psychologically insupportable to those making them—are readily denied through the creation of a fantasy world, whether it be the written one described in *The Turner Diaries* or the one that Bob played out in real life.

40 | What Else I Learned about the Jews

At the time Cutler was spinning out his murderous plot with Smith and Bowyer, I was enjoying a measure of happiness for the first time since the early days of my marriage.

It came about despite the continuing unusual circumstances of our lives. Susan and I still were not permitted to hold jobs; the Bureau was adamant on that. Though thwarted in its efforts to get us into the Federal Witness Protection Program, it still wanted to keep us under wraps as much as possible, and going off to work every day would make surveillance of us difficult.

We had also been placed in an environment foreign to our K&A background. By the summer, we had shed our motel existence and were settled into a $1,000-a-month apartment in a complex that came equipped with swimming pool and tennis courts. That allowed us to see—if not participate—in a way of life we had previously glimpsed only on television. In the complex, the average family income was around $75,000 a year; ours was less than a third of that. Although the government was paying the rent and the utilities for the apartment, our only cash income was our FBI "salary" of $379 a week—

less than $20,000 a year—or exactly what we had been bringing home from our jobs before we had been forced to leave them. From that, I paid the mortgage and utilities on my house, car payments, insurance, groceries, and all the other usual family expenses. We got by, but we were constantly aware of being interlopers among the well-to-do who, for the most part, kept their distance.

We also had no idea how long our new way of life would last. Theoretically, the cutoff date would come when I had completed giving testimony at The Order trial, which might or might not take place in August—from my own experience, I now knew that trials have a way of getting postponed—but that was not certain; there could be additional trials or further threats against me that would necessitate continued protection. On the other side, it was also possible that our support would end before any trial; the Bureau had made quite clear to us that we could be summarily cut off from all funding and evicted from the apartment at any time. It is difficult to make plans for a future that has no known beginning.

Neither was it normal for me to have to see my parents on the sly, yet that was what I had to do, the Bureau having given me strict orders to go nowhere near them. I understood the reasoning and agreed with it. When I had been in the racist movement, I had made no secret of where my parents lived, which meant that anyone out to murder me might well set up a stakeout near their house. For that reason, I could possibly be endangering them as well as myself by visiting. Yet I felt a need to be with them, as they did with me, perhaps more so on their part. Never, for a moment, had either my mother or father approved of my beliefs—they thought I'd outgrow them, which, in a sense, I had—and they were pleased I was now making an attempt to undo the harm I had caused. At the same time, they were frightened for me. Speaking to me on the phone wasn't sufficient to allay that. They wanted to be able to see and touch me, and my own sense of security—of normality—was bolstered whenever I saw them.

My enjoyment of life that summer, however, had its primary wellspring in my wife and children. My enforced idleness permitted me to get to know Diane and Tom, Jr., as I never had before. And they me: For them, Diane especially, I had too long been a distant and wrathful figure who must be left alone of an evening as he sat in his corner sopping up his racist literature. On weekends I had rarely been home. When not off to a Klan meeting, later a National Alliance meeting, I was out distributing literature at K&A. My domestic appearances had been the hurried and distracted ones of the father who had much more important things to do than loving and caring for his own children. Now I did have time to play with them, to take them on day trips—usually little drives about the countryside—and our affection for and awareness of one another blossomed.

I was also able, during this interval, to find a way back to Susan, which, because of our bond, became a giving of myself back to me. It was a time for intimacy and love to be established and re-established.

The rejuvenation of those months, I believe, did much to give me the courage to take a step that had first crossed my mind back in January but that I had then dismissed as unrealistic. It had to do with the Jews.

Specifically, it had to do with the Anti-Defamation League of B'nai B'rith. I was no longer suffering under the delusion, fostered on me by my years in the racist movement, that the ADL was all-powerful, controlling the media, forming the policies of government, but I did recognize it to be influential, well financed, and that it and I now had a cause in common. Its enemies had become my enemies. Perhaps, I thought, I can give the ADL information it can use, in that indirect way helping me get my warning message out to the public.

But I had held back, principally because I didn't think I would be welcome. I didn't think I should be welcome. What they'll see you as, I thought, is a slimy ex-Nazi who became an informant only because he was scared for his own skin. They would have no reason to trust me. I wouldn't have.

Practical considerations, as I thought of them, also had deterred me. Although some of the racist papers had for some time been describing me as a "long-time ADL mole," should it become known—in reality rather than fantasy—that I was talking to the ADL, I could well be encouraging attempts on my life that were not already under way. A more immediate worry was the FBI. I was never quite sure what terrible thing I might do that could cause the Bureau to cut us adrift, but I had no doubt that I was expected to be obedient and—

most important—keep out of sight. If the Bureau got word that I was occasionally sneaking off to see my parents, I doubted that would be considered more than a venial sin, but to endanger myself by going to the ADL and, worse yet, share with it the information the Bureau wanted to keep to itself could have, I feared, dire consequences. We'd be thrown out on the street, jobless—as a convicted felon, where would I find a job?—and no longer with the protection, such as it was, that we had been receiving. (Oddly enough, it never occurred to me—possibly because I was still in awe of the Bureau's power—that the threats I was hearing were hollow, that, in fact, no matter what I did, I wouldn't be disowned. I was needed alive and cooperative for the trial.)

Despite my worries about displeasing my masters, by July I had asked myself over and over again all the Don Miller questions and kept arriving at the same single answer: By going to the ADL, I would be attempting an act of redemption that was not contaminated by being part of a self-serving plea bargain as my trial testimony would be. I began to see the ADL contact as a measuring stick of my own sincerity, the thing I didn't have to do that I could do.

On the last Thursday of July, I went into Philadelphia—I still lived near there then—and walked into its ADL office. I told the secretary I was Tom Martinez and that I'd like to talk to the person in charge. The man who came out to greet me was wiry, intense, with dark wavy hair. "I'm Barry Morrison," he said. He knew who I was. My name had come up in the ADL's investigations of The Order. "Why don't we sit and talk?" he asked as he shook my hand.

We did, that day and many days afterward. Through Morrison and the people he introduced me to at the national headquarters in New York City—men like Irwin Suall and David Lowe, who head the terrorism research unit—I was exposed to a way of thinking about the world that was new to me.

My assumption, in considering going to the ADL, had been that its sole purpose was to help Jews, which was as I thought it should be. People, in my experience, looked out primarily and usually exclusively for themselves. When they saw themselves oppressed, as I had, they might join organizations that claim to fight against the inequities they are suffering, but they join nothing unless a benefit for them personally can be foreseen, harm to others irrelevant. Society, in that view, is held to consist entirely of competing self-interests. Bob Mathews had expressed that philosophy when he spoke enviously to me of how well the Jews finance their causes and how it was up to us to learn how to finance ours. But the ADL and the people who work for it, I discovered, didn't believe that interests necessarily have to be in collision or in competition with one another, nor did they see that the purpose of an organization designed to help oppressed people should be to gain supremacy for its beneficiaries, as the racists desired. The ADL, in carrying out its purpose of fighting discrimination against Jews, rather, perceived that effort as part of a broader program to assure that everyone's civil rights and liberties were protected. If self-interest led to mutual interest, that was good; if not, not. I came to this realization about the ADL only gradually. No one there ever described it to me as a credo, nor was I ever showered with propaganda leaflets to attempt to educate me into believing what a fine organization it was. Instead, my understanding of the concept of mutuality seeped into me through the way people like Suall and Lowe and Morrison conducted themselves, even in casual conversations. From that perception, I realized for the first time that racism, and the terrorism that springs from it, has as its ultimate victim not the announced victim but our common sense of humanity.

I would suppose—I would hope—for many people that would be a lesson that didn't have to be learned; for me, it was an important part of my reeducation as a man.

When I told the people at the ADL about the message I wanted them to spread for me, they said to me: But don't you think you should tell your story yourself?

I have. Through ADL auspices, I have traveled the country, speaking to groups in synagogues, at national conferences, Jewish and Christian, on television, on radio. And never have I mounted a stage before a Jewish group that I don't, at that moment, remember how, in the National Alliance, I would stand around with my friends, listening with approval and sometimes participating in the talk about what we would do to the Jews if we ever got the chance. And never have I had hate returned from them for that I had demonstrated toward them. Never has a single person in an audience shrugged me away or walked out on me in anger when hearing what I'd been. They accept my story which, I guess, isn't surprising, but they accept me, too; after I've talked, they shake my hand or put a hand on my shoulder, and I've been given phone numbers to call if they can ever be of help to me. God be with you is what they say to me, in those words, and in their faces.

When, not long before she died, I tried to explain to my mother the feelings I had during and after these speeches, she said to me: "But, Tom, I always told you the Jewish people were good."

CHAPTER

41 | How I Lost My Head

"One of our men has been hired to kill you." That was Libby. On the phone.

His name was Thomas R. Norris, known to Cutler as Dave Smith. The FBI had learned from an Aryan Nations informant—one of dozens who have infiltrated that organization—that Cutler was planning to have me murdered, my head removed from my body, as Bob had ordained. When Norris, his bloodthirsty record vouched for by the informant, arranged to meet with Cutler, the videotape record that was made had incriminated Cutler. The Bureau, however, in order to make the case airtight, also wanted evidence of him paying the balance owed after the deed was committed. Suspecting that Cutler would want proof, someone, possibly Wayne Manis, who was in charge of the investigation, had come up with the idea that Norris should offer to provide photographs of me decapitated.

To create that proof, the day following Libby's call, I accompanied her, Lou Vizi, and their superior, Frank Stokes, to FBI headquarters in Washington, D.C. My mood during the trip, as it had been since receiving Libby's call, was a mixed one. That the Bureau's intelligence was such that it had been able to uncover the plot and insert one of its own as the gunman had to some degree reestablished my shaken confidence in its ability to protect me, but my main reaction was one of renewed fear. I had developed my brave thoughts about standing up to my enemies when I knew of no immediate danger from them. The news about Cutler didn't shake my resolve to speak out—I hoped it didn't—but my realization that a Bud Cutler was actually out there, lunatic and evil enough to want to carry out Bob's demands literally, left me badly shaken. I knew I had no guarantee that the next time a hatchet-carrying killer was hired he would again be an FBI agent.

When we entered the FBI building, I was sent to a lavatory to change from the suit I was wearing into the clothes I had been told to bring along with me, the street kind I'd be likely to be wearing when I was killed. They consisted of dungarees, sneakers, and a white *Soldier of Fortune* T-shirt I frequently wore when I had been in the right wing.

Appropriately dressed, I was escorted to a spacious office from which all the furniture had been removed. Several agents were present, along with a photographer and a woman who, I was told, was an artist. Her function wasn't explained to me at first.

The office had a dark carpet to provide a neutral background for the photographing. While I watched, several agents got to their hands and knees to smooth out indentations the furniture legs had made on the carpeting, and to pick up little pieces of fuzz, so that nothing suspicious would show in the pictures. As they were working on that task and the photographer was setting up the cameras, I was shown two color slides. One was of a black woman whose head had been chopped off by her boyfriend, the other of a white man who had committed suicide by laying his head on a subway track where it had been sheared off by a train.

As if giving me a kind of guided tour, an agent lectured me on the weirdly contorted positions of the two bodies, the pictures of which were making me ill. He invited me to duplicate them. I laid down on the rug, tried to do as I was told. It took a while, photographing me from this angle and that, stretched this way and that, but finally they were satisfied. I arose. It struck me as funny, in a morbid way, how stiff my neck was.

Once my pictures were developed, I was told, those that most closely matched the postures of the decapitated people in the slides I had been shown, would be selected, after which my pictures would be cut apart so that my head was separated from my body. The resulting composites would be shot up to maximum size. The next step explained the role of the artist, and possibly why she studied my throat with such attention. She was to draw onto the composites a flow of blood and gore from the separated parts of my neck, using the slides of the actual decapitated people as a guideline. That portrait would be reduced and rephotographed by a Polaroid camera, a necessary precaution since anything but Polaroid snaps might arouse Cutler's suspicions; after all, these were not pictures one would ordinarily send to one's corner Fotomat to have developed.

Perhaps a month or so later, I was offered an opportunity to view the completed handiwork. I refused.

42 | The Condition of Cutler's Crops

Norris, who can speak English a great deal better than he indicated in the conversation at the Red Lion Inn, had his second meeting with Cutler on August 12 in Room 582 of the Northshore Resort Hotel in Coeur d'Alene, Idaho. As with the first one, the proceedings were videotaped. At the beginning of the film, Cutler strides into the room and almost immediately gives Norris the $1,000 he still owes him for carrying out the contract. Norris then hands him the pictures of me. "Jeez. Looks good," says Cutler lasciviously.

"That what you wanted?" Norris asks.

"You bet!" says Cutler.

With the exchange of the cash and Cutler's response upon seeing the photos, the case against him was completed as far as the attempted murder of me was concerned. Norris, however, also wanted to try to find out who, if anyone, besides Cutler was involved in the scheme. From the content of the succeeding conversation, it is clear, the hope was that Cutler would implicate Butler. But Cutler maintained that "the pastor actually knows nothing about this," and that the only person to whom he was going to show the pictures, before destroying them, was David Dorr, a member of the Aryan Nations security force.

In another part of the conversation, Cutler indicates that he would next like to hire Norris to murder Ken Loff, who, he had heard, was talking to the FBI and was believed to be under protection somewhere in New York.

Norris says he would be happy to accommodate him, but the Loff hit will be more expensive, $15,000 to $20,000. Cutler opines it will be "at the earliest around three months" before he can come up with that kind of money, and Norris sympathetically agrees that it "is not a, ah, drop in the bucket, that's, that's a sizable amount," after which Cutler observes temptingly: "I strongly suspicion that Loff could tell where there was quite a little bit stashed away if he was pressed for it."

As the talk goes on, it becomes apparent that Cutler has become uneasy about Robert Bowyer, the man who introduced him to Norris.

CUTLER: Have you had any contact with Bob lately?

NORRIS: Yeah, I talked to Bob. He's gettin' ready, he's doing some movin' or something, he said.

CUTLER: Yeah, he just all of a sudden disappeared and don't show up anymore. Wonder what the devil is....

NORRIS: I know he's been real busy.

A few minutes later, as if on cue, the phone rings. Norris, hearing the voice, says over to Cutler: "Bob," and then, "Hello. Okay, you gonna be able to get here?...Yeah, yeah, ah, yeah....Okay, hmmm, you think you're gonna be tied up a little bit, huh?...Okay....All right." He hangs up. "Was Bob. He was gonna try and get over here today, but..."

To which a relieved Cutler cries, "Ah huh!"

The man on the other end of the phone wasn't Bowyer but a member of the surveillance team inquiring if the time had arrived for the arrest. Norris's "you're gonna be tied up a little bit," was a signal to him to hold up on the bust for a few more minutes to give Norris time to pump Cutler for additional information. As for Bowyer, or whatever his real name was, he had by then left for parts unknown, his work as an informant completed. When Bowyer introduced Norris to Cutler, Norris's frightening appearance, I believe, helped convince Cutler he was the hired killer he purported to be. (Norris, in fact, was a highly decorated veteran of the Vietnam War whose scarred face was the result of battle wounds.)

After the supposed call from Bowyer, the conversation drifts over to David Tate's arrest for killing the state trooper, but Cutler appears to have no first-hand information about it. Having by then covered all the bases, Norris has entered into a waiting pattern. The tape ends this way:

NORRIS: Well, that's okay. Didn't have t'change any flight reservations or anything so—I'm pretty good there. So—what, how's your crops doin' this time of year, anyway? The crops, yep.

CUTLER: Damn poor this year.

NORRIS: (All sympathy again) Is that right?

CUTLER: We go about, ah, two-thirds of the crops.

NORRIS: Two-thirds?

CUTLER: (He says something but his words are unintelligible)

By then, the door has opened and a man with a gun is standing in it. He says, "Mr. Cutler, I'm Wayne Manis with the FBI. Stand on your feet and put your hands on your head. Now. Up. Hands on your head. Okay."

A newspaper picture of Cutler after his arrest shows him in a cowboy shirt, his hands manacled in front of him, staring expressionlessly at the camera.

43 | Out of My Corner

It was five months later, toward the end of January 1986, and I was on an airplane heading for Boise, Idaho, where I was to testify at Cutler's trial.

As I sat back in my seat, I was trying to concentrate on Cutler, too, to conceive of him, the man they called "Bud," a friendly name, a country boy grown old, the farmer with his failing crops, sipping iced tea while he plotted murdering me. But my mind rejected him. Maybe it was the way the newspaper photographer caught his eyes. I couldn't get beyond them, and I wasn't quite sure why.

Unlike the turbulence that had marked my flight to Portland when I was heading there for my meeting with Bob, this ride was smooth, and as we darted through the clouds, I could sometimes see below me the vast and vacant and achingly beautiful land of the American West. The New Eden Bob had told me of: "You'll see the deer come out to play, buddy," he had said. "You'll see that."

A deer had been nibbling at leaves, just visible in the woods behind Bob's house when we left it that morning, he carrying the briefcase that had Zillah's picture in it, I lugging his machine gun for him, the day Walter West was killed.

By the time Cutler's trial began, that of The Order members, which took place in a federal courtroom in Seattle, had been over for nearly a month. That prosecution began in early September, with the jurors not retiring to begin their deliberations until nearly the end of December. Altogether, the government had introduced 1,528 pieces of evidence and had put 295 witnesses on the stand. One of them was me.

When I entered the courtroom on the morning of October 15, I saw ahead of me the defendants, their backs to me, seated at tables, their lawyers interspersed among them. Five of them—Bruce Pierce, Ardie McBrearty, Frank Silva, Randall Evans, and Zillah's mother, Jean Craig—I had never met. I knew the other five—David Lane, who had bragged to me of killing; the boyish desperado Andy Barnhill; nervous Randy Duey, with his Hitler moustache; the foul-mouthed Gary Yarbrough; and the youth who had once so admired me, Richie Kemp—but they seemed hardly real to me anymore, had become dream figures moving stealthily through my memory, most frequently there when I didn't want them to be. Now, as I passed them on my way to the witness stand, giving each a quick glance, it was startling for me to see them, still with flesh, still with blood, with feelings of this moment, not from my past with them.

But as I took my oath and sat down on the witness chair to face them, the only one who visibly reacted to me was Jean Craig. She nodded to me and gave me the most pleasant smile, as if she would love nothing better than to have a pleasant little chat with me, if only there was time. As my testimony went on, she continued to give me her most careful attention (much as she had Alan Berg when she was trailing him); my impression was that she would have thought it impolite of her to do otherwise. The others, however, with only one exception, rarely looked at me. The walls were interesting, the ceiling was interesting, anything was more interesting to look at than Tom Martinez. The exception was David Lane. As the hours went on, so did his glare, an evil-eye performance that struck me as pathetic. I barely recognized him; he seemed to have aged twenty years since I last saw him, driving away from my house the day following his contemptuous description of the man he said he had helped murder.

Because there is no such crime as murder on the federal statute books, neither Lane nor any of the other defendants was charged with it. Not directly: The ten of them had been indicted under a federal racketeering law—Bob called it a revolution; the government called it a racket—in which each was charged with conspiring with the others to commit illegal acts (one of which could be murder) as part of an ongoing criminal enterprise. Under that statute's umbrella, therefore, I could testify about Lane's role in the Berg assassination but he could be convicted only of the conspiracy to kill Berg, not the actual act.

Yet murder was much in the air in that courtroom. Witness after witness—most of them Order members who had received reduced sentences in return for their testimony—told of how the Berg killers had bragged to them of their deeds, much as Lane had to me. For one, a morose and now repentant Denver Parmenter—he who had drunk his way through a viewing of *Birth of a Nation* at my house the night he and Barnhill were on their way to meet Glenn Miller—told how Pierce said to him that Berg "went down as though a rug had been pulled out from under him" when he shot him. The murder of the luckless Walter West was told too, how he had trustingly followed his best friend, Randy Duey, into the woods where the killers waited for him. Jimmy Dye told the jury that story in almost the same words he had told me. But there was more: Other witnesses stated that West had not been blabbing about Gary's army, had not known anything of the counterfeiting, had not even known there was such a thing as The Order. Luckless Walter West had been killed through a mistake, but the defendants only stared at the ceiling. "Nothing but a Jew-kike," David Lane had said to me of Berg. "You can count on me, Bob; I'll take care of it," Richie Kemp had said stoutly about West. The subject of the trial was murder.

As my plane began its approach to the Boise airfield, the Cutler trial ahead of me the next day, I was recalling myself in the witness chair at Seattle. I was not at that moment remembering what I'd said, or Jean Craig's smile, or David Lane's glare, but rather my own emotions as I was testifying. They had not been what I had expected. For more than a year, beginning on the day I agreed to cooperate with the government, I had known the time would almost certainly come when I'd be facing the people I was giving information against. I had believed I would have difficulty looking at them, those whom I once had considered my friends, my allies. (It never occurred to me that they wouldn't be able to look at me.) At times, I worried that I would make some terrible blunder, misstate a fact that their lawyers would leap upon, and I'd be responsible for their going free. None of that happened. Instead, beginning at an early moment in my testimony and becoming increasingly clear to me as it went on, my principal awareness was of calmly carrying out a duty. I was not only, I began to perceive, a witness; I was bearing witness to the jury and to myself as to what I had been through. When, after two days, I was done, I felt satisfied, unburdened.

Save in one way: I realized to my surprise—for I had not thought about him recently—that one defendant, Richie Kemp, disturbed me. The others, those I knew and those I didn't, roused no special feelings in me, not even dislike, but Richie both saddened and horrified me. Of him I believed, had to believe, from Dye's recountal of the Walter West murder and from other evidence produced at the trial—to say nothing of the revelatory change in his code name from "Jolly" to "Hammer"—that he had, cowardly and cold-bloodedly, bashed in Walter West's head while standing behind him, which made him loathsome to me. Yet even as I felt that, I still saw him as the big, good-natured, sensitive boy he had been when I first knew him. Like Billy Soderquist, he had been a student in a gifted children's program in California, like him had come from an advantaged background, but unlike Billy, he had a natural gracefulness, a potential for largeness, I believe, that could have made of him a contributor to, rather than a despoiler of, society. I thought of him then and now, much as I do of Bob, as a sad loss of a human mind and spirit.

They were all found guilty. Described in his pre-sentence report as "an unrepentant armed robber and a cold-blooded murderer" in the West killing, Richie was given sixty years in prison; Randy Duey, a hundred years; Gary Yarbrough, sixty years on top of the twenty-five-year sentence he had already received for his shoot-out with the FBI agents; Jean Craig, forty years; McBrearty, forty years; Evans, forty years; Silva, forty years; David Lane, forty years; the gun-toting Mr. Closet, Andy Barnhill, forty years. Bruce Pierce, repeatedly identified as the gunman in the Berg murder, received 100 years. A few months later, the last Order member on the loose, Richard "Mr.

Black" Scutari was arrested, pleaded guilty to an array of charges; sixty years for him. In Arkansas, David Tate was convicted of the murder of Officer Linegar and sentenced to life imprisonment with no possibility of parole for fifty years; he'd be seventy-two then.

The Order defendants convicted in Seattle were still waiting to hear their sentences when I arrived in Boise. My trip had been a long one, but my testimony would require no more than five minutes. The sole reason for my appearance was to tell the jurors who I was and, I suppose, to prove to them I was still alive despite the photos they would see of me apparently decapitated. My opportunity to see Cutler, therefore, was of brief duration, but it proved long enough to bring me finally all the way out of my corner.

He looked much like his picture, conical-shaped head ending in quivering jowls, his body not so much overweight as flaccid. His eyes, which I had imagined from the newspaper picture of him were menacing in their very expressionlessness—a cold-blooded gaze, I'd thought—turned out, as I studied him from the witness stand, to be merely watery.

He didn't frighten me. That surprised me. I knew it wasn't really his appearance; Bob Mathews hadn't been dangerous looking either. While I answered the questions put to me—I had trouble concentrating on them; they seemed to be coming from a distance—I continued to look at him, trying to understand what my lack of fear meant. He blinked a lot, I noticed. A word—and I can't remember if it was in one of the questions asked me, in a reply of mine, or just a word that crossed my mind—provided a clue. The word was "idea." From that, I understood why I had thought I should be frightened of him, why I had been unable to come to grips even with the *idea* of him until I saw him. It was because he represented their last grip on me, the faceless man grip, the man with the bomb, the man with the gun, with the hatchet, coming down my street late at night. They wanted me to spend the rest of my life looking over my shoulder for the faceless man. As long as I continued to fear the idea of the faceless man, I still feared them. He doesn't frighten me anymore, I repeated to myself, a delicious moment. Perhaps from all I had been through, I'd learned more than I thought I had; I'd learned the meaning of fear of fearing. I shook my head, as though in negation of a question the prosecutor was asking me, but I intended it for Cutler, and from the way he quickly looked away, I think he may have understood what I meant.

"Thank you, Mr. Martinez. That will be all."

That was all. A day or two later he was convicted, sentenced to twelve years in prison. I left the witness stand. I walked by him. I walked out of the courtroom. I didn't look back, didn't have to; there was nothing there I needed to see anymore. Outside, the day was cold and bright and good. I was a free man in it.

The Future of
American Terrorism

The Order has been vanquished as an entity, but while it existed it represented a dramatic departure from previous outbreaks of racial violence in this country. Those historically have taken many forms, ranging from lynch mobs to the occasional lunatic who grabs a gun and starts shooting people. Organizationally, the Klan, the Aryan Nations, the National Alliance, among others, have preached violence, but have always done so in a public way to attract members, to keep them enthusiastic, and to keep them contributing money. The Order, however, organizationally never engaged in demonstrations—no cross burnings for it—nor did it create or plunge into racially tense situations to exploit them. Quite to the contrary, its instructions to its members were never to express their racist beliefs publicly. From the beginning to the end, The Order's goals were to be fulfilled through purely criminal means, always carried out in secrecy.

In creating The Order, Bob Mathews appeared to have paid close attention to Dr. William Pierce's theory of the cadre. Although Bob believed that an army would eventually be needed to carry out his revolution, at the beginning a core of elite, well-trained and absolutely obedient soldiers was all that was required. A comparison between the cadre-like Order and Glenn Miller's parading White Patriot Party is instructive on this point. Miller's operation, at its height, probably had several hundred members. For that reason, its activities were relatively visible—abetted by Miller himself, who avidly sought publicity—so that it also became relatively easy for the government to keep it under surveillance. As the government was doing that and Miller was bragging about being persecuted, Bob and the twenty-two brothers of his secret organization—of whom no more than a dozen or so were ever full-time activists—were able to murder and pillage, their existence not known until I revealed it to the government in October 1984, a year and $4 million after they began their operation.

I am not suggesting that without me The Order would have continued to escape detection. If nothing else, the clues the FBI developed following the Ukiah robbery put its investigators on the right track, and I think inevitably they would have begun to understand the dimensions of what they were dealing with and then acted vigorously and successfully to make arrests. There is also the possibility that if I had not become an informant, someone else would have—perhaps Soderquist when he realized he was marked for murder. My role, however, was hardly insignificant. Because I became an informant when I did and because I had Bob's trust—as Soderquist didn't—I was able to help prevent the Morris Dees assassination; because of me, the imminent plan to blow up Boundary Dam near Seattle was thwarted; because of me, the government learned of the plan to rob the Brink's vault in San Francisco—another crime in the offing—and was in a position to stop it if it had been attempted. I also alerted the government to the plan to disrupt the Los Angeles power supply. Therefore, if I had not been stupid enough to follow Bob and pass the counterfeit tens—with all that followed from that—the government would not have lucked into getting me as an informant when it did, and at least some of these crimes would have been carried out. That is not a comforting thought.

That The Order's collapse was inevitable, one way or another, sooner or later, however, is of no significance to those who would emulate its terrorist program. Such people ordinarily don't think in terms of being caught; even if they do, they see themselves as becoming martyrs for their cause. To them, consequently, The Order provides a model for success, not failure. That such is the case is proven by copycat acts of terrorism that have been either planned or carried out since the dismantling of The Order.

In September 1986, just a year after The Order trial, a group calling itself the Bruderschweigen Task Force II was taking credit for setting off four bombs in downtown Coeur d'Alene, Idaho. No deaths resulted. One of those arrested for the bombings was David Dorr, the man to whom Cutler said he was going to show the photos of my decapitation and who succeeded Cutler as security chief of the Aryan Nations. Dorr and his confederates allegedly have also emulated Bob's formula by engaging in counterfeiting, assassination plots, and in the murder of one of their members under circumstances reminiscent of that of Walter West.

Another Aryan Nations member, Thomas George Harrelson, was arrested in Fargo, North Dakota, in February 1987, after fleeing the scene of a bank robbery. At the time he was also wanted for another bank robbery in Illinois in 1985, in which the getaway car was registered under the name of Reverend Robert Miles' daughter, who was then Harrelson's fiancee. Two months later, Harrelson pleaded guilty to both robberies, as well as to a string of others committed in Indiana, Arkansas, Minnesota and Ohio. The proceeds from these holdups, according to the Justice Department, were to be used to carry out terrorist activities.

Also, in April 1987, following a series of courtroom setbacks, principally at Morris Dees' hands, Glenn Miller aped Bob's declaration of war by issuing one of his own. In it, he also adopted Beam's Aryan Warrior point system, with the highest number awarded to anyone who killed Dees, indicating, among other things, that Miller is a sore loser. He was arrested a few weeks later.

Seven months earlier, in October 1986, eight members of a group calling itself the Committee of the States were indicted in Nevada on charges of plotting the murder of Internal Revenue Service employees and other federal officials. Among those charged in the murder plot was an Identity minister, William Potter Gale, who, in a sermon on a Dodge City, Kansas, radio station, declared: "You're damn right, I'm teaching violence....God said you're gonna do it that way, and it's about time somebody is telling you to get violent, Whitey." When arrested in California, Gale, a former Army colonel, was allegedly involved with seven others in paramilitary training that included instruction in ambushing and garroting.

Two months later, in December 1986, seven members of the Arizona Patriots, which appears to have close ties to the Committee of the States and the Identity movement, were arrested before they could carry out Order-like crimes they had allegedly planned. Among those schemes, according to federal officials, were a projected bombing of the Anti-Defamation League office in Phoenix, the bombing of an Internal Revenue Service office, and the bombing and robbery of an armored car. Discovered in the possession of one of their leaders were blueprints for the electrical systems of two major cities, and the piping system for a third.

As the stratagems of the copycat groups indicate, the principal lesson they took to heart from The Order was that of funding. Banks were to be robbed, armored cars were to be robbed. That kind of activity marks a distinct departure from that of previous racist organizations, which, when their members committed crimes, did so to carry out their beliefs, not to raise money. (One of the major funding sources for the National Alliance, for example, was selling *The Turner Diaries*, but those sales probably never averaged more than a profit of $5,000 a year, compared to Bob's $4 million in one year.) None of the new groups, fortunately, has developed a leader of Bob's qualities, and each has quickly been brought to justice. But that doesn't mean such a leader or leaders won't come along in the future. Worrisome to the government on that score is the Aryan Youth Movement, which by 1986 had twenty chapters on college campuses across the United States. When its founder, 26-year-old Greg Withrow, withdrew from the organization in July 1987 because he no longer believed in its tenets, vengeful members nailed his hands crucifixion-style to a board. Withrow was replaced as president by John Metzger, son of Tom Metzger, Bob Mathews' friend who heads the White Aryan Resistance in California.

In whatever way it originates, the new leadership may be impressed not only with how much money can be obtained quickly by committing relatively few crimes, but also with what can be done with that money, how readily and rapidly—sometimes without a trace—it can be disbursed. The fate of The Order's booty is illustrative.

Of the $4 million it stole by 1987, only about $400,000 had been recovered by the government. Were we to assume, generously, that the "salaries" to Order members, the leasing of safe houses, the purchasing of property for paramilitary training, accounted for almost half of the remainder, that still leaves about $2 million unaccounted for. Although it is certainly conceivable that a portion of that stuck to individual members' hands, there is reason to believe that nearly half of it was forwarded to groups Bob believed had the potential for carrying on terrorist activities, each of which continue in existence, and each of which may still have the money—or the weapons purchased with it—stockpiled.

Our principal source for the donation figures is Bruce Pierce. In a statement he made to the FBI shortly after his arrest, but which he subsequently recanted, he recalled that $300,000 went to Miller in North Carolina and another $250,000 to Tom Metzger of the White Aryan Resistance. The contributions to Miller and Metzger, Pierce stated, were intended for use by them to purchase guns and explosives for participation as allies in Bob's war.

Another $100,000, according to Pierce's statement, was given to Bob's hero, Louis Beam. For that donation we have confirmation from Jimmy Dye, who testified at the Seattle trial that he was present in a house in Rathdrum, Idaho, when that amount of money was handed over to Beam. In the same trial, Kenneth Loff stated that, acting on Bob's instructions, he dug up $640,000 of the robbery loot he had buried on his property and handed it over to Richie Kemp and David Lane to distribute to various racist leaders, including $100,000 for Beam. Loff's $640,000 closely approximates the $650,000 total that Pierce says was distributed to these three individuals.

Butler's Aryan Nations also, at some point, allegedly got money but did not fare so well. Although, like Miller's and Metzger's, Butler's is a paramilitary operation, he received, based on Pierce's assertion, only $40,000. If so, that would be in keeping with the generally low regard in which Bob held Butler. He saw the Aryan Nations as a source for recruits, but he did not think Butler was capable of much beyond posturing.

Bruce Pierce also stated that Dr. William Pierce was given $50,000 by Bob, who confirmed the donation, although not its size, in his conversation with me in his Portland motel room in November 1984. That same month, Pierce purchased property in West Virginia with $90,000 in cash that he said came from a wealthy donor, which may very well be true.

Bob Miles, who doesn't run a paramilitary operation but who has been convicted of a crime of violence and who preaches racist revolution, allegedly received a contribution of $15,300, an odd figure. Pierce said Miles didn't ask him about the origin of the money when he gave it to him, but added that he told Miles, "Stout-hearted Aryan men risked their lives to get this." (As far as I know, everyone in this group has denied receiving the money Bruce Pierce said was given to him.)

Bruce Pierce's statement further noted that in September 1984, Bob ordered $100,000 to be paid to implement the so-called Reliance Project. According to the FBI summary of its interview with Pierce, Reliance developed when an unnamed Order member "claimed to be in contact with two former government scientists who had been involved in a secret United States scientific experiment dealing with the transmission of electronic signals or waves at particular frequencies which serve to render people more docile and subservient... [and] that scientific experiments were being conducted that will allow persons with the knowledge to take a lock of hair from another and by some scientific process, project a chemical imbalance in that person." Under the same scheme—and we're now back in the world of ominous reality—The Order, according to Denver Parmenter's testimony, was to gain access to sophisticated laser technology designed for battle purposes. (The Order member who proposed the Reliance Project appears to have been Daniel Bauer, who pleaded guilty to receiving money for it, though he denied any was to be used for criminal purposes. Bauer also admitted that he told Bob and others about "radionics," the supposed mind-control device Pierce described.)

As a sidelight, still another slice of money—apparently never sent— was to go to a tall, blond-haired, blue-eyed rock musician, who was to start a punk band with it. That plan was identical to one carried out in England by the National Front, a neo-Nazi organization, which financed a rock group called White Power. It is made up of so-called skinheads, who perform songs with pro-Hitler and anti-Semitic lyrics. White Power reputedly has sold tens of thousands of records.

Even when the contributions to other racist organizations and such oddities as the Reliance Project and the punk rockers are taken into consideration, probably close to $1 million is still outstanding in the accounting of The Order's expenditures. (By way of perspective, it may be useful to bear in mind that all these figures could be increased by twenty to thirty times if the Brink's vault robbery had taken place.) A sizable but unknown portion of the remaining million went to the purchase of weapons directly for The Order's use.

As one means to accomplish that, Bob set up the Mountain Man Supply Company, which, by the fall of 1984, had purchased 137 shipments of military-type gear and ammunition from various suppliers. As far as I know, all the Mountain Man equipment came from licensed weapons dealers in the United States, but it is also possible that Bob had a second, illegal source. An informant claimed Bob told him in October 1984 "that he had a newly acquired connection in South America, that they were selling drugs down there and raising funds for the movement."

Despite Bob's genuine loathing for drugs and his frequently expressed distress about the harm it was doing the Aryan youth of the nation, I have no doubt that he would have gladly engaged in narcotics trafficking here or abroad. I reach this conclusion because of an incident that occurred in the spring of 1984 when I still believed in the New Eden. Bob mentioned he was thinking of recruiting for our dream future a mutual acquaintance from the National Alliance. I told him I didn't think that would be a good idea, because the person had become involved with drugs and "man, he's hanging around with a dealer." Bob perked up at that, laying pressure on me to arrange for the friend to introduce him to the dealer. (I refused.)

The informant also said that "some very old German families [in South America] were giving [Bob] some money." Although those connections may have come too late to do Bob and The Order any good, there is no reason to think any relationships American racists have with drug trafficking and Nazi funding sources in South America— the two might be the same—would have ceased with the arrest of The Order members.

Whatever the role, if any, that drug sales played, contacts between neo-Nazis in the United States and Europe and their counterparts in Latin America are nothing new. For example, as long ago as 1978, Manfred Roeder, who heads the remnants of the German Nazi party, traveled to Brazil, where he apparently met with Dr. Josef Mengele and other former Nazi leaders. Immediately afterward, Roeder came to the United States, where—according to the ADL—he conferred with Dr. William Pierce, among others. (Roeder, whose writings are published in the United States by the Aryan Nations and by George Dietz, a former member of the Nazi Youth Organization, has not recently been in a position to do any visiting. He is serving a thirteen-year prison sentence for his role in the 1980 fire bombing of a shelter for Vietnamese boat people in Hamburg, Germany, in which two refugees were killed. Roeder blamed the victims, saying they shouldn't have been in the room where the "symbolic" bombing took place.)

The long-standing Latin American connections of both European and American terrorists—conceivably some from the Middle East, too—when combined with the ready manner in which drug profits can be translated into weapons, could present a new and marked threat to our national security and that of nations abroad. (American racists have attempted to establish relationships with countries that practice terrorism, including Syria, Iran and Libya. Based on an investigation by the Anti-Defamation League's terrorist unit, those efforts have not been fruitful, at least as of 1987.)

Quite apart from alternative sources The Order might have thought to use for weapons and support supply, it is abundantly clear that the means it did use—armed robbery—was spectacularly and dangerously successful, qualitatively and quantitatively. I have already listed the cache found at Gary Yarbrough's home following the raid in October 1984. That was nothing compared to the inventory of Bruce Pierce's possessions when he was arrested. He owned: two airplanes; a half-dozen motor vehicles; nine rifles; a shotgun; seven pistols, including one with a silencer; an assortment of various types of radio scanners, radar detectors, computer equipment and the like; nine fragmentation hand grenades; three gas grenades; fifty-nine regular grenades; nine sticks of dynamite; one jar of nitro-based dynamite and one bag of the same; a pipe bomb; two cans of black powder; four simulator projective ground burst explosives; and five boxes of booby-trap equipment.

He could have easily blown up Rossville, Georgia, where he was arrested with the stockpile, and still have had enough left over to do a spectacular job on Atlanta.

And all that was purchased with just a tiny slice of the unaccounted-for $2 million. With $30 million to $50 million from the Brink's vault, The Order would have been able to get enough equipment to blow up every major city on the West Coast if that was what interested them—and based on *The Turner Diaries* and some of Bob's comments to me, that is what interested them. We may have come that close to a catastrophe.

Perhaps even more frightening than the amount of weapons The Order obtained is the ease with which it got what it got, whether on the open market through the Mountain Man purchases or otherwise. I am not referring here to buying items that often have legal purposes, such as ordinary rifles and dynamite, but those that never do when in the hands of civilians: the hand grenades, the booby-trap equipment, the C-4 and other plastic explosives, the sniper rifles and the guns with silencers owned by Pierce and others, to say nothing of the laser weapons Bob was on the verge of purchasing at the time of his death.

A major source for illegal weapons for terrorists apparently has been the U.S. government. A 1986 report published by the Government Accounting Office of the U.S. Congress revealed that millions of dollars in equipment has been stolen from military bases, including land mines, rockets, mortar shells, C-4 and other powerful explosives. Between 1976 and 1985, illegally obtained military supplies, the report stated, were used in 445 bombings in the United States. At one point, in 1984, the Army instituted an amnesty program in which stolen equipment could be returned on a no-questions-asked basis; more than 200 tons of ammunition was recovered.

Hardly all the thefts lead to the arming of terrorist groups. Some standard items, such as rifles and bullets, are undoubtedly retained by soldiers for their personal use in hunting, or else are sold by them to friends or weapons dealers who may resell to anybody.

Nevertheless, according to testimony given in a North Carolina trial by ex-Marine Robert Norman Jones, an ordnance expert, a goodly amount of the weaponry stolen from Fort Bragg and a nearby armory found its way to Miller's White Patriot Party. Helping to arrange one of the early deals, Jones alleged, was Bob Mathews' emissary, David Lane. Altogether, Jones was given approximately $50,000 to make the purchases, supplying the White Patriots with ten Claymore mines, thirteen LAW rockets, riot grenades, ammunition, pistols, rifles, semi-automatic weapons, military radios, packs, boots, fatigues, and as an extra little bonus of between 100 and 200 pounds of C-4. (To give an idea of its potency, a little more than a pound of C-4 was sufficient, in 1985, to blow up a house in Philadelphia, leading to a conflagration that killed eleven people and left sixty-one families homeless.) Jones was also employed by the White Patriots, he said, to train ten-man teams of White Patriots Party members in military tactics—for which he was paid $100 a day—with active-duty soldiers from Fort Bragg assisting. Miller denied all the accusations, though he did admit: "We're building a white Christian army."

When the 224-acre Covenant, Sword and Arm of the Lord (CSA) encampment in Arkansas was raided in April 1985, the weapons there included: plastic explosives; pistols; rifles; grenades; an antitank rocket; 15,000 rounds of ammunition; fifteen machine guns, including a MAC-10 similar to the one that killed Berg and that Tate used to murder Officer Linegar; "a small but efficient bomb factory," according to a federal official; and an armored tank under construction. The compound itself was protected by booby traps and an electronically detonated mine field. Also on hand, in eerie resemblance to the Jonestown massacre, was a thirty-gallon vat of cyanide. James Ellison, the leader of the eighty-member group, explained all this by saying he was using the Bible as a road map for his life. "If you've read the Bible, you know it's there," right up to and including, one assumes, the armored tank. Ellison was subsequently convicted in federal court on a variety of charges and received a twenty-year sentence.

But it's not only advanced and conventional weapons to which the racist right has access. Their propaganda efforts in recent years have been bolstered by the development of computerized information networks, beginning in 1984 when Louis Beam installed his.

Anyone with a home computer and a phone link-up can reach either Beam's bulletin board or that operated in West Virginia by Nazi-literature publisher George Dietz. Dietz's board, according to an article published in the *Washington Post Magazine* in 1985, carries such messages as "The Case Against the Holocaust" and a truly weird one about "Negro Michael Jackson" who supposedly has had "extensive plastic surgery to make him appear more effeminate....Only the Jews could have thought up such a creature as Michael Jackson for the youthful 'goyim' to admire."

Dietz, the article said, claims that he gets twenty-five to thirty calls a day to his board, many from children. That pleases him. "The major reason," he is quoted as saying, "for computer bulletin boards is that you're reaching youth—high school, college, and even grade school youth." (Approximately 90 percent of all computer "hackers" fall into these age groups.)

Aside from hoping to attract impressionable youngsters, the computer system has other purposes. Beam has stated that his was set up specifically to get messages into Canada, where importation of literature that promotes hatred toward any religious, racial or ethnic group has been prohibited since 1970. The bulletin boards also deliver threats. On Beam's board, a compilation of addresses of ADL offices across the country are provided, to the approval of Glenn Miller, who advised his followers: "We have an up-to-date list of many of the Jew headquarters around the country so that you can pay them a friendly visit."

A similar, barely cloaked, call for violence comes from a computerized message authored, according to the ADL, by Reverend Miles. He says: "Soon our own version of the 'troubles' will be widespread. The pattern of operations of the IRA will be seen across this land.... Soon America becomes Ireland re-created....These dragons of God... know their duty...," and on and on.

The computer bulletin boards can get more personal, too. On Beam's, a "Know Your Enemies" section seems to call for murder: "According to the word of our God, Morris Dees has earned two death sentences." Heading the "Race Traitors" list is Tom Martinez.

Even if most of this is talk, even if the impressionable youths who reach the network aren't as impressionable as the controllers hope, the bulletin boards, at the very least, provide racist groups with an instantaneous means for coordinating terrorist actions that wasn't available to Bob and The Order.

The increasing frequency with which the radical right has turned to acts of terrorism may be in part a product of its sense of frustration. Studies by federal agencies and the ADL note that these organizations in recent years have suffered significant losses of membership—the Klan especially is in a precipitate decline—presumably leaving the remaining troops beleaguered and desperate. There may be some truth to that analysis, but I don't think it is the principal cause of the frustration. Based on my experience in the Klan and the National Alliance, and my observations of others who were there with me, the fewness of our numbers, far from making us despair, added to our sense of belonging to an elite. That reaction was one of which Bob was a victim and which he exploited when he formed The Order.

The frustration, rather, in my judgment, emanates largely from the sense the elitists have that nobody but themselves is listening to them. That was my growing response during my racist days, as I described earlier. It was never the people who opposed my beliefs that discouraged me—I relished having them to fight—but those who seemed to agree, who might even give us a dollar or two, but who would never join us in our battle, quite possibly because they saw it correctly as such an obviously losing one.

My big-city experiences can be equated to events in rural America in recent years, where farmers in large numbers have found themselves caught in a tragic spiral of losses leading to bankruptcies, foreclosures on the land they loved and tilled and which very often had been in their families for generations, so that their displacement is not only personal but a destruction of their very history as a people. If anyone should be ripe for revolution, it is they. Recognizing that, the racists have done their best to recruit them to their cause. They have told them they are victims of an "international banker" conspiracy, although the code name is frequently dropped and "Jew" or "Zionist" used in its place. At times, just as I did at K&A, they have found what appears to be receptive audiences, have caused some hitherto secret anti-Semites to become outspoken ones, and have, here and there, gained new converts. But apparently very few of them, causing their frustration to grow. For instance, in 1984, the racist Populist Party (which has no relationship to the original and respectable party of the same name) had a candidate for President on the ballot in four farm-belt states (Wisconsin, Minnesota, Kansas and North Dakota); he received a total of 10,000 votes out of 5.6 million cast, or one-fifth of 1 percent. A candidate can get that percentage of votes almost entirely by accident.

Should the farmers' plight ease, not only will the nonaccidental racist vote decline in subsequent elections, local and national, but, I have no doubt, the racists themselves will leave the field, in part in discouragement but also because their interest in the farmer's plight has never been genuine, but has been merely self-serving. The so-called legal advice they hand out has the effect, apparently calculatedly so, of worsening the situation in order to create more propaganda opportunities for themselves. In that regard, they appear to be following in the footsteps of the communists, who equally hypocritically claimed to be coming to the aid of the farmer during the Depression years of the 1930s.

The danger from American racism, therefore, in my judgment, is not that its organizations will succeed in convincing significant numbers of people of the correctness of their views, but rather the capacity they have to wreak carnage, as their frustration grows, in the form of terrorist groups like The Order.

As the history of The Order and the copycat groups shows, the victims of the violence will not necessarily or even primarily be the Jews and blacks who are the supposed targets. Of the three men murdered by The Order, only one was a Jew, none was black; the other two were a pitiful alcoholic and a police officer. The Bruderschweigen Task Force II's main target was a Roman Catholic priest. Following the trial of the CSA's Ellison, several of his followers were arrested on charges of plotting to assassinate the judge at his trial, who was neither black nor Jewish. Had Bob succeeded in blowing up Boundary Dam or disrupting the electric supply of the city of Los Angeles, the majority of the victims undoubtedly would have been the white people the racist movement supposedly speaks for. Neither when, as happened in Arizona and Nevada, IRS offices are targeted will it be only Jews and blacks who die, nor is that the intent. The intent of terrorism is to strike fear. It is acting out a fantasy, but its consequences are real maimings, real deaths in a promiscuous, miscellaneous way.

The maiming is also spiritual, and that evil is enacted on those it succeeds in recruiting. Racists lay waste to their own. I know. I lost most of the years of my youth, became curdled with hate, on the edge of violence myself, because of what they taught me. Our children are as much at risk as I was, with groups such as the violence-prone Aryan Youth Movement ready to welcome them. Social class seems no barrier; off the mean streets of K&A I listened to them, but so did Billy Soderquist from his home of material comfort in suburban California, Bob from his upright soldier's background in Arizona. I do not want any of our children crouching in the loneliness of a prison cell, crying, as some day Richie Kemp will cry: "What have I done to myself?" Too late the question then, too late the answer.

The number of Americans who will die or be maimed because of future terrorist groups depends in large part on the preventive measures we take legally and as a society.

In safeguarding us, the role of the justice system is a significant one. The U.S. government, when it began to act against racist terrorism after I became an informant, has done so with vigor and success. The stiff sentences The Order defendants received at the Seattle trial remove them as a menace to society for the foreseeable future, with the severity also presumably acting as a deterrent to those who might otherwise be encouraged to imitate them. However, even those sentences didn't satisfy the Justice Department, and rightly so. When the district attorney in Denver announced that he wasn't going to prosecute Bruce Pierce, Lane, Scutari and Craig for murdering Alan Berg—he said he was afraid he might not get a conviction—the U.S. government proceeded to indict them on charges of violating Berg's civil rights by killing him, the nearest it can come under federal law to a murder charge. Lane and Pierce were convicted; Scutari and Craig weren't. (There may never be a trial in the Walter West killing. He was murdered somewhere along the Idaho-Washington border, but his body has never been found. Until and if it is learned in which state the crime occurred, both lack jurisdiction to try it. Presumably, the alleged murderers could also be indicted under the federal civil rights violation statute, but the Justice Department ordinarily takes that step only when local authorities are unwilling to prosecute, as occurred in Denver in the Berg murder.)

A step taken by the Justice Department in 1987 may prove even more substantive than the Denver civil rights indictment. On April 24, the Department brought charges of conspiracy to overthrow the government by force and violence against Louis Beam, against the Aryan Nations' Butler, against Reverend Miles. (Also indicted were Order members Lane, Pierce, Scutari, Barnhill and McBrearty.) In the case of Beam, Butler and Miles, the government is saying that those who call the tune must pay for it just like those who play it out. The warning to unindicted racist organizations could not be more clear.

It is not only by criminal trials, however, that it may be possible to deter the racist leadership from promoting violence. Civil actions are also possible. A start has been made in that direction. In Mobile, Alabama, after two members of the United Klans of America were convicted of the murder of a black teenage boy, a suit was brought on the mother's behalf by Morris Dees against the United Klans. In February 1987, an all-white jury awarded her $7 million. The ultimate result was not only justice but poetic justice: The Klan had only one asset, a $200,000 office building in Tuscaloosa, Alabama; to settle the suit, it had to turn ownership of the building over to the mother of the black youngster its members had murdered.

As encouraging as these legal developments are as a means to curb racist groups by striking at their leadership, I doubt if even their authors think they offer a permanent or total solution to the problem. Fear of personal consequences may not have much effect on the type of mind that can come up with terrorism as a solution to its frustrations. Time also has a way of going by, and those who might be deterred today may not be deterred a year or two or five years from now; new generations come along. The danger, therefore, is not that those who cause new outbursts of violence won't meet the same fate as did The Order but rather, as I have tried to indicate throughout this book, rises from the havoc they can unleash until they are caught.

As one means of self-protection, we must do our best to limit their access to weapons. I am not referring here to conventional side-arms and rifles or explosives like dynamite. Even if I favored delegalizing legislation in that regard, as a practical matter I think it would be virtually impossible to pass it and completely impossible to enforce it. However, as The Order indicates, terrorists thrive not on conventional weapons—as ordinary criminals do—but on those that have no conceivable legal use beyond the military: mines, rockets, hand grenades, machine guns, rocket launchers, booby-trap equipment, and most plastic explosives. It should, I think, be within the capacity of our government to see to it that there is no repetition of the 1986 scandal in stolen ammunition and armaments from military bases. We spend a trillion dollars or more each year on national defense; certainly a tiny portion of that can be appropriated to assure that we won't be the victims of the very weapons we pay the government to produce with our taxes because those weapons fall into the hands of terrorists.

Another useful antiterrorism step already taken by eighteen states (as of 1987) makes participation in paramilitary activity a felony. One of them is North Carolina, where Miller's White Patriot Party was successfully prosecuted in 1986 for violation of its statute. The other thirty-two states should follow suit, or, alternatively, the U.S. Congress should pass such legislation.

The impact of inflammatory and threatening hate rhetoric on the impressionable—young and old—is an issue of long-range concern. The Morris Dees suit in Alabama moves in that direction, but a civil suit cannot be brought because something might happen, only if something has. (That is, the boy had to be killed before the mother could sue.) Similarly, the criminal indictment against Beam, Butler, Miles and the others is limited to proving an actual conspiracy to overthrow the government; the rhetoric is not an issue, what was done to put the rhetoric into action is. Attempting to curb inflammatory rhetoric prior to a criminal act flowing from it raises free speech questions, as I'm aware, and I believe, as a general principle, that if we have to err in that direction, it should be on the side of permitting it. Nevertheless, to allow a computer network like Beam's, which issues death threats against people, is to me so shocking that I can't imagine it coming under the protection of the First Amendment. I also wonder if this editorial statement found in William Pierce's *National Vanguard* (January–February 1985) qualifies: "No combination of clever lawyers, yuppies, and Joe Sixpacks will ever beat the Jews. Money will not beat them. Brains alone will not beat them. Votes will not beat them. But blood will, eventually."

Or this from a 1986 issue of the *Thunderbolt,* as reported by the

Center for Democratic Renewal, concerning Lyn Wells, Anne Braden and other staffers of the National Anti-Klan Network: "Can you help us find them? If you see them, follow them to their places of residence and report same back to us. A generous reward will be paid. . . . We want them questioned." And this about their enemies generally: "The time has come for us to fight with everything we can hit them with and we mean FIRE POWER. This time let there be no survivors. WIPE THEM OUT ONCE AND FOR ALL." (Capitals in the original.) They are not referring to overthrowing the government: They are talking about killing Jews and blacks.

Or what of this from that same radio station in Dodge City where Reverend Gale held forth: "You better start making dossiers, names, addresses, phone numbers, car license numbers on every damn Jew rabbi in this land, and every Anti-Defamation League leader or JDL leader in this land, and you better start doing it now. . . . If you have to be told any more than that you're too damn dumb to bother with. You get those road block locations, where you can set up ambushes, and get it all working now." Free speech? Protected by the First Amendment?

Then we have the books and pamphlets advertised and sold to anyone who has the money to buy them, which give instructions on how to go about sabotaging an armored car, build bombs, and offer advice on committing assassinations. Probably the best-known book in the "guerilla warfare" category is *The Road Back*, published in California by Noontide Press. *The Road Back*, according to Peter Lake, a journalist who infiltrated neo-Nazi movements, has been used as a textbook for seminars at the Aryan Nations. It includes an illustrated chapter on methods of mining roads and blowing up bridges. Free speech? Protected by the First Amendment? I wonder.

Canada, as I noted earlier, refuses to allow hate literature into its country. Perhaps we ought at least take a look to see how they are doing it.

Another free speech issue that presents itself is not one for which I would suggest any change in the law, but rather the application of common sense. It concerns the media. For the most part, I think both the print and the electronic media act properly and responsibly in their coverage of the actions of extremists. It is, however, also true that I probably never would have joined the Ku Klux Klan were it not for the David Duke interview on Tom Snyder's show. Alan Berg gave huge amounts of air time to racists so that he could satisfy his ego by responding to them and ridiculing them. The racists know they will be ridiculed when they go on such programs, and assume they will be despised by more than 99 percent of the people who hear them spout their venom. But none of that is of any matter to them. The fraction of 1 percent is. There they will find the malcontents, the embittered, the bigots, and the sincerely concerned but ignorant people like I was. The numbers are in their favor, and they know it. Snyder's program may have reached 2 million listeners; if only one-tenth of 1 percent of them respond favorably, they have recruited 2,000 people, no doubt swelling the ranks of their group ten- or twentyfold. One-hundredth of 1 percent would make them happy. Perhaps there's some legitimate reason—other than ratings—for giving these hate peddlers free air time, but I'm at a loss to think what it might be.

It's not just air time either. The newspaper *USA Today*, in what to me was a disgraceful example of editorial irresponsibility, gave the Aryan Nations' Butler free and equal editorial space to respond to its editorial against racism. That's like giving Hitler a column to praise genocide.

I also think that our mainstream Christian churches, Catholic and Protestant, don't do enough to warn their parishioners about the betrayal of Christ's message that can come beaming at them and their children through computer bulletin boards, through hate literature in any of its forms, and through so-called Christian Identity churches. The announced object of the assault may be the Jews, but it's Christianity, as Christ taught it, that's also under attack by these zealots.

Finally, I believe our schools have an obligation to our children that many of them are not fulfilling. The problem may be most prevalent in inner-city schools, such as those I attended, where getting through the day alive is more important than learning. However, I am far from sure that the problem I have in mind is not also to be found in more peaceful atmospheres. Based on my own experience, as well as on a number of studies of the American educational system, the teaching of history, both of our nation and that of others—I never even heard of the Holocaust when I was in school—has become relegated to an insignificant status in the curriculum. As a result, we are releasing from our schools generations of young people who know little or nothing about how their country came to be, its relationship to the rest of the world, the meaning and the reasons for its democratic form of government. If you don't know where you came from, I do not know how you can understand where you are.

Knowledge, in the end, may be our strongest weapon.

Acknowledgments

Two organizations that have long been courageous in battling bigotry in the United States are the Anti-Defamation League of B'nai B'rith and the Southern Poverty Law Center. Both were enormously helpful in providing resource material for this book. My best hope is that my contribution in the fight against racist terrorism will, in some small measure, help theirs.

The Anti-Defamation League's Director of Fact Finding, Irwin Suall, his assistant David Lowe, and Barry Morrison, Director of the Eastern Pennsylvania and Delaware Region of B'nai B'rith, have given me support and guidance both in my personal life and in this undertaking; my gratitude to them cannot be measured.

Morris Dees, the founder of the Southern Poverty Law Center and its inspirational force, has been an inspiration to me, helping me define the meaning of the word "courage." William Stanton, former Director of the Southern Poverty Law Center's publication, *Klanwatch*, and Pat Clark, Director, have been both friends and colleagues in putting this book together.

Gene Wilson, the U.S. Attorney who prosecuted The Order trial in Seattle in 1985, has made important contributions to this book, as have Robert D. Ward, the chief of the Criminal Division of the U.S.

Attorney's Office in San Francisco, and Ronald D. Howen of the U.S. Attorney's Office in Boise, Idaho.

Anath White, producer of the Alan Berg radio show at station KOA in Denver, has given selflessly of her time. Additional background on Berg's turbulent career came from a splendid article by J. Anthony Lukas, "The Man Who Talked Himself to Death," (GQ *Quarterly*, July 1985).

Peter Lake's "An Exegesis of the Radical Right" (*California Magazine*, April 1985) was helpful on aspects of Bob Mathews' career with which I was not familiar. L. J. Davis's "Ballad of an American Terrorist" (*Harper's Magazine*, July 1986) was of inestimable value in providing information about the Christian Identity movement, and for some of the events that occurred on Whidbey Island in December 1984. Mr. Davis also gave generously of his time at a crucial point in the book's writing.

I also wish to acknowledge the role played in my life by various federal law enforcement agents. They helped me when I badly needed help. Some of their names I never learned, but I do especially wish to single out for their support: Robert J. McDonough of the Secret Service; Wayne Manis, Thomas R. Norris, Elizabeth Pierciey, Frank Stokes, and Lou Vizi of the FBI; also, Bucky P. Mansuy of the U.S. Attorney's Office in Philadelphia.

My thanks are also extended to: Stan Lacks and Larry Bailine, who did so much to formulate the idea of the book; Edward F. Borden, Jr.; Perry DeMarco, to whom I should have listened earlier; my editor at McGraw-Hill, Elisabeth Jakab; and my agent, Elizabeth Knappman.

My entire family supported me with love and hope when I gave them little cause for either; to them my endless gratitude.

Finally, there is Don Miller, who did more than any other person, at a desperate time in my life, to make it possible for me to begin to understand myself and see the way I could travel to making amends for the wrong I did.

T.M.